RACE AND
THE EDUCATION
OF DESIRE

D1459700

Race and the Education of Desire

FOUCAULT'S HISTORY OF SEXUALITY

AND THE COLONIAL ORDER OF THINGS

BY ANN LAURA STOLER

DUKE UNIVERSITY PRESS   Durham and London 1995

Third printing, 1997
© 1995 Duke University Press
All rights reserved
Printed in the United States of America on acid-free paper ∞
Typeset in Joanna by Tseng Information Systems, Inc.
Library of Congress Cataloging-in-Publication Data appear
on the last printed page of this book.

Contents

Preface

This book emerged out of a number of questions I began mulling over some fifteen years ago when I first read Michel Foucault's *The History of Sexuality* while writing my dissertation in Paris. As my own work has focused over the last decade more squarely on the sexual politics of race, those questions have felt more pressing than ever before. At a time when Foucault's work has had such an enormous impact on anthropology and on the discursive and historic turns within it, why have contemporary scholars dealt in such an oblique way with the slimmest and, some might argue, the most accessible of his major works, volume 1 of *The History of Sexuality*? More precisely, why has colonial studies, where issues of sexuality and power are now so high on the intellectual and political agenda, had so little to say about it? In a field in which reading that volume seems *de rigueur* and reference to it confers intellectual authority, what accounts for this striking absence of an engagement that is analytically critical and historically grounded at the same time?

This study begins with some obvious questions: Why, for Foucault, colonial bodies never figure as a possible site of the articulation of nineteenth-century European sexuality? And given this omission, what are the consequences for his treatment of racism in the making of the European bourgeois self? More troubling still are the implications for those of us who have sought to extend Foucault's approach to sexuality and power into imperial settings. Do we run the risk of reproducing precisely the terms of colonial discourse itself where any and everything could be attributed to and/or reduced to the dangers, contaminations, and enticements of sex?

This book is an effort to address some of these questions, to redress that absence of reflection, and to reread volume 1 of *The History of Sexuality* in what I think is an unexplored light. It questions both Foucault's account of the technologies of sexuality that pervaded Western Europe's nineteenth-century bourgeois order and his marginalization of that order's imperial coordinates and their effects. But it also sets out to do something more, to register a part of Foucault's analysis that seems to have eluded those of us in colonial studies: namely how he conceived the discourses of sexuality to articulate with the discourse of race. Empire may be absent from *The History of Sexuality*, but racism is certainly not. How do we reckon both with the book's categorical effacement of colonialism and our overwhelming silence about Foucault's at once conventional and idiosyncratic handling of racism in it?

Contrary to the evidence from most other commentators, race is not a subject marginal to Foucault's work. As I argue here, it is far more central than has been acknowledged or explored. It is certainly more integral to his thinking than I first imagined when I began this book as an essay on *The History of Sexuality* two years ago. At the time, my assessment of Foucault's interest in race was based solely on his written work. Later in Paris, I had the opportunity to listen to the French recordings and read the Italian transcripts of the lectures Foucault gave in 1976 at the Collège de France. Some have cast those lectures as an elaboration of the final chapter of *The History of Sexuality*, others as a foray into political theory. But I was startled by what else they contained, for they also represent Foucault's equivocal effort to sketch out a genealogy of the discourse of race. I draw on them here, not to provide a "clue" to what Foucault "really" thought, but rather to investigate the tensions between what he wrote and what he said. As importantly, I want to ask how these tensions might help us rethink the connection between European and colonial historiography, between a European bourgeois order and the colonial management of sexuality, as well as how those tensions might bear upon how we go about writing genealogies of race today.

This is neither the celebration of the canonical text of Foucault as culture hero. Nor is this a subtle effort to undermine his powerful conceptual claims. My task is both more humble and ambitious: namely, to read Foucault's work against issues with which he grappled for years, sometimes with prescience and great acumen, other times with what he characterized as only marginal success. I am interested in identifying the impulse of his venture, the contingent space of ideas, the precluded venues of enquiry, the selective genealogies by which his—and our—writing of history has been constrained.

In response to the Italian journalist, Duccio Trombadori, who asked Foucault about the relationship between his earlier work and his then recently published volume 1 of *The History of Sexuality*, Foucault answered:

> If I had to write a book to communicate what I have already thought, I'd never have courage to begin it. I write precisely because I don't know yet what to think about a subject that attracts my interest. . . . As a consequence, each new work profoundly changes the terms of thinking which I had reached with the previous work. In this sense I consider myself more an "experimenter" than a theorist; I don't develop deductive systems to apply uniformly in different fields of research. When I write, I do it above all to change myself and not to think the same thing as before.[1]

If Foucault thought it took courage to write what he already knew, most of us might think it takes more courage to admit a lack of sure-footed intent, that in beginning few of us are sure what will come out at all. Some might argue that such an admission could only be enjoyed by someone whose innovative contribution was already secured. Others might be inclined to look more askance, to dismiss the statement as a disingenuous disclaimer, a display of false modesty by France's then leading intellectual whose master plan was evident in a patterned corpus that spanned nearly twenty-five prolific years. Either reading would do an injustice to Foucault by missing the tenor of his work, the persistent questioning that compelled his ventures. It would be to misrecognize how much his recursive style, his serial framings of what something was through concentric negations about what it was not, were part of a "thinking out loud" that not only transformed his books but has allowed his readers a unique sort of engagement with them.

Certainly any close reading of volume 1 of *The History of Sexuality* would support his methodological claims. For that volume is at once a recuperation of and departure from themes addressed in his earlier work. It represents both a renewal of a concern with how discursive forma-

---

1. Michel Foucault, *Remarks on Marx* (New York: Semiotext(e), 1991) 27.

tions are shaped and a reconception of power and how power transforms those formations. It takes us from an earlier focus on the normalization of power described in Discipline and Punish to a broader concern with the power of normalization. It replays themes of disciplinary regimes, but distinguishes between individual disciplines and social regulation in new strategic ways. It first introduces the "cultivation of the self" as a defining feature of the nineteenth-century bourgeoisie. Later, as Foucault shifted course in volumes two and three, that self-cultivation is recast as part of a deeper genealogy of ethics that pushes him back to antiquity, away from nineteenth-century France which had long been his preoccupation—a move that some historians have seen as a limit to the larger applicability of his speculations. Volume 1 of The History of Sexuality introduces the question of racism in a muted way that resurfaces at the core of his 1976 Collège de France lectures the following year.

In the Trombadori interview, Foucault describes his books as a "network of scaffolding" that carried him from one to another.[2] But that imagery is misleading. There is nothing fixed about how he saw the relationship between his projects, nor what girded the very scaffolding itself. Thus, in one place he refers to volume 1 of The History of Sexuality as a "twin project" with Madness and Civilization and elsewhere as a "sequel" to Discipline and Punish.[3] In the first of his lectures in 1976 at the Collège de France, volume 1 is somewhat disturbingly cast as one of several "fragmentary researches," that "failed to develop into any continuous or coherent whole."[4] It is also, as Dreyfus and Rabinow note, "a broad overview of a larger project." Foucault's project changed radically in the undertaking; the six volumes initially planned were never written. The volumes he did write became a very different kind of study of "desiring man," of a very different "pseudo-object."[5] These later volumes are obviously related to the first, but it is also clear that in 1976 Foucault shifted his analytic tactics, if not his critical trajectory. By 1983, Foucault would contend, in his favored role as provocateur, that "sex [was] boring", that he was "much more interested in

2. Foucault 29.

3. Interview in L'Express 24–30, January 1977, quoted in David Macey, The Lives of Michel Foucault (New York: Pantheon, 1993) 354. Foucault refers to it as a "sequel" to Discipline and Punish in page one of his unpublished talk on infantile sexuality available at the Saulchoir Library.

4. Reproduced in Nicholas Dirks, Geoff Eley, and Sherry Ortner, eds., Culture/Power/History (Princeton: Princeton UP, 1993) 200.

5. John Rajchman, Michel Foucault: The Freedom of Philosphy (New York: Columbia UP, 1985) 52.

problems about the technology of the self".[6] Thus, just as many of us were beginning to digest how we might use his insights on the relationship between the "truth" of the self and the discourse on sexuality, Foucault seemed to dismiss the value of such a project. But laying bare the scope and limits of his work is impossible if we think about it in linear terms as the abandonment of, for example, the "archaeological" method as he developed his new genealogical project.

By my reading, what is striking are his recursive folds. It may be awing, but it is no accident that Foucault, as Daniel Defert tells it, began the last chapter of volume 1 of *The History of Sexuality* on the very same day that he finished *Discipline and Punish*; both are concerned in different ways with biopolitics and normalization.[7] Nor is it insignificant that that final chapter of volume 1 should reappear the following year in revised form as the last Collège de France lecture, entitled "The Birth of State Racism": both focus on the relationship between biopower and race. Foucault was the quintessential *bricoleur*.[8] While many of the components of his analysis remain, they appear with different conceptual weight in different projects and with a function that is never quite the same. As I discuss later, this tension between rupture and recuperation is more than a stylistic quirk. It is at the very basis of how Foucault worked and understood the nature of discursive transformations.

It should no longer be possible in the current state of colonial scholarship to imagine the research process, either the consumption or production of knowledge, as an individuated, private affair. Changes in the anthropology of colonialism over the last decade require new recognition of the collective nature of what we do. As many of us try to heed our own advice to treat metropole and colony in a single analytic field and to abandon those contained units of analysis once so cherished, we are confronted with a

6. Herbert Dreyfus and Paul Rabinow, *Michel Foucault: Beyond Structuralism and Hermeneutics* (Chicago: Chicago UP, 1983) 229.

7. James Miller, *The Passion of Michel Foucault* (New York: Simon and Schuster, 1993) 240–241.

8. The term "*bricoleur*" is often loosely translated as "handyman" but I have more in mind Levi-Strauss' use of the term in *The Savage Mind* (London: Wiedenfeld and Nicolson, 1966, esp. 16–36). There he uses it to describe an adeptness (of mythical as opposed to scientific reflection in his case) at manipulating and reworking a finite field of intellectual and/or material resources to carry out a varied set of tasks. To me, it aptly captures a feature of Foucault's work in that concepts from his earlier books reappear in later ones to perform new sorts of analytic tasks.

daunting task. In dismantling the careful bracketing that contained metro-politan and colonial history, research has not only become unwieldy as an individual effort, but difficult for either fledgling graduate student or seasoned scholar to sustain. As part of that new scholarship, this book reflects the collective insights and expertise of students, colleagues, and friends I have called upon with a new frequency and urgency. This is not to relinquish blame or excuse the shortcomings in my evidence or argu-ment. It is, however, to recognize that the license I have allowed myself in posing more questions than I can answer and in glaringly omitting others, is grounded on the support of those who thought the questions them-selves worth asking. My hope is that this undertaking will both clear and complicate the space in which others might draw on Foucault and move beyond him to pose questions that his insights and omissions provoke us to address.

This book was originally conceived as an essay in another book I am writing on bourgeois civilities and the cultivation of racial categories in colonial Southeast Asia. Unwittingly, and in part due to the promptings of students and colleagues, it took on a life of its own. I thank the students in my 1991 graduate seminar, "The Body Politics of Empire," in which I first taught The History of Sexuality and fellows with whom I contentiously hashed out questions concerning histories of sexuality in that same year at the Institute of the Humanities at the University of Michigan.

I owe special thanks to a number of people whose careful readings were both a challenge and an inspiration: Julia Adams, whose healthy scepti-cism about Foucault's work forced me to confront his lapses as well as his contribution; Gwen Wright, whose enthusiasm and intellectual generosity sustained me throughout, who convinced me how much Foucault might have relished this project and made me both bolder and more tempered by doing so; Nancy Lutkehaus, who listened with patience and perspi-cacity to the first draft as it was being written; Val Daniel, whose meticu-lous and discerning eye took me through its final form; Nick Dirks, who urged me to turn the original essay into a book; Jean Comaroff, Frederick Cooper, Fernando Coronil, Brinkley Messick, David Scobey, Bill Sewell, Julie Skurski, Luise White, and an anonymous, Duke University Press re-viewer, whose comments on the book prompted me to do more—and less—and who kept me from major gaffes in content and form; Etienne Balibar, for his support and for wisely sending me to the Saulchoir Library;

Lila Abu-Lughod, Laura Bear, Lauren Berlant, Dennis Cordell, Victoria Ebin, Geoff Eley, Julie Elison, Nancy Florida, Webb Keane, Mely Ivy, Tom Laqueur, Rena Lederman, Marjorie Levenson, Bruce Mannheim, Hazel Markus, Uday Mehta, Sherry Ortner, Chris Schmidt-Nowara, John Pemberton, Doris Sommer, Jean Taylor, and Susan Thorne, for sharing with me their regional and other sorts of expertise—and for helping me sustain my enthusiasm for the project.

Earlier and much truncated versions of this book were presented as talks at the University of Washington, New York University, and at a session of the 1993 American Anthropological Association meetings organized by Bruce Knaupt and Gil Herdt. I thank the organizers, participants, and audience in these events for their comments. Ken Wissoker is an exemplary editor whose insights combine a critical eye, timely advice, and well-tempered enthusiasm. Melissa Solomon's copyediting skills smoothed and clarified the book's final form.

I thank Daniela Gobetti and Setraq Manoukian for their studied translations of the Italian and Remco van Eeuwijk for helping me with some particularly difficult Dutch passages. Samia Meziane shared with me the delights and frustrations of deciphering Foucault's lectures from scratchy cassettes. Madame Judith Revel formerly of the Saulchoir Library in Paris and the Père Albaric, its present director, graciously facilitated my task. Lisa Lindsay deftly compiled the bibliography. Carole McGranahan and Javier Morillo-Alicea labored swiftly through the index. Grants from the John Simon Guggenheim Foundation, the National Endowment for the Humanities, and generous support from the University of Michigan in the form of extended leave and a research award allowed me the luxury, unfettered by other obligations, of gratifying my obsession with Foucault's work.

I thank my daughter Tessa for rereading The Secret Garden with me and for persistently asking me why I have so many books on this person Foucault and why he was so important. I thank my son Bruno who pressed me to talk to him about the book and to write it in an accessible manner. I have tried to heed his sound advice in a way that will make this book useful both to those with only a healthy if skeptical curiosity about Foucault's work and for those, like myself, who have long been smitten with him. Finally, I thank Lawrence Hirschfeld, whose work on children and racism has prompted me to hurl my epithets about "psychologism" with much more care and to see how implicitly our post-colonial and postmodern analyses are both enabled and muffled by psychological insights, as we broach the politics of sentiment and the psychology of domination.

This book is dedicated to my sister, Barbara Stoler Miller, who died with such grace sixteen months ago on a cold, sunny, snowy day. I began writing it just after she died with an intensity that could only have been born out of my grief over the loss of the person whose passion for knowledge and life has sustained and guided my own. When I was just a small girl, she taught me that it matters what one says and how one says it, that the power of words is both in their message and their form. She took pleasure in our differences and encouraged my first forays into the history and politics of knowledge. I offer her this book, on her birthday today, the only piece of work that we did not have the chance to share, with my love, respect, and admiration.

8 August 1994, Ann Arbor

Postscript: As this manuscript was going to press in December 1994, I received the long anticipated four volumes of Foucault's complete published works (excluding his books), *Dits et écrits, 1954–1988*, under the direction of Daniel Defert, François Ewald and Jacques LaGrange (Paris: Gallimard, 1994). While I had read many of these interviews and articles in their earlier published form, it was too late to consider this entire new corpus of collected materials here.

RACE AND
THE EDUCATION
OF DESIRE

I

COLONIAL STUDIES AND THE HISTORY OF SEXUALITY

There are several possible ways to think about a colonial reading of Foucault. And at one level, anthropologists and historians have been doing such readings for some time. No single analytic framework has saturated the field of colonial studies so completely over the last decade as that of Foucault. His claims for the discursive construction of regimes of power have prompted us to explore both the production of colonial discourses and their effects;[1] inspired, in part, by Edward Said's forceful lead, students of colonialism have tracked the ties that bound the production of anthropological knowledge to colonial authority, to trace the disciplinary regimes that have produced subjugated bodies and the sorts of identities created by them. Some have sought to describe how discourses on hygiene, education, confession, architecture, and urbanism have shaped the social geography of colonies and specific strategies of rule.[2]

1. I use "us" and "we" throughout this book to identify students of colonialism, whether they be anthropologists, historians, specialists in comparative literature or none of the above. Differences in profession and geopolitical locale are less central to my analysis than the fact of an overwhelming response that Foucault has elicited from those in a wide range of political locations. Where appropriate, I identify the "we" as Euro-American scholars although some of my generalizations about the nature of colonial studies apply to a wider shared community of scholarship than those who would identify themselves with that which is Euro-American.
2. Among those studies of colonial history and historiography that draw on various Foucauldian concepts to different (and varying critical) degrees see, for example, Jean Comaroff, *Body of Power, Spirit of Resistance: The Culture and history of a South African People* (Chicago: Chicago UP, 1985); Ann Laura Stoler, *Capitalism and Confrontation in Sumatra's Plantation Belt, 1870–1987* (New Haven, Yale UP, 1985); Nicholas B. Dirks, *The Hollow Crown* (Cambridge: Cambridge UP, 1987); Aihwa Ong, *Spirits of Resistance and Capitalist Discipline* (Binghamton: SUNY Press, 1987); Vincente Rafael, *Contracting Colonialism* (Ithaca: Cornell UP, 1988); Guari Viswanathan, *Masks of Conquest: Literary Study*

Nor have we done so in blind faith. Our ethnographic sensibilities have pushed us to challenge the limits of Foucault's discursive emphasis and his diffuse conceptions of power, to flesh out the localized, quotidian practices of people who authorized and resisted European authority, to expose the tensions of that project and its inherent vulnerabilities.[3] These readings, for the most part, have been of a particular kind: by and large, applying the *general principles* of a Foucauldian frame to specific ethnographic time and place, drawing on the conceptual apparatus more than engaging the historical content of his analysis.[4]

This sort of passion for Foucault's general strategies is apparent in readings of his specific texts as well—particularly in treatments of volume 1 of *The History of Sexuality*. His book engages a disarmingly simple thesis: if in nineteenth-century Europe sexuality was indeed something to be silenced, hidden, and repressed, why was there such a proliferating dis-

---

and *British Rule in India* (New York: Columbia UP, 1989); Lamont Lindstrom, *Knowledge and Power in a South Pacific Society* (Washington, D.C.: Smithsonian Institution Press, 1990); Jean and John Comaroff, *Of Revelation and Revolution* (Chicago: Chicago UP, 1991); Tim Mitchell, *Colonising Egypt* (Berkeley: U of California P, 1991); Gwendolyn Wright, *The Politics of Design in French Colonial Urbanism* (Chicago: Chicago UP, 1991); David Arnold, *Colonizing the Body: State Medicine and Epidemic Disease in Nineteenth-Century India* (Berkeley: U of California P, 1993); Dipesh Chakrabarty, "Postcoloniality and the Artifice of History: Who Speaks for the 'Indian' Pasts?" *Representations* 37 (Winter 1992): 1–26. Nicholas Thomas, *Colonialism's Culture: Anthropology, Travel and Government* (Princeton: Princeton UP, 1994); David Scott, *Formations of Ritual: Colonial and Anthropological Discourses on the Sinhala Yaktovil* (Minneapolis: U of Minnesota P, 1994).

3. See Megan Vaughan, *Curing their Ills: Colonial Power and African Illness* (London: Polity Press, 1991) x. Vaughan makes an explicit effort "to explore the limitations of a Foucauldian account of 'biopower'" with respect to the discourse of colonial medicine.

4. In addition to the citations above see, for example, Ranjait Guha and Gayatri Spivak, eds., *Selected Subaltern Studies* (New York: Oxford UP, 1988), where the final two articles by Partha Chatterjee and David Arnold are grouped under the rubric "Developing Foucault." Chatterjee's otherwise excellent piece makes only implicit reference to Foucault, while Arnold's Foucauldian impulse is defined by his attention to bodies, discourse, and power. The engagement is conceptual, not historical, while the "development" of Foucault is unclear. Arnold's analysis of the distinctive response of the Indian middle-classes to the plague for example makes no effort to address how "cultivation" of an Indian bourgeois identity did or did not conform to Foucault's European model.

An important exception is Paul Rabinow's *French Modern: Norms and Forms of the Social Environment* (Cambridge: MIT, 1989), that "continues the exploration, in its own way, of some of the contours of modern power and knowledge Foucault had begun to map" on colonial terrain (8–9).

course about it? Foucault argues that we have gotten the story wrong: that the "image of the imperial prude . . . emblazoned on our restrained, mute and hypocritical sexuality" (HS:3) misses what that regime of sexuality was all about: not restriction of a biological instinct, a "stubborn drive" to be overcome, nor an "exterior domain to which power is applied" (HS:152). Sexuality was "a result and an instrument of power's design," a social construction of a historical moment (HS:152).

For Foucault, sexuality is not opposed to and subversive of power. On the contrary, sexuality is a "dense transfer point" of power, charged with "instrumentality" (HS:103). Thus, "far from being repressed in [nineteenth-century] society [sexuality] was constantly aroused" (HS:148). This is no dismissal of repression as a "ruse" of the nineteenth-century bourgeois order or a denial that sex was prohibited and masked, as critics and followers have sometimes claimed (HS:12). Foucault rejected, not the fact of repression, but the notion that it was the organizing principle of sexual discourse, that repression could account for its silences and prolific emanations. At the heart of his enquiry are neither sexual practices nor the moral codes that have given rise to them. Foucault's questions are of a very different order. Why has there been such a protracted search for the "truth" about sex? Why should an identification and assessment of our real and hidden selves be sought in our sexual desires, fantasies, and behavior? Not least why did that search become such a riveting obsession of the nineteenth-century bourgeois order, and why does it remain so tenacious today?

His answer is one that reconceives both the notion of power and how sexuality is tied to it. For Foucault, the history of sexuality is defined, not as a Freudian account of Victorian prudery would have it, by injunctions against talk about sex and specific sexual couplings in the bourgeois family, but by patterned discursive incitements and stimulations that facilitated the penetration of social and self-disciplinary regimes into the most intimate domains of modern life. Nor was that discourse initially designed to sublimate the sexual energy of exploited classes into productive labor, but first and foremost to set out the distinctions of bourgeois identity rooted in the sexual politics of the home. Central to Foucault's account of proliferating sexualities and discourses about them is the emergence of "biopower," a political technology that "brought life and its mechanisms into the realm of explicit calculations and made knowledge/power an agent of transformation of human life" (HS:143). In its specific nineteenth-century form, the disciplining of individual bodies and the regulations of the life processes of aggregate human populations "constituted the two poles around which the organization of power over life was deployed" (HS:139). Within this schema, technologies of sex played a critical role; sex occupied the discursive interface, linking the life of the individual to the life of the species as a whole (HS:146).

   While we have caught the gist of that message well—that discourses of sexuality and specific forms of power are inextricably bound, engagement with *The History of Sexuality* has been more formal than substantive, more suggestive than concrete. This is not to say that the parallels between the management of sexuality and the management of empire have been left unexplored.[5] Many students of colonialism have been quick to note that another crucial "Victorian" project—ruling colonies—entailed colonizing both bodies and minds. A number of studies, including my own, have turned on a similar premise that the discursive management of the sexual practices of colonizer and colonized was fundamental to the colonial order of things. We have been able to show how discourses of sexuality at once classified colonial subjects into distinct human kinds, while policing the domestic recesses of imperial rule.[6] But again, such readings take seriously the fact of a relationship between colonial power and the discourses of sexuality, without confirming or seriously challenging the specific chronologies Foucault offers, his critique of the repressive hypothesis, or the selective genealogical maps that his work suggests.

   In taking up each of these themes, this book both draws on Foucault

5. See, for example, John Kelly, *Politics of Virtue: Hinduism, Sexuality, and Countercolonial Discourse in Fiji* (Chicago: Chicago UP, 1991); Ronald Hyam, *Empire and Sexuality: The British Experience* (Manchester: Manchester UP, 1990); Vron Ware, *Beyond the Pale: White Women, Racism and History* (London: Verso, 1992); Luise White, *Comforts of Home: Prostitution in Colonial Nairobi* (Chicago: Chicago UP, 1990); and my own work on the sexual politics of Europeans in colonial Southeast Asia, "Carnal Knowledge and Imperial Power: Gender, Race and Morality in Colonial Asia" in Micaela di Leonardo, ed., *Gender at the Crossroads of Knowledge: Feminist Anthropology in a Postmodern Era* (Berkeley: U of California P, 1991): 51–101, and "Sexual Affronts and Racial Frontiers: European Identities and the Cultural Politics of Exclusion in Colonial Southeast Asia," *Comparative Studies in Society and History* 34.2 (July 1992): 514–51.

6. Also see Asuncion Lavrin, ed., *Sexuality and Marriage in Colonial Latin America* (Lincoln: U of Nebraska P, 1989); Mary Louise Pratt, *Imperial Eyes: Travel Writing and Transculturation* (London: Routledge, 1992) esp. chapter 5; and Vincente Rafael, *Contracting Colonialism* (Ithaca: Cornell UP, 1988) that deals specifically with sexuality and confession in the Philippines under Spanish rule.

and extends his analysis.[7] On the one hand, I look to how his insights play out in a colonial setting; on the other, I suggest that a wider imperial context resituates the work of racial thinking in the making of European bourgeois identity in a number of specific ways. While many historians have dismissed Foucault's empirical work as hopelessly wrong, and anthropologists, as well as other social analysts, taken with his theoretical insights have tended to treat his specific historical claims as less relevant, I question whether issues of historiography and theory can be so neatly disengaged. I pursue here a critique of Foucault's chronologies, a species of the empirical, not to quibble over dates but rather to argue that the discursive and practical field in which nineteenth-century bourgeois sexuality emerged was situated on an imperial landscape where the cultural accoutrements of bourgeois distinction were partially shaped through contrasts forged in the politics and language of race. I trace how certain colonial prefigurings contest and force a reconceptualizing of Foucault's sexual history of the Occident and, more generally, a rethinking of the historiographic conventions that have bracketed histories of "the West."

Clearly the latter is not my venture alone. A collective impulse of the last decade of post-colonial scholarship has been precisely to disassemble the neat divisions that could imagine a European history and its unified collectivities apart from the externalized Others on whom it was founded and which it produced. And Foucault's metatheory has played no small part in that project, animating a critique of how specific and competing forms of knowledge have carved out the exclusionary principles of imperial power in the first place. What is striking is how consistently Foucault's own framing of the European bourgeois order has been exempt from the very sorts of criticism that his insistence on the fused regimes of knowledge/power would seem to encourage and allow.[8] Why have we been so willing to

---

7. While more clarity might have been achieved by separating out these efforts, I have chosen to treat them simultaneously throughout this book, signaling where appropriate my different stances vis-à-vis Foucault's analysis: where I think his analysis opens or precludes a discussion of racism, where he allows for it but does not pursue it himself, and where my analysis challenges his own.

8. Although Edward Said, for example, notes that "Foucault ignores the imperial context of his own theories," his critique of Foucault's "imagination of power" and its "minimization of resistance" takes on the theoretical imbalances of the work less than the historical skewing of his European-bound frame. See "Foucault and the Imagination of Power," *Foucault: A Critical Reader*,

accept his story of a nineteenth-century sexual order that systematically excludes and/or subsumes the fact of colonialism within it? To say that Foucault was a product of his discipline, his locale, his time may be generous, but beside the point. Colonial studies in the 1970s in England, the U.S., and France may have had little as yet to say about the relationship between colonial power and sexuality, but it had a lot to say about western imperial expansion, culture, and the production of disciplinary knowledge.[9]

Several basic questions remain. What happens to Foucault's chronologies when the technologies of sexuality are refigured in an imperial field? Was the obsessive search for the "truth about sex" in the eighteenth and nineteenth centuries directly culled from earlier confessional models, as Foucault claims, or was this "truth about sex" recast around the invention of other truth claims, specifically those working through the language of race? While we might comfortably concur with Foucault that a discourse of sexuality was incited and activated as an instrument of power in the nineteenth century, we might still raise a basic question: a discourse about whom? His answer is clear: it was a discourse that produced four "objects of knowledge that were also targets and anchorage points of the ventures of knowledge" (HS:105), with specific technologies around them: the masturbating child of the bourgeois family, the "hysterical woman," the Malthusian couple, and the perverse adult. But students of empire would surely add at least one more. Did any of these figures exist as objects of knowledge and discourse in the nineteenth century without a racially erotic counterpoint, without reference to the libidinal energies of

ed. David C. Hoy (London: Basil Blackwell, 1986). Similarly, Robert Young's carefully argued assault on "white mythologies" of the West graciously lets Foucault off the hook by suggesting that his "position on the relations of Western humanism to colonialism would no doubt be similar to that outlined in his discussion of the relation of ethnography to colonialism in The Order of Things" (376–7). Robert Young, White Mythologies: Writing History and the West (London: Routledge, 1990) 195. For others who draw on Foucault's discursive analysis for treating empire and its discourses of sexuality without querying the specific historicity assumed for those discourses see Lisa Lowe, Critical Terrains: French and British Orientalisms (Ithaca: Cornell UP, 1991); Sara Mills, Discourses of Differences: An Analysis of Women's Travel Writing and Colonialism (London: Routledge, 1991); and Ronald Hyam, Empire and Sexual Opportunity (Manchester: Manchester UP, 1991).

9. See, among others, Dell Hymes, ed. Reinventing Anthropology (New York: Random House, 1969); Talal Asad, ed. Anthropology and the Colonial Encounter (New York: Humanities Press, 1973); Gerard LeClerc, Anthropologie et Colonialisme (Paris: Fayard, 1972); and Gerald Berreman, The Politics of Truth: Essays in Critical Anthropology (New Delhi: South Asian Publishers, 1981), especially chapter 2, written in 1970.

the savage, the primitive, the colonized—reference points of difference, critique, and desire? At one level, these are clearly contrapuntal as well as indexical referents, serving to bolster Europe's bourgeois society and to underscore what might befall it in moral decline. But they were not that alone. The sexual discourse of empire and of the biopolitic state in Europe were mutually constitutive: their "targets" were broadly imperial, their regimes of power synthetically bound.

My rereading of The History of Sexuality thus rests on two basic contentions, central to much recent work in colonial studies. First, that Europe's eighteenth- and nineteenth-century discourses on sexuality, like other cultural, political, or economic assertions, cannot be charted in Europe alone. In short-circuiting empire, Foucault's history of European sexuality misses key sites in the production of that discourse, discounts the practices that racialized bodies, and thus elides a field of knowledge that provided the contrasts for what a "healthy, vigorous, bourgeois body" was all about. Europe's eighteenth-century discourses on sexuality can—indeed must—be traced along a more circuitous imperial route that leads to nineteenth-century technologies of sex. They were refracted through the discourses of empire and its exigencies, by men and women whose affirmations of a bourgeois self, and the racialized contexts in which those confidences were built, could not be disentangled. I thus approach The History of Sexuality through several venues by comparing its chronologies and strategic ruptures to those in the colonies and by looking at these inflections on a racially charged ground. But, as importantly, I argue that a "comparison" between these two seemingly dispersed technologies of sex in colony and in metropole may miss the extent to which these technologies were bound.

My second contention is that the racial obsessions and refractions of imperial discourses on sexuality have not been restricted to bourgeois culture in the colonies alone. By bringing the discursive anxieties and practical struggles over citizenship and national identities in the nineteenth century back more squarely within Foucault's frame, bourgeois identities in both metropole and colony emerge tacitly and emphatically coded by race. Discourses of sexuality do more than define the distinctions of the bourgeois self; in identifying marginal members of the body politic, they have mapped the moral parameters of European nations. These deeply sedimented discourses on sexual morality could redraw the "interior frontiers" of national communities, frontiers that were secured through—and sometimes in collision with—the boundaries of race. These nationalist discourses were predicated on exclusionary cultural principles that did more than divide the middle class from the poor. They marked out those whose claims to property rights, citizenship, and public relief were worthy of recognition and whose were not.

Nationalist discourse drew on and gave force to a wider politics of exclusion. This version was not concerned solely with the visual markers of difference, but with the relationship between visible characteristics and invisible properties, outer form and inner essence. Assessment of these untraceable identity markers could seal economic, political, and social fates. Imperial discourses that divided colonizer from colonized, metropolitan observers from colonial agents, and bourgeois colonizers from their subaltern compatriots designated certain cultural competencies, sexual proclivities, psychological dispositions, and cultivated habits. These in turn defined the hidden fault lines—both fixed and fluid—along which gendered assessments of class and racial membership were drawn. Within the lexicon of bourgeois civility, self-control, self-discipline, and self-determination were defining features of bourgeois selves in the colonies. These features, affirmed in the ideal family milieu, were often transgressed by sexual, moral, and racial contaminations in those same European colonial homes. Repression was clearly part of this story, but as Foucault argues, it was subsumed by something more. These discourses on self-mastery were productive of racial distinctions, of clarified notions of "whiteness" and what it meant to be truly European. These discourses provided the working categories in which an imperial division of labor was clarified, legitimated, and—when under threat—restored.

If this rerouting of the history of sexuality through the history of empire makes analytic sense, then we must ask whether the racial configurations of that imperial world, rather than being peripheral to the cultivation of the nineteenth-century bourgeois self, were not constitutive of it. In this perspective, racism in the nineteenth century may not have been "anchored" in European technologies of sex as Foucault claims. If sexuality and the social taxonomies of race were mutually built out of a "more comprehensive history of exclusive biological categories,"[10] as Tom Laqueur

10. Tom Laqueur, *Making Sex: Body and Gender from the Greeks to Freud* (Cambridge: Harvard UP, 1990) 155. Also see Collette Guillaumin's "The Idea of Race and its Elevation to Autonomous Scientific and Legal Status," *Sociological Theories: Race and Colonialism* (Paris: UNESCO, 1980), which makes a

claims, then we should see race and sexuality as ordering mechanisms that shared their emergence with the bourgeois order of the early nineteenth century, "that beginning of the modern age."[11] Such a perspective figures race, racism, and its representations as structured entailments of post-enlightenment universals, as formative features of modernity, as deeply embedded in bourgeois liberalism, not as aberrant offshoots of them.[12] My concern here is not to isolate racism's originary moment, much less to claim that all racisms are fundamentally the same. On the contrary, I grant slippage among the projects that modernity, the enlightenment and bourgeois liberalism embraced to make another sort of point, one that appreciates both how racial thinking harnesses itself to varied progressive projects and shapes the social taxonomies defining who will be excluded from them.

My colonial reading is of a particular kind, neither definitive nor comprehensive. It is not a reading of alternative cultural conceptions of sexuality, nor an encyclopedic account of how colonized bodies were shaped by the sexual policies of colonial states. It does not track the subversive ways in which different segments of colonized populations have appropriated the civilities imposed upon them and reread those moral injunctions against their European grain, a task that others have done so well.[13] My

---

similar point while arguing more generally that the historical rise of legal individuality gave rise to the legal notion of race, see esp. 46–49.

11. Foucault, The Order of Things xxii.

12. See Henry Louis Gates, Jr., introduction, "Race," Writing, and Difference (Chicago: U of Chicago P, 1986) 3; Michael Banton, The Idea of Race (London: Tavistock, 1977) esp. chapter 2, "The intellectual inheritance," 12–26; Collette Guillaumin, "Idea of Race"; George Mosse, Toward the Final Solution: A History of European Racism (Madison: U of Wisconsin P, 1978); Leon Poliakov, The Aryan Myth: A History of Racist and Nationalist Ideas in Europe (London: Heineman, 1974); Zygmunt Bauman, Modernity and the Holocaust (Ithaca: Cornell UP, 1989). Many of these arguments have been recently synthesized by David Goldberg in Racist Culture: Philosophy and the Politics of Meaning (Oxford: Blackwell, 1993).

13. While in this project colonialism is seen through a European optic but not determined by it, it is still a limitation imposed by the particular circuits I have set out to view. For a different treatment that more fully explores imperial taxonomies and their colonized appropriations see my introduction with Frederick Cooper, "Between metropole and colony: Rethinking a Research Agenda," Tensions of Empire: Colonial Cultures in a Bourgeois World, eds. Frederick Cooper and Ann Laura Stoler (Berkeley: U of California P, forthcoming) and Ann Stoler, "In Cold Blood: Hierarchies of Credibility and the Politics of Colonial Narratives," Representations 37 (1992): 151–189. It is important to underscore that I am making no claim that Foucault's history of European

task is more specifically focused and constrained. It is an effort to see what Foucault's work adds to our understanding of the bourgeois casting of European colonials and their categories of rule and in turn what ways the political configurations of European colonial cultures might bring a new understanding to *The History of Sexuality.*

In exploring the making of a European colonial bourgeois order, I draw primarily on a colonial context with which I am most familiar: the Dutch East Indies in the nineteenth and early twentieth centuries. But Dutch colonial anxieties over the meanings of "Dutchness" and its bourgeois underpinnings also provide a touchstone for wider claims. Well aware of the peculiarities that distinguish Dutch, French, and British notions of what it meant to be bourgeois, I am nevertheless convinced that the construction of bourgeois sensibilities in these varied contexts are comparable in some fundamental ways. In chapter 4, I argue that each defined their unique civilities through a language of difference that drew on images of racial purity and sexual virtue. That language of difference conjured up the supposed moral bankruptcy of culturally dissonant populations, distinguishing them from the interests of those who ruled. For each, bourgeois morality was strategically allied with the moral authority of nineteenth-century liberal states. European bourgeois orders produced a multiplicity of discourses that turned on the dangers of "internal enemies," of class, sexual and racial origin, an argument that Foucault will also make as he traces the genealogy of racism in his Collège de France lectures. As Geoff Eley notes, in nineteenth-century Europe's bourgeois discourse

---

bourgeois sexuality nor my reworking of his genealogy of that history is generalizable to other cultural contexts, or could be mapped on to the histories of sexuality, power, and truth claims about the self among specific subjugated populations in the nineteenth-century colonized world. Those histories cannot be "read off" European ones. This does not mean, however, that consideration of these imperial articulations are irrelevant to these other cultural and political configurations. On the contrary, the particular distribution of differences that helped construct what was dominant and bourgeois for imperial Europe may be important for understanding how colonized populations claimed entitlements and strategically moved against the colonial state. It is not these imperial framings that are mirrored but the ways that concepts are organized within them that become available for oppositional political projects. Partha Chatterjee's analyses of such appropriations in *Nationalist Thought and the Colonial World: A Derivative Discourse* (London: Zed, 1986) and *The Nation and Its Fragments* (Princeton: Princeton UP, 1993) are obvious and exemplary cases in point.

citizenship was "a faculty to be learned and a privilege to be earned."[14] These discourses were peopled with surreptitious invaders in the body politic, "fictive" Frenchmen, "fabricated" Dutchmen, anglicized but not "true" British citizens who threatened to traverse both the colonial and metropolitan "interior frontiers" of nation-states.[15] In short, that discourse on bourgeois selves was founded on what Foucault would call a particular "grid of intelligibility," a hierarchy of distinctions in perception and practice that conflated, substituted, and collapsed the categories of racial, class and sexual Others strategically and at different times. Nor is this attention to the working of race through the language of class as dissonant with Foucault's project as his published legacy of writings might suggest. In his Collège de France lectures discussed in chapter 3, Foucault traces the derivation of a nineteenth-century language of class from an earlier discourse of races as a key element in the changing historiography of Europe itself.

In outlining some of the genealogical shifts eclipsed in Foucault's tunnel vision of the West, I focus on certain specific domains in which a discourse of sexuality articulated with the politics of race. I use the Indies to illustrate—and really only to hint at here—how a cultivation of the European self (and specifically a Dutch bourgeois identity) was affirmed in the proliferating discourses around pedagogy, parenting, children's sexuality, servants, and tropical hygiene: micro-sites where designations of racial membership were subject to gendered appraisals and where "character," "good breeding," and proper rearing were implicitly raced. These discourses do more than prescribe suitable behavior; they locate how fundamentally bourgeois identity has been tied to notions of being "European" and being "white" and how sexual prescriptions served to secure and delineate the authentic, first-class citizens of the nation-state. Crucial to my argument, and distinct from Foucault's self-referential conception

14. See Geoff Eley's "Liberalism, Europe, and the Bourgeoisie" in David Blackburn and Richard Evans, eds., *The German Bourgeoisie* (London: Routledge, 1991) 300.

15. See Etienne Balibar, "Paradoxes of Universality" in David Goldberg, ed., *Anatomy of Racism* (Minneapolis: U of Minnesota P, 1990), where he discusses how racism "embarks on the obsessive quest for a [national] 'core,'" based largely on "criteria of social class," 284–5. Also see Balibar, "Fichte and the Internal Border: On *Addresses to the German Nation*," in *Masses, Classes, Idea: Studies on Politics and Philosophy before and after Marx* (London: Routledge, 1994) 61–86 where the political ambiguities of Fichte's notion of an "interior frontier" are spelled out.

of bourgeois identity, I stress the *relational* terms in which bourgeois selves have been conceived.

In short, I make three sorts of arguments. The first concerns chronology: why Foucault situates "the birth of racism" in the late nineteenth century and what the consequences of that placement are. Part of the answer can be found in *The History of Sexuality*, but more of it in the lectures delivered in 1976 at the Collège de France when that volume was in press. Second, I argue that an implicit racial grammar underwrote the sexual regimes of bourgeois culture in more ways than Foucault explored and at an earlier date. Here, I cast a wide net drawing on an emergent post-colonial scholarship whose forays into what were once construed as the margins of Western historiography have begun to unravel its core. I draw my argument in part from the Dutch colonial archival record. In that record, the ambiguities of racial categories and the uncertainties of Dutch identity in the nineteenth-century Indies were explicitly debated in terms setting out the racial dangers of desire, the class coordinates of "true" Europeans, and the cultural competencies which the conferral of European status required.

Third, in attending to "tensions of empire" that cut across the dichotomies of colonizer and colonized, colony and core, I reconnect a range of domains that have been treated discretely in colonial scripts, divisions that students of colonialism have often subscribed to themselves. How, for example, have Dutch historians come to think that the racial mapping of state-funded relief for poor whites in the Indies is irrelevant to liberal discourse on poor relief in nineteenth-century Holland? What allows French historians to dissect the anxieties over French national identity at the turn of the century without tackling the heated debates waged over the legal category of mixed-bloods in French Indochina in the same period? Why have both students of European and colonial histories treated bourgeois "civilizing missions" in metropole and colony as though they were independent projects for so long?

One might argue, as Robert Young does, that the collective vision in Euro-American scholarship has been blurred by "white mythologies" of history writing in the West.[16] But what would constitute a successful effort to write against those mythologies is not self-evident. It could not, for example, merely "compare" metropolitan and colonial reform to show that

16. Young, *White Mythologies*.

their political meanings are the same. It would not be to assume that the discourse on paternity suits in Haiphong and Paris and the debates over "child abandonment" in Amsterdam and Batavia have the same political valence. Rather, I think we should ask, as Foucault did in other contexts, how seemingly shared vocabularies of sexual and social reform may sometimes remain the same and sometimes diverge and/or transpose into distinct and oppositional political meanings. Foucault turns to this process in *The History of Sexuality* with respect to the discourses of sexuality and again even more boldly as he traces the strategic mobility of racial discourses in his lectures. In each of these projects, Foucault offers ways to rethink the colonial order of things, ways that challenge—and sometimes derive from—him.

Tracking Empire in The History of Sexuality

For a long time, the story goes, we supported a Victorian regime, and we continue to be dominated by it even today. Thus the image of the imperial prude is emblazoned on our restrained, mute, and hypocritical sexuality. (HS:3)

Students of empire have shown little interest in the historical ruptures and periodicities in which new technologies of sex develop and in Foucault's rejection of Freud's repressive hypothesis. If anything, as I show later, we have had contradictory allegiances on the one hand, to a Foucauldian perspective on power, and on the other, to implicit Freudian assumptions about the psychodynamics of empire, the sexual energies "released," and the ways such regimes extend and work. We have been profoundly silent on the "four strategic unities" that Foucault placed at the core of eighteenth-century technologies of sex: the hysterizing of women's bodies, the pedagogic expertise applied to children's sexuality, the socialization of procreative life, and the psychiatric analytics of perverse pleasure (HS:104–105). Are these intense sites of power relevant to imperial history or beside the point? And, if they are relevant, why has so little been said about them? More strikingly, in a thematic close to the ethnological turf of kinship, Foucault identifies an eighteenth-century shift from a "deployment of alliance" to a "deployment of sexuality" that marks the modern character of power. Yet this too has fallen quietly and nearly without comment on an anthropological audience.

Some of the problems reside in Foucault's work, some are lodged in our own. *The History of Sexuality* at one level seems to impede such a venture. Foucault explicitly traces the deployment of sexuality within an analytic field confined to the metropole—to "modern western sexuality." We are offered a distinction between "erotic art" (*ars erotica*) of the Orient, and a "science of sexuality" (*scientia sexualis*) of the West. (HS:70–71) The image of the "imperial prude" in the opening paragraph, cited earlier, of volume 1, is the first and only reference to the fact of empire. For Foucault, the image of the prude is a mainstay of our misguided reading of nineteenth-century sexuality. Empire is a backdrop of Victorian ideology, and contemporary stories about it, easily dismissed and not further discussed.[17] The "prude" is replaced; empire disappears along with its caricature. The incitement to sexual discourse in eighteenth- and nineteenth-century Europe historicizes a European matter *tout court*. Foucault traces the biopolitics that emerged in the early 1700s and flourished in nineteenth-century Europe along axes that are sui generis to Europe, what Gayatri Spivak rightly has dismissed as a self-contained version of history, only about the West.[18] James Clifford's observation that Foucault was "scrupulously ethnocentric"[19] might give some confidence that he assiduously confined himself to the epistemic field of Europe, but when dealing with the issue of race, such careful containment should give us pause. His genealogies of nineteenth-century bourgeois identity are not only deeply rooted in a self-referential western culture but bounded by Europe's geographic parameters.[20]

Such origin myths of European culture are less credible today, as the bracketed domain of European history has been pried open, its sources reassessed, its boundaries blurred. Nearly two decades after *The History of Sexuality* first appeared, as colonial studies has moved from a delimited concern with colonialism's consequences for the colonized to tensions

17. See Edward Said, *Culture and Imperialism* (New York: Knopf, 1993) where he explores this presence/absence of empire in European literature.
18. Gayatri Spivak, "Can the Subaltern Speak" in Cary Nelson and Lawrence Grossberg, eds., *Marxism and the Interpretation of Culture* (Urbana: U of Illinois P, 1988).
19. James Clifford, *The Predicament of Culture* (Cambridge: Harvard UP, 1988) 265.
20. It is not only that empire is excluded, but Europe itself is defined by those powerfully situated within it, i.e. by its *northern* European parameters. Thus Spain and Portugal are sometimes eclipsed while Europe largely refers to England, Germany and France. See Fernando Coronil's "Beyond Occidentalism: Towards Non-Imperial Geohistorical Categories" *Cultural Anthropology* (forthcoming) where he deals with the skewed geopolitics that has constituted what we conceive of as "Europe" and the proper domain of European history. Also see Deny Hay, *Europe: The Emergence of an Idea* (Edinburgh: Edinburgh UP, 1957).

that cut across metropolitan and colonial sites of imperial rule, we are prompted to query whether the shaping of nineteenth-century bourgeois subjects can be located outside those force fields in which imperial knowledge was promoted and desiring subjects were made. It was after all Foucault who placed the connections among the production of specific knowledges, forms of power, and expressions of desire at the center of his work.[21] Armed with Foucault's impulse to write a history of Western desire that rejects desire as biological instinct or as a response to repressive prohibitions, we should be pushed to ask what other desires are excluded from his account, to question how shifts in the imperial distributions of desiring male subjects and desired female objects might reshape that story as well.[22]

As we have begun to explore the colonies as more than sites of exploitation but as "laboratories of modernity," the genealogical trajectories mapping what constitutes metropolitan versus colonial inventions have precipitously shifted course.[23] With this redirection, the hallmarks of European cultural production have been sighted in earlier ventures of empire and sometimes in the colonies first. Thus, Sidney Mintz has suggested that the disciplinary strategies of large-scale industrial production may have been worked out in the colonies before they were tried out in European contexts.[24] Timothy Mitchell has placed the panopticon, that supreme model institution of disciplinary power, as a colonial invention that first appeared in the Ottoman Empire, not Northern Europe.[25] French

21. As Arnold Davidson notes in "Sex and the Emergence of Sexuality," *Critical Inquiry* 17 (1987): 16–48.
22. Feminist critics of Foucault have posed this question more generally, but without specific reference to empire. See, for example, Teresa de Lauretis, *Technologies of Gender* (Bloomington: Indiana UP, 1987); Judith Butler, *Gender Trouble* (London: Routledge, 1990); Biddy Martin, "Feminism, Criticism, and Foucault," *New German Critique* 27 (Fall 1987): 3–30; Edith Kurzweil, "Michel Foucault's History of Sexuality as Interpreted by Feminists and Marxists," *Social Research* 53.4 (Winter 1986): 647–63; Caroline Ramazanoglu, ed., *Up Against Foucault: Explorations of Some Tensions between Foucault and Feminism* (New York: Routledge, 1993); Lois McNay, *Foucault and Feminism* (Boston: Northeastern UP, 1992); Jana Sawicki, *Disciplining Foucault: Feminism, Power and the Body* (New York: Routledge,1991).
23. See Gwendolyn Wright, *The Politics of Design in French Colonial Urbanism* (Chicago: U of Chicago P, 1991) and Paul Rabinow's *French Modern* (Berkeley: U of California P, 1989) for different elaborations of this notion.
24. Sidney Mintz, *Sweetness and Power* (New York: Viking, 1985).
25. Timothy Mitchell, *Colonising Egypt* (Berkeley: U of California P, 1991) 35.

policies on urban planning were certainly experimented with in Paris and
Toulouse, but as both Gwendolyn Wright and Paul Rabinow have each so
artfully shown, probably in Rabat and Haiphong first.[26] Mary Louise Pratt
stretches back further and argues that modes of social discipline taken
to be quintessentially European may have been inspired by seventeenth-
century imperial ventures and only then refashioned for the eighteenth-
century bourgeois order.[27] Nicholas Dirks has raised the possibility that
the very concept of "culture is a colonial formation."[28] These reconfigured
histories have pushed us to rethink European cultural genealogies across
the board and to question whether the key symbols of modern western societies—liberalism, nationalism, state welfare, citizenship, culture,
and "Europeanness" itself—were not clarified among Europe's colonial
exiles and by those colonized classes caught in their pedagogic net in Asia,
Africa and Latin America, and only then brought "home."[29] In sorting out
these colonial etiologies of Western culture and its reformist gestures, one
cannot help but ask whether Foucault's genealogy of bourgeois identity
and its biopolitics might also be traced through imperial maps of wider
breadth that locate racial thinking and notions of "whiteness" as formative
and formidable coordinates of them.

In an interview in 1976, responding to a question posed by the Italian
journalist, Duccio Trombadori, as to whether he saw his books as a set of
"teachings," as a "discourse that prescribes," Foucault answered:

> In my case it's another matter entirely; my books don't have this kind
> of value. They function as invitations, as public gestures, for those

26. Wright, The Politics of Design; Rabinow, French Modern.

27. Pratt, Imperial Eyes: 36.

28. Nicholas Dirks, Colonialism and Culture (Ann Arbor: U of Michigan P, 1991) 3.

29. On liberalism and British India see Uday Mehta's "Liberal Strategies of Exclusion," Politics and Society 18.4 (Dec. 1990): 427–454; on "culture as a colonial formation" see Nicholas Dirks, "Intro-duction: Colonialism and Culture" in Colonialism and Culture; on urban planning see Rabinow, French Modern and Wright, Politics of Design; on empire, citizenship and emergent welfare politics see my "Sexual Affronts and Racial Frontiers," Comparative Studies in Society and History 34.2 (July 1992): 514–51 and "The Politics of Mothercare: Poor Whites and the Subversion of the Colo-nial State," Chapter 5 of Carnal Knowledge and Imperial Power: Bourgeois Civilities and the Cultivation of Racial Categories in Colonial Southeast Asia (Berkeley: U of California P, forthcoming); on national-ism see Benedict Anderson, Imagined Communities (London: Verso, 1983) and "Fax Nationalism" (manuscript); on Europeanness see Stoler, "Rethinking Colonial Categories," Comparative Studies in Society and History 13.1 (1989): 134–61 and Daniel Segal, " 'The European': Allegories of Racial

who may want eventually to do the same thing, or something like it, or, in any case, who intend to slip into this kind of experience.[30]

The History of Sexuality is a schematic blueprint for what Foucault had intended to write but chose not to complete. Thus even more than The Order of Things which Foucault hoped would be read as an "open site," in volume 1 he extends that invitation for openness more explicitly than in many of his other works.[31] However prescriptive that may be, it leaves us with more provocations than closely crafted arguments and a surprising number of conventions to wade through should we accept his invitation. My own response to Foucault's "public gesture" has been to do "something like it," something which, as he might have anticipated, would not come out at all the same. In rereading The History of Sexuality in an unexplored colonial light, "off center court" as Ben Anderson once put it, I suppose there is some implicit desire to cast this book as an opening, as a provocation, as an invitation of my own.[32]

In that spirit, I turn in the beginning of chapter 2, to the proliferation of sexualities and racisms that underwrote Europe's nineteenth-century bourgeois orders in an effort to address a basic question: how Foucault could write an effective history of sexuality, one that earmarks racism as one of its crucial products, but that has had so little resonance for theorizing racial formations today. The bulk of that chapter attends to the place of racism in volume 1 and offers a colonial mapping of it. Chapter 3 focuses almost exclusively on his 1976 lectures on race at the Collège de France. I look at how the lectures inform his treatment of racism in The History of Sexuality and in what unexpected ways they allow a rethinking of his broader analytic project. Chapter 4 takes up one of Foucault's central concerns in The History of Sexuality; namely, his claim that technologies of sexuality were a core component in the making and cultivation of the bourgeois self. I question less that assumption than the racialized making of it.[33] Chap-

Purity," Anthropology Today 7.5 (Oct. 1991): 7–9. On the flattened histories that "occidentalism" has produced (with Sidney Mintz's and Eric Wolf's work offered as striking examples) see Fernando Coronil, "Beyond Occidentalism: Toward Non-Imperial Geohistorical Categories," Cultural Anthropology, (forthcoming).

30. Foucault, Remarks on Marx (New York: Semiotext(e), 1991) 40.
31. Foucault, The Order of Things, xii.
32. Anderson, Imagined Communities.
33. Foucault uses the term "bourgeoisie," "bourgeois class," and "bourgeois affirmation of self"

ter 5 expands on a theme to which Foucault had planned to devote an entire volume; namely, the discourse on masturbating children and why it so concerned the bourgeoisie. I take up the discourse on masturbation with a different emphasis than Foucault's that in turn leads my discussion toward another end. The colonial variant of that discourse on children and their sexual desires was more about the cultural transgressions of women servants and native mothers than about children themselves, less about the pedagogy surrounding children's sexuality than the racialization of it. Chapter 6 engages Foucault and colonial studies on a subject which at once underwrites *The History of Sexuality* and is absent from it: namely, the production of desire. My interest is in the distributions of desire, an issue which Foucault's apparent dismissal of Freud's focus on sexual desire would seem to preclude. In the concluding chapter, I pose two sorts of questions: first, how *The History of Sexuality* and the lectures on race might be differently located within Foucault's broader projects, and second, how such locations inform new ways we might write "effective histories of the present" in colonial studies today.

throughout volume 1 of *The History of Sexuality* without ever defining what he means by those terms. I use these terms as well but resist the impulse to fill in for Foucault or provide a fixed alternative definition on the argument that what constituted the "bourgeois self" and its "self affirmation" was relational and tied to historically specific notions of gender, nation, and race, not class alone. This book may be seen as an effort to identify the changing parameters of a bourgeois self that were contingent on a racially, sexually, and morally distinct range of other human kinds. While this may be frustrating to the reader, it serves to underscore the mobile discourses of dominance in which bourgeois priorities were defined and defended and in which cultural and economic vulnerabilities were perceived.

II

PLACING RACE IN THE HISTORY OF SEXUALITY

An inducement for students of colonialism to work out Foucault's genealogies on a broader imperial map should be spurred simply by their
glaring absence. It is even more disturbing that such a crucial element of
The History of Sexuality that does speak directly to the nineteenth-century
imperial world has been so conspicuously ignored. This is Foucault's strategic linking of the history of sexuality to the construction of race. The
omission is not that by students of colonialism alone. While references to
racism appear in virtually every chapter, few of Foucault's interlocutors
have considered them for comment or review.[1] None of the three recent

1. Among the many well-argued reviews and articles that deal critically with volume 1 of *The
History of Sexuality* but with no reference to its treatment of race see, for example, Eloise Buker,
"Hidden Desires and Missing Persons: A Feminist Deconstruction of Sexuality," *Western Politi-
cal Quarterly* 43 (1990): 811–32; Manthia Diawara, "Reading Africa through Foucault: Mudimbe's
Reaffirmation of the Subject," *October* 55 (1990): 79–92; Lucette Finas, "Michel Foucault: Les
Rapport de pouvoir passent à l'intérieur des corps," *La Quinzaine Littérature* 247 (1977): 4–6; Al-
thar Hussain, "Foucault's History of Sexuality," *M/F* 5 (1981): 169–91; Edith Kurzweil, "Michel
Foucault's History of Sexuality as Interpreted by Feminists and Marxists," *Social Research* 53.4
(Winter 1986): 647–63; Bernard-Henry Levy, "Non au sexe roi," interview with Foucault, *Nouvel
Observateur* 644 (1977); Biddy Martin, "Feminism, Criticism, and Foucault," *New German Critique* 27
(Fall 1987): 3–30; Alec McHoul, "The Getting of Sexuality: Foucault, Garfinkel and the Analysis
of Sexual Discourse," *Theory, Culture and Society* 3.2 (1986): 65–79; Allan Megill, *Prophets of Extremity:
Nietzsche, Heidegger, Foucault, Derrida* (Berkeley: U of California P, 1987); Claire O'Farrell, *Foucault:
Historian or Philospher* (London: Macmillan, 1989); Robert Padgug, "Sexual Matters: On Conceptu-
alizing Sexuality in History," *Passion and Power: Sexuality in History*, eds. Kathy Peiss and Christina
Simmons with Robert Padgug (Philadelphia: Temple UP, 1989); Carol A. Pollis, "The Apparatus of
Sexuality: Reflections on Foucault's Contributions to the Study of Sex in History," *Adversaria* 23.3
(1987): 401–14; Roy Porter, "Is Foucault Useful for Understanding Eighteenth and Nineteenth
Century Sexuality?" *Contention* 1 (1991): 61–82; Mark Poster, *Foucault, Marxism and History: Mode of

biographies of Foucault even index the subject of "racism."[2] From a wide range of interviews, book reviews and *explications du texte*, by philosophers, anthropologists, historians, journalists, and literary critics of varied critical persuasions, few address Foucault's attention to the "instrumentality" of sexuality in the making of race.[3] Even David Goldberg's recent study, *Racist Culture*, explicitly inspired by Foucault's analysis of discursive formations, never mentions Foucault's treatment of that subject.[4] Given this resounding silence, one might rightfully be more suspect of my peculiar reading of Foucault than of these prevailing omissions. There are, however, I think some good reasons to pursue the question further.

The silence seems unwarranted on several counts; most strikingly because the final two sections of *The History of Sexuality* deal directly with the intersection of sexuality, degeneracy, and racism within the emergence of the "biopolitical" state. In a 1977 interview, a rare instance when Foucault was asked to address the issue of racism directly, he somewhat cynically responded:

Production vs. Mode of Information (Cambridge: Polity Press, 1984); Uta Liebmann Schaub, "Foucault's Oriental Subtext," PMLA 104 (1989): 306–16; Victor Seidler, "Reason, Desire and Male Sexuality," The Cultural Construction of Sexuality, ed. Pat Caplan (London: Tavistock, 1987); Elinor Shaffer, "Book Review of The History of Sexuality, Vol.I," Signs (Summer 1980): 812–20; Pierre Sullivan, "Historie et sexualité: à propos de l'oeuvre de Michel Foucault," Revue Française de Psychoanalyse 5 (1984): 1441–1453; Jeffrey Weeks, Sex, Politics, and Society: The Regulation of Sexuality Since 1800 (London: Longman, 1981). Also see the interviews collected in Power/Knowledge: Selected Interviews and Other Writings 1972–1977. This list does not include those works I cite elsewhere. Alan Sheridan, Michel Foucault: The Will to Truth (London: Tavistock, 1980) 191–93, David R. Shumway, Michel Foucault (Boston: Twayne, 1989) 151, and Herbert Dreyfus and Paul Rabinow, Michel Foucault: Beyond Structuralism and Hermeneutics (Chicago: Chicago UP, 1983) 141 mention Foucault's discussion of racism in passing.

2. See Didier Eribon, Michel Foucault (Cambridge: Harvard UP, 1991); James Miller, The Passion of Michel Foucault (New York: Simon & Schuster, 1993); David Macey, The Lives of Michel Foucault (New York: Pantheon, 1993).

3. Etienne Balibar, "Foucault and Marx," delivered in 1988 at a Conference on Foucault in Paris. As Balibar notes "the place occupied by the problem of racism [in Foucault's work] . . . was considerable" (58).

4. David Theo Goldberg, Racist Culture: Philosophy and the Politics of Meaning (London: Blackwell, 1993). Also see Frank Dikötter's The Discourse of Race in Modern China (Stanford: Stanford UP, 1992) which, albeit far more influenced by Michael Banton's treatment of racial thinking, makes no reference to Foucault on race.

Yes, no one wants to talk about that last part. Even though the book is a short one, but I suspect people never got as far as this last chapter. All the same, it's the fundamental part of the book.[5]

Secondly, references to racism in The History of Sexuality are neither incidental nor perfunctory. They are carefully positioned, signposted if not elaborated, in parts 2, 3, 4, and 5. Nor should this be surprising. Volume 1 was, in its inception, a schematic overview of the six volumes Foucault had intended to write, with volume 6 (as advertised on the back cover of the first French edition) to be devoted to "Populations and Races."[6] That project was put aside by 1977 when Foucault turned back to Hellenic conceptions of sexuality and cultivations of the self that contrast modern forms. Even as a plan de recherche, volume 1 offers compelling insights into how Foucault conjoined the rise of racism and technologies of sex. But there is stronger evidence still that the subject of racism was of more than passing concern to Foucault's larger project. The lectures he gave at the Collège de France in 1976, when that first volume was just completed, were explicitly devoted to the nature of racial discourses and their shifting political semantics.

Thus from either the vantage point of Foucault's project or contemporary studies of racism, the silence of his interlocutors is strange. Etienne Balibar is one of the few to note Foucault's central concern with racism as "the most revealing concrete effect" of a biopolitics that bore on the species and its reproduction. In Balibar's reading, racism was the "crucial phenomenon" that biopolitics set out to explain.[7] John Rajchman similarly has remarked on Foucault's focus on the "scientific" notion of "degeneracy" as a category racially inflected through the technologies of sex.[8] Others, however, such as Abdul JanMohamed, have invoked Foucault's

5. Quoted in Michel Foucault, Power/Knowledge: Selected Interviews and Other Writings, 1972–1977 (New York: Pantheon, 1977) 222.

6. The six volumes were to be titled: 1. La volonté du savoir (The will to knowledge) 2. La chair et le corps (The flesh and the body) 3. La croisade des enfants (The children's crusade), 4. La femme, la mère et l'hystérique (The woman, the mother and the hysteric) 5. Les pervers (perverts) 6. Populations et races (populations and races).

7. Etienne Balibar, "Foucault et Marx: L'enjeu du nominalisme," Michel Foucault: Philosophe (Paris: Seuil, 1990), see esp. 58;66.

8. John Rajchman, Truth and Eros: Foucault, Lacan, and the Question of Ethics (New York: Routledge, 1991) 106–7.

analysis of bourgeois sexuality only to quickly dismiss it out of hand. JanMohamed's contention that Foucault's exclusive focus on the bourgeois forms of sexuality precludes an understanding of racialized sexuality seems to miss the very force of Foucault's argument. If the technologies of sexuality that shape bourgeois identity account for the rise of racism in its statist form, then it would seem that racialized sexuality is not outside this "class body" in the making, but, on the contrary, part and parcel of it.[9]

Without digressing at length into a social history of French intellectual pursuits of the 1970s, it still seems worth noting some of the contours of the political field in which Foucault's reflections could be heard at the time.[10] First of all, The History of Sexuality is not, of course, a book about racism. Its critique is directed against Marxist and Freudian analyses of society and its discontents and particularly against the repressive notion of power that he saw embraced in those accounts. More pointedly, it targeted Wilhelm Reich's and Herbert Marcuse's Freudian-Marxist celebration of sex as liberation from the repressive power of capitalism and its restrictive institutions. Foucault contested both of these interpretations. For him, on the contrary, power must be seen in its affirmative, knowledge-producing form, prompting a proliferation of discourses on sexuality and their effects, not their attenuation. It is the form of power generated by these discourses that shape his project; racism here is a consequence of them. In short, racism is not the subject of The History of Sexuality. Instead, it analyzes how a discourse of sexuality articulates and eventually incorporates a racist logic. This is the book's end-product. Racisms are not what Foucault analyzed; he looked rather to the ways in which a prior technology of sexuality provided a cultural susceptibility and discursive field for them.

Foucault's somewhat oblique treatment of the issue of racism may account for its lack of resonance. But then he was not the only one who failed to enlist the French intellectual left to take on these issues—nor is

9. Abdul R. JanMohamed, "Sexuality on/of the Racial Border, Foucault, Wright and the Articulation of 'Racialized Sexuality,'" Discourses of Sexuality, ed. Domna Stanton (Ann Arbor: U of Michigan P, 1992) 94–116.

10. For the most recent effort to map out the intellectual and political field in which Foucault's work was situated see Didier Eribon, Michel Foucault et ses contemporains (Paris: Gallimard, 1994). While Eribon marks 1970 and 1976 as two key moments when Foucault's project changed course, he makes no reference to the 1976 Collège de France lectures on race and Foucault's turn away from that subject in subsequent years.

it clear that such a task would have been his intent.[11] Although opposed to the wars in Indochina and Algeria, there is no indication that Foucault sought to situate his analysis of racism with respect to these political interventions.[12] He belonged to a generation whose political energies had been massively mobilized against the French government's efforts to keep Algeria under its tutelage. Many loudly supported France's colonized populations in the Algerian war.[13] While Albert Memmi, Frantz Fanon and Jean-Paul Sartre were among those who explicitly addressed colonial racism, they did not prompt a general theoretical engagement with racism nor a confrontation with the racial underpinnings of French society itself.[14] The concept of class and the sorts of social transformations to which capitalism gave rise remained foundational in critical social and political theory; race and racial theory was not.

But one could easily argue that such an effort to situate Foucault's knowledge and his reception are at best speculative, perhaps irrelevant. We might do better to look, not at the politics of intellectuals, but at the muted presence—some might argue, the absence—of a politics of race in Europe in the 1970s. Could Foucault have written an effective history of racism (as he had done for prisons, madness, and sexuality) in a political environment in which racial identity was accorded no positive force nor race a strategic space? In contrast to the United States, where the civil rights movement

11. Mark Lilla, in a review of Eribon's and Miller's biographies of Foucault, criticizes both for missing the crucial point that "Foucault was never a political leader: he was what the French call a suiviste." See "A Taste for Pain: Michel Foucault and the Outer Reaches of Human Experience," Times Literary Supplement 26 March 1993: 3–4.

12. On Foucault's opposition to French interventions in Indochina and the Algerian war, Miller makes passing reference. James Miller, The Passion of Michel Foucault (New York: Simon and Schuster, 1993) 57, 136.

13. Clearly the French left was not unambiguously anticolonial during the Algerian war—the left version of the civilizing mission was hard to overcome. On the different sorts of political engagements and positions taken on by French intellectuals during the Indochinese and Algerian wars see Paul Clay Sorum, Intellectuals and Decolonization in France (Chapel Hill: U of North Carolina P, 1977) and J.-P. Rioux and J.-F. Sirinelli, eds., La Guerre d'Algerie et les intellectuels français (Paris: Editions Complexe, 1991). Note that while intellectuals of the right who fought for a "French Algeria" identified their position with 19th century racist thinkers such as Renan and Vacher LaPouge, the left's defense of an independent Algeria was framed as an assault on imperialism more than on racism per se.

14. Albert Memmi, Portrait du colonisé (Paris: Payot, 1957); Frantz Fanon, The Wretched of the Earth (New York: Grove, 1963); Jean-Paul Sartre, La Critique de la Raison Dialectique (Paris: Gallimard, 1960).

prompted a generation of scholars to resituate racism as inherent to the inclusionary myths and exclusionary practices of democracy and freedom,[15] histories of European racism took a very different course. Such histories remained bracketed in specific stories: as a subtheme in the history of totalitarianism as in the influential work of Hannah Arendt, as a politically anesthetized, ahistorical field of "race relations" as in Britain, and perhaps most notably as a history of the horror of recent Nazi memory (as in Leon Poliakov's *The Aryan Myth*)—a cordoned off history of archaic origins, a history to dispose of, a narrative of the past.[16]

A radical rethinking of racism as inherent in the deep structure of Europe's *contemporary* social order has only emerged with the political force of "new racism" in the 1980s and in dialogue with the multiple constituencies voicing opposition. The "immigration problem" of England, Germany, Holland, and France, most vicious in the LePenist fears about its defiling of French cultural identity, has brought racist violence and a virulent discourse on racial contamination, "rootless" foreigners, and internal aliens back home.[17] But in this analysis too, Foucault is granted no part. Even the more recent wave of German scholarship that resituates Nazism as part of the " 'normal' achievement of respectable science" accords him no place. As Geoff Eley notes, Foucault could easily have been its "patron saint," but he is not.[18]

Leaving the psychodynamics of Foucault's choice of subject to his biographers, one might still argue that the absence of any reference to his work on race may in part derive from his own abrupt shifts in trajectory. While his forays in his 1976 lectures into "the origins of state racism" were both bold and counter-intuitive, they were shortlived. After a sabbatical

---

15. For the best example of an effort to tie the history of racism to the rise of democracy in the U.S. see Edmund Morgan, *American Slavery, American Freedom: The Ordeal of Colonial Virginia* (New York: Norton, 1975).

16. See Hannah Arendt, *The Origins of Totalitarianism* (New York: Harcourt and Brace, 1948). On the depoliticization of the "race relations" literature in Britain see Robert Miles, "Marxism Versus the 'Sociology of Race Relations'?" *Ethnic and Racial Studies* 7.2 (1984): 217–37. For the originary approach of Leon Poliakov see *The Aryan Myth* (London: Heineman, 1974).

17. See, most notably, Pierre-André Taguieff, *La force du préjugé: essai sur le racisme et ses doubles* (Paris: La Découverte, 1988); and "The National Front in France," *New Political Science* 16–17 (Fall/Winter 1989): 29–70. Also see Tore Björgo and Rob Witte, eds., *Racist Violence in Europe* (London: St. Martin's Press, 1993).

18. Geoff Eley, "Scholarship Serving the Nazi State I; Studying the East," *Ethnic and Racial Studies* 12.4 (1989): 576.

in 1977, his 1977–78 course at the Collège de France surprised associates, students, and friends.[19] The transformation he had explored in 1976 from a "discourse on the war of races" to "state racism" never appears again, and the genealogy of racism was not pursued further. By 1978, "governmentality" took its place entirely, leading Foucault back to sex in the governing and care of the self. As one of Foucault's associates told James Miller, "the [1978] course did not go as planned."[20] This may have been a period of "crisis" for Foucault, as some have claimed, following the "quiet" reception of volume 1 by some, and its more scathing dismissal by others, the latter reflected in extremis by Baudrillard's 1977 piece, Forget Foucault.[21] What we do know is that there was a radical shift in the historical period on which he worked, a different weighting of his analytic focus, marked by a clean erasure of the question of racism from his project.

The suggestion of one of Foucault's close associates that he was possibly "deadlocked" on thinking about race may be on the mark.[22] The discrepancy between The History of Sexuality and the lectures on racism is striking. While the former alludes to linkages between racism and technologies of sexuality (that were to be pursued in later volumes), in the lectures biopower, not sexuality, frames his argument. The explicit link between racism and the bourgeois order is no longer there. The lectures take off from another vantage point entirely. They trace the "polyvalent mobility" of a discourse of races through a number of minor and major figures in European historiography. On the other hand, Foucault centrally positions the discourses of race in a way he had never done before. The specificity of the late nineteenth-century racism alluded to in The History of Sexuality is no longer assumed but engaged directly.

Even if we could account for the reception of this part of his work two decades ago, it does not explain the silence now. Today, when critiques of the essentialist underpinnings of racial and sexual identities are so well incorporated into intellectual and political agendas, few have drawn directly from him. I return to the lectures in the following chapter. Here I invoke them to make a specific point; namely, that the attribution to Foucault of a concern with racism is not merely a presentist reading of his work.

19. Miller, The Passion of Michel Foucault 299.

20. Miller 299.

21. See Macey, Lives of Michel Foucault, 358 on the "quiet welcome," and Jean Baudrillard, Forget Foucault (New York: Semiotext, 1977).

22. Personal communication, January 1994.

Racism is a complex, if elusive subtext of it. Before turning to the lectures in chapter 3, I outline how Foucault saw the relationship between racism and discourses of sexuality in The History of Sexuality and suggest some of the dissonances that emerge when the economics of colonial racism is joined with his account.

Discourses of Sexuality and Racism in The History of Sexuality

Foucault's engagement with issues of racism is not easy to untangle. While references to racism appear sparingly throughout volume 1, the fact of modern racism is fundamental to its project. Racism is first mentioned in a discussion of the earliest technologies of sex that arose in the eighteenth century around the political economy of population, regulating the modes of sexual conduct by which populations could be expanded and controlled. It was, "these new measures that would become the anchorage points for the different varieties of racism of the nineteenth and twentieth centuries" (HS:26). In describing the rupture between a medicine of sex and the biology of reproduction in the nineteenth century, Foucault describes how the scientific arbitrators of sex authorized the "hygienic necessity" of cleansing and invigorating the social body in forms that "justified the racisms of the state, which at the time were on the horizon" (HS:54). Note that here racism is a potential waiting to be born, not yet on the terra firma that produced the rigid racial taxonomies of the late nineteenth century.

In colonial perspective, we could easily offer a different chronology with other prefigurings, of which Foucault was clearly aware. Colonial technologies of rule bear witness to earlier, explicit racially-based policies once in widespread use. Discriminations based on color divided black slaves from indentured poor whites in the American south in the early 1600s just as religion and color served to delineate status in the Dutch East Indies a half century later.[23] By 1680, those of "mixed-blood" were systematically

23. Ernest van den Boogaart, "Colour Prejudice and the Yardstick of Civility: the Initial Dutch Confrontation with Black Africans, 1590–1635," Racism and Colonialism, ed. Robert Ross (Leiden: Martinus Nijhoff, 1982). Boogaart's effort to distinguish "color prejudice" of the early seventeenth century from the racism of a later period belies how early both color and religion were the joint criteria on which access to office and residence was based. For the Dutch East Indies see Willem Mastenbroek, De Historische Ontwikkeling van de Staatsrechtelijke Indeeling der Bevolking van Nederlandsch-Indie (Wageningen: Veenman, 1934) 35. On the force of racism in eighteenth-century

denied entry to the upper echelons of the Indies bureaucratic service.[24] When Spain is brought back within the "European" picture, the "undisguised contempt" for *criollos* and "half-breeds" that peninsular Spaniards and metropolitan authorities displayed is evident even earlier.[25]

Students of U.S., French, British, and Dutch colonial history have debated whether these were emergent racisms of a different order, not yet as firmly biologized as in the nineteenth century. Some argue that racism was systematically embraced by the seventeenth century, others hold that it had not yet emerged in its consolidated, pure somatic form.[26] In either case, there is good evidence that discourses of race did not have to await mid-nineteenth-century science for their verification. Distinctions of color joined with those of religion and culture to distinguish the rulers from the ruled, invoked in varied measures in the governing strategies of colonial states. In the nineteenth century, on the other hand, race becomes the organizing grammar of an imperial order in which modernity, the civilizing mission and the "measure of man" were framed. And with it, "culture" was harnessed to do more specific political work; not only to mark difference, but to rationalize the hierarchies of privilege and profit, to consolidate the labor regimes of expanding capitalism, to provide the psychological scaffolding for the exploitative structures of colonial rule.

France and its colonies see Pierre Pluchon (*Nègres et Juifs au XVIIIe siècle: Le racisme au siècle des Lumières* [Paris: Tallandier, 1984]).

24. C. Fasseur, *De Indologen: Ambtenaren voor de Oost, 1825–1950* (Amsterdam: Bert Bakker, 1993) 119.

25. See Anthony Pagden's "Identity Formation in Spanish America" (*Colonial Identity in the Atlantic World* Nicholas Canny and Anthony Pagden, eds. Princeton: Princeton UP, 1987), where he argues that, "within a few years of the conquest the mestizos, far from being the bearers of a new mixed culture, had become a despised breed, contemptuous of their own Indian origins and rejected by a white elite that had come to fear racial contamination too much to wish to acknowledge direct association with them" (71).

26. This debate has been most sharply defined in the U.S. over the relationship between racism and slavery in the seventeenth century. It has been treated in depth in other contexts and I will not review them here. See Winthrop Jordan, *White over Black: American Attitudes toward the Negro, 1550–1812* (Chapel Hill: U of North Carolina P, 1968); George Fredrickson, *The Black Image in the White Mind: The Debate on Afro-American Character and Destiny, 1817–1914* (New York: Harper and Row, 1972); Alden Vaugh, "The Origins Debate: Slavery and Racism in 17th Century Virginia," *Virginia Magazine of History and Biography* 97 (July 1989): 347–49; and David Roediger, *Wages of Whiteness* (London: Verso, 1991) esp. 23–36. For a sample of the wide range of contributors to this debate from philosophy, history and comparative literature see Harold Pagliaro, ed., *Racism in the Eighteenth Century* (Cleveland: Case Western Reserve UP, 1973).

But even among historians who place the emergence of modern racism in the nineteenth century, this emergence is often dated earlier than does Foucault, around 1800—coterminous with an anxious and uncertain bourgeois order—not subsequent to it.[27] Why, then, does Foucault embrace this particular version of the nineteenth-century history of race but categorically reject the standard story of nineteenth-century sexuality? The History of Sexuality hints at some reasons, but the lectures offer more guidance. Colonialism was clearly outside Foucault's analytic concern, to him a byproduct of Europe's internal and permanent state of war with itself, not formative of those conflicts. In lectures, he would state only that racism was elaborated with colonization, to allow and account for "la genocide colonisateur." Colonial genocide is then one manifestation of a much more protracted discourse on the war of races, an elaborative moment of it.

Foucault's focus on the second half of the nineteenth century has other motivations as well. His concern was with state racism, not its popular forms. Racism is a state affair, confirmed by a set of scientific discourses that bear witness to it (HS:147). This latter may seem like a curious formulation, given the common rendering of Foucault's position that the state is not a privileged site for the discursive construction of power. But reading the lectures against The History of Sexuality provides a more subtle insight. The state is not written off as a locus of power. Rather, Foucault locates how state institutions foster and draw on new independent disciplines of knowledge and in turn harness these micro-fields of power as they permeate the body politic at large.

Another issue informs his chronology, a point we can only vaguely discern from The History of Sexuality: the principal form of state racism which concerned Foucault was that of the Nazi state and its "Final Solution." As such, there is an implicit teleology to how he treats what racist discourse "does." It must account for a set of practices that allow a state to identify not primarily its external foes, but its enemies within. In both the lectures and volume one, the focus is on the internal dynamics of European states

27. See George Mosse, Toward the Final Solution: A History of European Racism (Madison: U of Wisconsin P, 1978); Michael Banton, The Idea of Race (London: Tavistock, 1977); Collette Guillaumin, "Idea of Race"; Roediger, Wages of Whiteness, 23. Tom Holt places racism as a "creature of the ostensibly nonracist ideology that had undermined and destroyed slavery." Holt, The Problem of Freedom: Race, Labor, and Politics in Jamaica and Britain, 1832–1938 (Baltimore: Johns Hopkins Press, 1992) xx.

and their disciplinary biopolitical strategies. Contiguous empires figure in Foucault's genealogy of racism in his lectures, but imperial expansion outside Europe does not. In short, the genealogy of racist discourse is sui generis to Europe: colonial genocide is subsumed, dependent, accounted for, and explained in absentia.

For Foucault, racism is embedded in early discourses on sexuality, but not yet in explicit form. In the making of a bourgeois "class" body in the eighteenth century, a new field of discourse emerged concerned with "body hygiene, the art of longevity, ways of having healthy children and of keeping them alive as long as possible" that "attest to the correlation of this concern with the body and sex to a type of 'racism'" (HS:125). But "racism" is still bracketed here with inverted commas. This was not, he warns us, the familiar racism of the blue-blood aristocracy, invested in a conservative status quo. On the contrary it was a "dynamic racism, a racism of expansion, even if it was still in a budding state, awaiting the second half of the nineteenth century to bear the fruits that we have tasted" (HS:125). Two important issues emerge here. First, this is the only place in The History of Sexuality where Foucault alludes both to different historical moments of racism and to its different varieties. Up to this point, racism has been presented as a nineteenth-century invention. Here, however, he specifies an earlier racism that preceded its bourgeois form, one "manifested by the nobility" and organized for different ends. But note again, racism remains both internal to northern Europe and of elite derivation.[28]

This is not a unique story of racism's origin.[29] Benedict Anderson offers an account that, at first glance, would seem very much the same. In Imagined Communities, he writes:

28. Foucault's only mention of "inquisitions" is in the context of the spread of the confessional in the Middle Ages (HS:58). The sort of "state racism" that one might argue was entailed in the Spanish Inquisition and the policies of mass expulsion and extermination based on "purity of blood" is perhaps assumed, but unaddressed. On the Inquisition's part in accenting issues of race and a discourse on the "purity of blood" see Henry Kamen, Inquisition and Society in Spain in the Sixteenth and Seventeenth Centuries (Bloomington: Indiana UP, 1985) esp. 101–133. For support of the argument that the early Spanish history of racism was salient to the making of national identities in nineteenth-century northern Europe, see Michael Ragussis, "The Birth of a Nation in Victorian Culture: The Spanish Inquisition, the Converted Daughter, and the 'Secret Race'" Critical Inquiry 20 (Spring 1994): 477–508.

29. Joseph Schumpeter, Imperialism and Social Class (New York: Augustus Kelley, 1951) for example, argued that imperialist policy was not at odds with the interests of the aristocracy, but "rested on it" (35).

dreams of racism have their origin in ideologies of *class*, rather than in those of nation; above all in claims to divinity among rulers and to 'blue' or 'white' blood and 'breeding' among aristocracies. No surprise . . . that on the whole, racism and anti-semitism manifest themselves, not across national boundaries, but within them. In other words, they justify not so much foreign wars as domestic repression and domination.[30]

While Anderson and Foucault concur on racism's aristocratic etymology, they differ on two fundamental counts. For Anderson, racism derives from class. For Foucault, as we shall see in chapter 3, it is the other way around: a discourse of class derives from an earlier discourse of races. Also, for Foucault, these racisms of the nobility and the bourgeoisie are distinct, discontinuous, and qualitatively different in kind. For Anderson, on the contrary, racism is not only continuous but serves the hybrid "upper class" political project of "official nationalism." These two racisms become one and the same, welded by a nineteenth-century "conception of empire" in which "colonial racism was a major element."[31] By his account "late colonial empires even served to shore up domestic aristocratic bastions, since they appeared to confirm on a global, modern stage antique conceptions of power and privilege."[32] In short, colonial racism was of "aristocratic or pseudo-aristocratic derivation," but not confined to those class interests. Colonial empires "permitted sizeable numbers of bourgeois and petty bourgeois to play aristocrat off center court: i.e. anywhere in the empire except at home"[33] (my emphasis). We will have occasion to question Anderson's portrayal of European colonial communities as comprised of a "bourgeois aristocracy" in chapter 4. Here, I invoke him to underscore the basic point that notions of "a purity of blood" and the racisms that they expressed circulated through empire and back through Europe. They were never contained in Europe alone.

While Foucault's description of this "familiar" earlier aristocratic racism is at best vague, his account of its later "dynamic" variant has more specific referents. It is in the late nineteenth century that technologies of sex

30. Anderson, *Imagined Communities* 136.
31. Anderson 137.
32. Anderson 137.
33. Anderson 137.

are most fully mobilized around issues of race with the pseudo-scientific theory of degeneration at their core. He writes:

> The series composed of perversion-heredity-degenerescence formed the solid nucleus of the new technologies of sex. . . . Its application was widespread and its implantation went deep. Psychiatry, to be sure, but also jurisprudence, legal medicine, agencies of social control, the surveillance of dangerous or endangered children, all functioned for a long time on the basis of 'degenerescence' and the heredity-perversion system. An entire social practice, which took the exasperated but coherent form of a state-directed racism, furnished this technology of sex with a formidable power and far-reaching consequences. (HS:118-119)

That "vast theoretical and legislative edifice" that was the theory of degeneracy secured the relationship between racism and sexuality. It conferred abnormality on individual bodies, casting certain deviations as both internal dangers to the body politic and as inheritable legacies that threatened the well-being of a race (PK:204).

There is nothing particularly innovative in this formulation. Sander Gilman, Daniel Pick, and Anna Davin, among others, have treated the discourse of degeneracy with more nuance and far more historical depth than Foucault.[34] Pick argues that degeneracy was a "European disorder" that "above all [evoked] danger from internal transgressions rather than inter-racial 'pollution'."[35] Crystallizing in eugenics, nineteenth-century degeneracy theory developed as a national and a class-specific project that converged with wider purity campaigns for improved natality and selective sterilization. While Pick rejects what he calls the more conventional portrayal of degeneracy as part of the racist construction of empire, for Foucault, empire never comes up. Only Nazism is mentioned as, "doubtless the most cunning and the most naive combination of the fantasies of blood and the paroxysms of disciplinary power" (HS:149).

---

34. Sander Gilman, *Difference and Pathology: Stereotypes of Sexuality, Race, and Madness* (Ithaca: Cornell, 1985) 191–216; Anna Davin, "Motherhood and Imperialism," *History Workshop* 8 (1978); Daniel Pick, *The Faces of Degeneration: A European Disorder, c.1848-c.1918* (New York: Cambridge, 1989). Cf. Dain Borges, " 'Puffy, Ugly, Slothful and Inert': Degeneration in Brazilian Social Thought, 1880–1940," *Journal of Latin American Studies* 25 (1993): 235–256 who looks at the discourse on degeneration as a "major vehicle of social criticism . . . for Brazilian intellectuals" in this period.

35. Pick, *Faces of Degeneration* 39.

Pick differs with Foucault on a crucial point. The discourse of degeneracy was not an instrumental vehicle of bourgeois empowerment as for Foucault, but quite the opposite, an expression of "social anxiety," "internal disorder," and political fear; in short, a representation of "powerlessness" within a "seemingly self-possessed imperious discourse."[36] From a colonial perspective, this makes much more sense. As we will see in chapter 4, notions of degeneracy were directed at multiple targets and had wide applications.[37] They not only targeted colonized populations as Pick assumes, but also the indigent, supposedly *décivilisé*, racially-hybrid members within the European community. Degeneracy characterized those who were seen to veer off bourgeois course in their choice of language, domestic arrangement, and cultural affiliation. Notions of degeneracy registered dissension among Europeans and basic uncertainties about who would be granted that privileged status.[38] Thus, in the Dutch Indies, "degenerate" was an adjective that invariably preceded those labelled as poor and white. It could be invoked to protect the schools of "full-blooded" Dutch children from their poor Indo-European compatriots, as well as from those children who were "purely" Javanese. Similarly, the notion of degeneracy appears repeatedly in the 1898 Indies legal code on mixed-marriages to justify why European women who choose native men as their husbands should not be entitled to Dutch citizenship. The point is this was not a "European" disorder or a specifically colonial one, but a "mobile" discourse of empire that designated eligibility for citizenship, class membership, and gendered assignments to race.

Biopower, Sexuality and Race

While the references cited above suggest a progressive story of racism emerging out of earlier technologies of sex, Foucault's story, not surprisingly, is far more complicated. It is in the book's final chapter where the welding of racism to "biopower" confers on racism its most viru-

36. Pick 237.

37. This was, of course, true in Europe and the U.S. as well, where a discourse of degeneracy was used by feminist and left wing birth control advocates such as Emma Goldman as well as those adamantly against them. See Daniel Kevles, *In the Name of Eugenics: Genetics and the Uses of Human Heredity* (Berkeley: U of California P, 1985) 90 and Linda Gordon, *Woman's Body, Woman's Right: A Social History of Birth Control in America* (New York: Grossman, 1976).

38. Pick, *Faces of Degeneration* 39.

lent form. It is not biopower per se that produces racism, but rather the "calculated management of life" consolidated in the nineteenth century bringing together the two "poles" of biopower that emerged separately two centuries earlier (HS:140). One pole centers on the disciplining of the individual, on the "anatomo-politics of the human body"; the second centers on a set of "regulatory controls" over the life of the species in a "biopolitics of the population" (HS:139).[39]

What marks nineteenth-century biopower as unique then is not its focus on the individual body and the species alone, although this is the feature that most commentators have rightly pointed out.[40] It also joins two distinct technologies of power operating at different levels; one addresses the disciplining of individual bodies, the other addresses the "global" regulation of the biological processes of human beings.[41] It is this "technology of power centered on life" that produces a normalizing society and a new form of racism inscribed within it. Foucault would explore these connections in more detail in his 1976 lectures, but this concern with normality is already prefigured in volume 1 of The History of Sexuality, in Discipline and Punish, earlier still in Madness and Civilization, and The Birth of the Clinic, as well.[42]

39. In Curing their Ills: Colonial Power and African Illness (London: Polity Press, 1991), Megan Vaughan explores "the limitations of a Foucauldian account of biopower," arguing that colonial medical discourse and practice differed substantially from that described by Foucault because it conceptualized Africans "first and foremost, as members of groups and it was these groups, rather than individuals who were said to possess distinctive psychologies and bodies. In contrast to the developments described by Foucault, in colonial Africa group classification was a far more important construction than individualization" (11). In this otherwise rich study on colonial power, medicine and African subjectivity, Vaughan misses just this point that nineteenth-century biopower represented a shift toward the regulation of the social body, toward the normalization of collective identities, and away from individualizing disciplinary regimes. Vaughan dismisses Foucault's account precisely because she understands biopower to be a form of individualization rather than collective regulation.

40. See, for example, Dreyfus and Rabinow, Michel Foucault 140.

41. Michel Foucault, Temps Modernes 45.

42. Colin Gordon makes a similar observation:

Whether out of a polemical appetite for indications of unstable oscillation and damaging retreat, or through an inclination to apply the (often misunderstood) Foucauldian thematic of discontinuity to Foucault's own thought, or simply out of the need for a striking story-line, the evidences of a strong continuity from Histoire de la folie through to the end of Foucault's output have generally been paid too little critical attention."

See Colin Gordon, "Histoire de la folie: An Unknown Book of Michel Foucault," History of the Social Sciences 3.1 (1990): 5.

In *Discipline and Punish*, he identifies 1840, when the children's rural reformatory was established at Mettray, as the start of a "new era" in the "normalization of power." It was a key moment when what he calls the "carceral archipelago" of the nineteenth century produced a "slow, continuous, imperceptible gradation" that allowed the "social enemy" to be defined at once by irregularities, departures from the norm, anomaly and criminal deviations (DP:298–9). In the French language edition of *Madness and Civilization*, he already has set out "to write a history of boundaries . . . by which a culture rejects something that it will designate for itself as Exterior."[43] In each of these projects, Foucault first explores the "normalization of power." By the time he writes *The History of Sexuality* and the lectures on racism, his focus has shifted to a wider concern with the power of normalization.[44] And with this shift, the underpinnings of his approach to modern racism are close at hand. This creation of the "internal enemy" and of "the dangerous individual," both framed within a "theory of social defense," will be fundamental, as we shall see in the following chapter, to how Foucault will explain the racisms of modern states.[45] As George Mosse, among others, has noted, the distinction between normality and abnormality, between bourgeois respectability and sexual deviance, and between moral degeneracy and eugenic cleansing were the elements of a discourse that made unconventional sex a national threat and thus put a premium on managed sexuality for the health of a state.[46] Foucault writes, "Sex was a means of access both to the life of the body and the life of the species. It was employed as a standard for the disciplines and as a basis of regulation (HS:146)." Through this new biopolitic "management of life,"

---

43. *Folie et Déraison: Historie de la Folie à l'âge classique* (Paris: Plon, 1961). The French quote reads: "On pourrait faire une histoire des limites,—de ces gestes obscurs, nécessairement oubliés dès qu'accomplis, par lesquels une culture rejette quelque chose qui sera pour elle l'Exterieur," III.
44. In agreement with Miller's biography of Foucault, Mark Lilla notes: ". . . it was the idea of social boundaries and their trangression, not homoeroticism as such, that dominated [Foucault's] mature outlook." "A Taste of Pain," *Times Literary Supplement* 26 March 1993: 3. Also see John Rajchman's discussion (*Truth and Eros*, 105–106) of Foucault's reflections on the "technology of exclusion."
45. On this creation of "the dangerous individual" as an enemy of society within a "theory of social defense" see his seldom referenced but fascinating piece, "About the Concept of the 'Dangerous Individual' in 19th century Legal Psychiatry," *International Journal of Law and Psychiatry* I (1978): 1–18.
46. George Mosse, *Nationalism and Sexuality* (Madison: U of Wisconsin P, 1985) esp. 10–22.

sex not only stamped individuality; it emerged as "the theme of political operations" and as an "index of a society's strength, revealing of both its political energy and biological vigor" (HS:146).

Thus surveillance of sexuality and insistence on racial supremacy are played out at several levels that, in the wake of feminist history, are now familiar. The sexualization of children "was accomplished in the form of a campaign for the health of the race" (HS:146), while the medicalization of women's bodies was carried out "in the name of the responsibility they owed to the health of their children, the solidity of the family institution and the safeguarding of society" (HS:147). In Foucault's abridged rendering of these processes in volume 1, the two crucial elements of gender and empire are missing from his account. But it is imperial-wide discourses that linked children's health programs to racial survival, tied increased campaigns for domestic hygiene to colonial expansion, made child-rearing an imperial and class duty, and cast white women as the bearers of a more racist imperial order and the custodians of their desire-driven, immoral men.[47]

If the connections among sexuality, race, and biopower outlined above seem only loosely articulated it is because in Foucault's story they remain so. He links racism and the technologies of sexuality directly to biopower, without linking racism and sexuality explicitly to each other. Their relationship is mediated through what he would later call, "a sort of statisation of the biological," a biopolitical state in which sex was an instrumental "target" and racism an effect. What is implicit, however, is important. If "a normalizing society is the historical outcome of a technology of power centered on life" (HS:144), then, as we shall see from his lectures, modern racism is the historical outcome of a normalizing society. It is no coincidence that his Collège de France lectures given in 1974–75 were devoted to les anormaux (abnormals) and to racism and the biopolitical state the following year. Both dealt with the burden of normality and its biological technologies and with how these "relations of subjugation can produce

47. See Davin, "Imperialism and Motherhood" for one of the earliest and still best, accounts of an imperial "biohistory" that does not use the term. Also see Nancy Hunt, "Le bébé en brousse': European Women, African Birth Spacing and Colonial Intervention in Breastfeeding in the Belgian Congo," The International Journal of African Historical Studies 21.3 (1988): 401–432; my "Carnal Knowledge and Imperial Power"; and Carol Summers, "Intimate Colonialism: The Imperial Production of Reproduction in Uganda, 1907–1925," Signs 16.4 (1991): 787–807.

subjects," defined by their varied transgressions as "internal enemies" of society and state.[48]

Deployments of Alliance, Deployments of Sexuality and Race

Distinctions between the technologies of bodily discipline and mass regulation are not the only distinctions Foucault explores. Two other fundamental oppositions mark the rise of biopower in modern European history. One is the distinction between a deployment or device ("*dispositif*") of alliance and a deployment of sexuality.[49] The other is the distinction between a "symbolics of blood" and an "analytics of sexuality," each initially grounded in distinct regimes of power. How do these contrasting terms relate? What do they have to do with racism, and what kind of colonial sense can we make of them?

In skeletal form, his argument runs something like this. Prior to the end of the eighteenth century, the regulation of social life was mediated through a "deployment of alliance," in which control over sexual practices centered on matrimonial relations (HS:37) and on legal and religious codes of conduct that distinguished between the lawful and illicit sexual practices. This system, centered on "legitimate alliance" (HS:38), was "attuned to a homeostasis of the social body" (HS:107), to the sexual behavior of the conjugal couple, and to "maintain[ing] the laws that govern" those relations (HS:106). Foucault writes, "This deployment of alliance, with the mechanisms of constraint that ensured its existence and the complex knowledge it often required, lost some of its importance as economic processes and political structures could no longer rely on it as an adequate instrument or sufficient support" (HS:106). This failure to maintain elite control within an alliance-based system of power is not fleshed out, nor does Foucault seem to consider that such an explication is required. He only hints at those "economic processes and political structures" in which the decline of absolutism and monarchy and the rise of liberalism

48. Michel Foucault, *Resumé des cours: 1970–1982* (Paris: Julliard, 1984): 85.

49. "Dispositif" is a loaded theoretical concept for Foucault that is notoriously difficult to translate. Hubert Dreyfus and Paul Rabinow prefer to translate it as "deployment," Gilles Deleuze as "[social] apparatus," Alan Sheridan chooses "machinery." I prefer "deployment," "device," and "apparatus" and use them interchangeably. See Gilles Deleuze's "What is a dispositif?" (in *Michel Foucault: Philospher*, Timothy Armstrong, ed. [New York: Routledge, 1992] 159–168), the most lucid explanation I know of that captures the complexity of meaning and movement in the term.

undermined the social hierarchies based on lines of descent and called for new ways of naturalizing the inequities on which an emergent bourgeois order was based. Whereas for Foucault, racism has not yet appeared in its modern form, this is precisely that moment when others have sought its emergence. Collette Guillaumin, for example, argues that the rise of individualism and the decline of monarchy prompted new theories about how "individuals might be linked together by their natural character." [50] In replacing alliance as an organizing principle of society, these theories of new naturalized collectivities would prompt the production of new disciplines giving truth-value to the belief that these were organic collectivities with distinct somatic and psychological traits. John Rex, Edmund Morgan, and, more recently, David Goldberg have made similar arguments that economic liberalism, commitments to "freedom," and modernity have produced structured inequities and distinctions of difference on which nineteenth-century racism was based. [51]

Foucault neither explores these issues, nor really accounts for them. Instead, he pursues another sort of argument. With the "discursive explosion" around sexuality in the eighteenth and nineteenth centuries, he identifies a split between the laws of matrimony and the rules of sexuality when each began "to be recorded on two separate registers" (HS:40). The social apparatus of alliance and that of sexuality are contrasted term by term; the former being a maintenance system, the latter "engender[ing] continual extension of areas and forms of control"; the former concerned with reproduction, the latter with penetrating and annexing individual bodies in ever more comprehensive and intrusive ways (HS:106).

50. Guillaumin, "Idea of Race" 30.

51. Rex argues that with the decline of a legal system that upheld inequalities and specific sanctions to back it, racist beliefs took hold . . . "that the doctrine of equality of economic opportunity [of economic liberalism] and that of racial superiority and inferiority are complements of one another." "The Theory of Race Relations—a Weberian Approach," *Sociological Theories: Race and Colonialism* (Paris: UNESCO, 1980) 131. David Goldberg skillfully draws on the earlier insights of Zgyman Bauman, Etienne Balibar and others to analyze race as "one of the central conceptual inventions of modernity." As he states it, the "liberal paradox" is that as "modernity commits itself progressively to idealized principles of liberty, equality and fraternity . . . there is a multiplication of racial identities and the sets of exclusions they prompt and rationalize, enable and sustain." Also see Harry Bracken ("Essence, Accident and Race" *Hermathena* 116 [Winter 1973] 81–96) who argues that empiricism and "the rise of manipulative models of man" emerging with Locke in the late seventeenth century made it more possible to think about different species of humans and to conceive of them in racist terms.

The model here seems disturbingly conventional. Is Foucault a modernization theorist in disguise? Has he constructed a model of modernity that is all too familiar: a premodern system of power predicated on legal codes, "on a system of marriage, of fixation and development of kinship ties, of transmission of names and possessions" (HS:106)? In it, the privileges and "symbolics of blood" are replaced by a system of power that regulates through normalization rather than legal codes, that enlists the individual to monitor itself, that turns away from the sexuality of the conjugal couple to those peripheral sexualities where "abnormality" can be scrutinized, pluralized, and controlled. But such a developmentalist reading misses his point. The deployment of sexuality is "superimposed," it does not "supplant" the deployment of alliance, but is constructed out of the latter, imbuing it with a new tactic of power. The family is the site of this convergence, not a structure of alliance that restrains sexuality, as the conventional account would have it, but that which provides its most crucial support (HS:108).

One could read Foucault as a master at the art of crafting bold dichotomies that he recants as quickly as he sets them up. He notes a "shift" or "transition" from a deployment of alliance to one of sexuality and then quickly debunks the assumption that there were ever any such clear breaks. He writes that the "symbolics of blood" and the "analytics of sexuality" developed out of "two distinct regimes of power" (HS:149), though he earlier disclaims the notion that these were "the organizing principle[s] of two cultural forms" (HS:148). These read as contradictions, however, only if we assume that Foucault construed history in terms of such clean breaks. While a notion of epistemic rupture does frame the Order of Things, The History of Sexuality seems to operate under different analytic emphasis.[52] At issue here is not rupture, but the tension between rupture and recuperation.[53] Thus, just as a reader may think that the thematics of blood disappears with the analytics of sexuality, Foucault reveals the symbolics

52. There seems more affinity with The Archaeology of Knowledge where he states his willingness to "accept the groupings that history suggests only to subject them at once to interrogation; to break them up and then to see whether they can be legitimately reformed" (AK:26). There he explores how existing themes are reanimated, asking whether it is "possible, with a particular set of concepts, to play different games?" (AK:37–38).

53. See Jonathan Goldberg, who notes that the apparatus of sexuality contains within it a "strange continuity with the old supposedly outmoded regimes of alliance." Sodometries: Renaissance Texts, Modern Sexualities (Stanford: Stanford UP, 1992) 16.

of blood as a living discourse that "lent its weight" to a power exercised through the deployment of sexuality (HS:149). Foucault did not reject the identification of continuities, but only those "false" ones, as one of his less sympathetic readers, Jurgen Habermas, has rightly noted.[54] Appreciating Foucault's sustained concern with this tension will be critical when we turn to his treatment of racism in the lectures.

Foucault traces a distinct discourse of sexuality appearing in the early eighteenth century and a "completely new technology of sex" by its end (HS:116). This new technology expanded along the three axes of pedagogy, medicine, and demography that "made sex not only a secular concern but a concern of the state as well. . . . sex became a matter that required the social body as a whole, and virtually all of its individuals to place themselves under surveillance." When "sex became a police matter" (HS:24), the administrative concerns of the state became riveted not on a "people, but on a 'population' as an economic and political problem." It is that moment when governments began to enumerate "legitimate and illegitimate births," frequency of illnesses, patterns of diet and habitation . . . the effects of unmarried life or of the prohibitions" (HS:25). This "policing of sex" was not a matter of enforcing a "taboo" so much as it was an apparatus for the "ordered maximization of collective and individual forces" (HS:24–25).

In colonial perspective, we can recognize some of this pattern, but some parts of the formulation are questionable, and the eighteenth century dating seems in some places too early, in others too late. For one thing, it is not clear that this shift from a "people" to a "population" makes metahistorical sense. What is striking about colonial projects is that both the notions of a "population" and a "people" often were being crafted by administrators cum ethnographers at the same time.[55] As populations were being enumerated, classified, and fixed, "peoples" were being regrouped and reconfigured according to somatic, cultural, and psychological criteria that would make such administrative interventions necessary and credible. The heightened British interest in cataloguing the "peoples of India" in the eighteenth and nineteenth centuries was part of what Bernard Cohn has described as, a "vast documentation project" that created forms of

54. Jurgen Habermas, *The Philosophical Discourse of Modernity: Twelve Lectures* (Cambridge: MIT Press, 1990) 251.
55. I thank Val Daniel for pushing me to clarify this connection.

ethnological knowledge in the service of colonial control.[56] The concept of a "population" did not substitute for a "people": both conceptions represent state-building *and* nation-building projects in which a racial grammar tying certain physical attributes to specific hidden dispositions played a crucial role.

Secondly, sex becomes an "issue" between the administrative apparatus and European colonists nearly one hundred years earlier. Granted these are not discourses of sexuality with comparable breadth and intensity to those in the nineteenth century. Nevertheless, they were repeatedly linked to the potentialities of colonial settlement and to the production of populations that would be made loyal to emerging colonial states. But it was not "sex" that "required the social body as a whole and virtually all of its individuals to place themselves under surveillance" (HS:116); it was specific individuals and those in authority who identified sex as a domain of control.

In the case of the Indies, the Dutch East India Company's management of sexual arrangements condoned certain kinds of liaisons and not others. The Indies' early Dutch rulers debated long and hard over the best means to cultivate a Dutch settler population on Java, and issues of sexual management were high on their agenda. As early as 1612, the East Indies' first governor general refused to allow Dutch women to emigrate because of their scandalous sexual promiscuity "to the shame of our nation."[57] By 1642, there was already a women's prison in Batavia to confine those married and unmarried European women "whose scandalous lives were debauching the [European] young men and children of honorable homes."[58] Managed sex was on the state agenda, but it would be disingenuous to assume this to be the sort of surveillance Foucault had in mind. Still, the management of non-conjugal sex was implicated in a discourse on "the defense of society" much earlier than he suggests, not as a coherent and comprehensive regime of biopower, but with many of its incipient ele-

56. See Bernard Cohn, "Past in the Present: As Museum of Mankind," *An Anthropologist among the Historians and Other Essays* (Delhi: Oxford, 1987), "The Peoples of India: From the Picturesque to the Museum of Mankind," n.d., and "The Census, Social Structure and Objectification in South Asia," in *An Anthropologist among the Historians and Other Essays.*

57. See C. R. Boxer, *The Dutch Seaborne Empire 1600–1800* (London: Hutchinson, 1965) and Jean Taylor, *The Social World of Batavia* (Madison: U of Wisconsin P, 1983).

58. Mr. J. A. van der Chijs, Nederlandsche-Indisch Plakaatboek, 1602–1811, Part I, 1602–1642 (Batavia: Landsdrukkerij, 1885) 461–65.

ments. Sexual arrangements of company officials, subaltern military, and free burghers was monitored, if not successfully regulated early on.

Dutch anxieties over the sexual proclivities of European subjects were paralleled in North America as well. What George Fredrickson has called the "first clear-cut example of statutory racial discrimination" in the Virginia law of 1662 fined "interracial fornicators," followed by a ban on all forms of interracial marriage in 1691.[59] While these injunctions were clearly legal and concerned with the conjugal couple—features that Foucault attributes to the apparatus of alliance—they also linked individual desires to social reproduction in ways that he dates for Europe a century later.

Rabinow and Dreyfus note that Foucault linked individual sexualities and the security of the social body as nineteenth-century inventions when "appeals to the very fate of the race and the nation seemed to turn in large part on its sexual practices."[60] But the "fate of the race and the nation" were also tied in colonial discourses to individual sexual practices in Africa, Asia, and the Americas at an earlier date. Maryland legislators had already made such connections in 1664 when they focused on the sexual inclinations of white women who bedded with "non-white" men as targets of concern, accusing them, as in the Indies, of causing a "disgrace not only to the English but also of many other Christian nations."[61] Male sexual anxiety focused on more than suitable Christian marriage partners for European women and on the transmission of property, but on the unmanaged desires of women themselves. Thus, the Maryland law of 1681 regulating interracial unions justified its injunctions by the fact that white women were giving in to their "lascivious and lustful desires" with "negroes and slaves."[62] In both the Dutch and British accounts, the sexual choices of white women were at issue; they are desired objects, but unruly desiring subjects as well. While the notion of a "Christian nation" in the

---

59. Fredrickson, *White Supremacy* 101.

60. Dreyfus and Rabinow, *Michel Foucault* 141.

61. Fredrickson, *White Supremacy* 101, 103.

62. Fredrickson 104. Clearly the notion of race in the seventeenth- and eighteenth-century colonies did not bear the same explanatory weight as it does in the nineteenth century. In the former, race is folded into Christian hierarchies of civility, a piece of a larger narrative in which the economics of slavery played a crucial role. By the nineteenth century, race organizes the grammar of difference. Christianity is no longer a defining feature, but subsumed as a form of distinction that varied with specific strategies of imperial control.

seventeenth century and the bourgeois nation of the nineteenth century were clearly not the same, in both contexts unmanaged sexuality was considered a threat to these different social bodies. The pointed control over women's sexuality, as well as over the "natural inclinations" of men, was a shared effect.[63]

Foucault's story may eclipse the extent to which colonial regimes anticipated the policing of sexuality in modern Europe. Nevertheless, the distinctions he draws between deployments of alliance and sexuality make some sense when applied to the colonial society of the Dutch East Indies. Jean Taylor's fine-grained study of the changes in the colonial culture of the Indies between the seventeenth and early twentieth centuries makes a similar argument, if to a different end.[64] She describes how colonial authority in the seventeenth and eighteenth centuries was secured through a pervasive system of political and familial alliance.[65] This "deployment of alliance," to use Foucault's terms, allowed Dutch men access to privilege and profits through a calculated series of marriage links to Asian and creole women. She writes:

> The glue that held this society together was the family system. Under the VOC [Dutch East Indies company] political and economic structure, promotions were largely controlled by patronage in which family relationship played a key part . . . At the heart of the Indies clan were women, locally born and raised, who brought men into relationships of patron and protégé as father-in-law, son-in-law, and brothers-in-law. Such alliances could be far-reaching when high death rates and remarriage meant that spouses circulated. And since, under Dutch law, women could be named sole inheritor of a man's property, widows were sought after for the fortune they brought to a marriage . . . The VOC's Asian empire . . . used marriage to cement alliances.[66]

63. Again, this is not to suggest that they were the same. In the latter, the bourgeoisie's engagement with a discourse of universality and progress opened up possibilities that social boundaries might be loosened in ways that heightened anxiety about that very question.

64. Taylor, The Social World of Batavia.

65. Also see Julia Adams, "The Familial State: Elite Family Practices and State-Making in the Early Modern Netherlands," Theory and Society (Summer 1994): 505–539; and F. S. Gaastra, "The Independent Fiscaals of the VOC, 1689–1719," All of One Company: the VOC in Biographical Perspective (Utrecht: Hes, 1986) 92–107 who argues that by the end of the seventeenth century family ties among the VOC's higher servants were "growing closer and closer" (96).

66. Taylor, Social World of Batavia 71–72.

This legally secured system of alliance was a power structure of limited reign. Dutch metropolitan authorities saw these strong mestizo and creole connections, produced out of interracial unions, threatening the metropolitan hold on colonial authority and sought specific cultural measures to remedy the situation. By the mid-nineteenth century, "assaults on mestizo culture" were expressed in concerted efforts to make the colony more clearly of a "Dutch character" in a number of domains.[67] Most notable were attempts to enforce spoken Dutch in newly established private schools for European children. But these met with little success. With even the strongest advocates of enlightenment ideals still securing their connections and wealth through mestiza marriages, the elite in the Dutch stronghold of Batavia remained as removed from the *burgerlijk* order of the Netherlands as ever.[68]

This was to change radically in the early nineteenth century when a streamlined Dutch administration took over from the collapsed VOC after a brief British interregnum.[69] The bureaucratic engine of the colony was set on a new course with much more stringent guidelines established for entry into the colonial service. "Foreigners" as well as "undesirable persons drawn from impoverished families" no longer had a place.[70] A "sound" education in the Netherlands was required. This implied not only a fluency in Dutch, but the elimination of those who might form a " 'pernicious middle-race' between Europeans and natives," lacking the morality of cultivated Europeans.[71] If "inappropriate" Europeans were mildly suspect, the large population of "creoles," "colored," and the mixed population of so-called "*inlandsche kinderen*" were placed under administrative spotlight as never before.[72] By 1838 all *inlandsche kinderen* were banned from posts that might bring them in direct contact with Javanese.[73] Although explicit discrimination against Indo-Europeans was to be abolished from the Indies civil service requirements in the following decades,

67. Taylor 78–113.

68. Taylor 90, 93. On the term *burgerlijk* see fn. 50, chp. 4.

69. See C. Fasseur, *De Indologen: Ambtenaren voor de Oost, 1825–1950* (Amsterdam: Bert Bakker, 1993).

70. Fasseur 41.

71. Fasseur 43–44.

72. See also C. Fasseur, "De 'adeldom' van de huid: De role van de Indische Nederlander in het Nederlands-Indisch bestuur," *Sporen van een Indische Verleden* (1600-1942), ed. Wim Willem (Leiden: Rijkuniversiteit, 1992) 14.

73. Fasseur, *De Indologen* 17.

it did not disappear.[74] It was merely substituted with a criteria of "quality" that explicitly sought recruits from the Dutch "*beschaafde stand*" (the "cultivated classes") which served the same purpose: Indo-Europeans were effectively barred.[75] With this mandate, a more visible European-oriented, Dutch middle class was recruited and encouraged to make its presence felt. Revised managements of sexuality thus *followed* from efforts to secure a Dutch national identity and creole compliance with a metropolitan-controlled colonial project.

As the Dutch colonial bureaucracy grew, an expanding class of civil servants, born and educated in Holland, took over as the new scientific, administrative, and cultural arbitrators on hygiene, education, morality, and sex. This transformation not only instilled a more explicitly bourgeois morality. It also made the formalization of racial categories contingent on the management of sex, but more directly on a legal system that was sharply attuned to the conditions in which "mixed-blood" children were born: out of prostitution, concubinage, and marriage. It refused children born in concubinary relations between European men and native women rights to European status without acknowledgment by their fathers, thereby allowing or compelling men to relinquish responsibility for them. The "social apparatus of alliance" did not disappear as issues of sexual morality and bourgeois convention came to define who was eligible for European status and who was not. It rather resurfaced in a new form as European-born wives, and white endogamy came to define the new style of a modern colony that would efface its mestizo connections and culturally hybrid roots.

From a Foucauldian perspective, there are three striking features of this shift. The first is how quickly the power structure based on mestizo alliance broke down, as prestige and coveted administrative posts were increasingly accessible only to the European educated and the European-born.[76] The second is that the emergence in the nineteenth-century Indies

---

74. Fasseur, "De 'adeldom' van de huid," 19.

75. Fasseur, "De 'adeldom' van de huid": 21, Fasseur, De Indologen: 76.

76. This is not to suggest that kinship alliances did not continue to play an important part in how offices were procured and assigned, only that other powerful criteria of selection, namely wealth, education and standardized exams now intervened. If we trace the family ties in the Indies nineteenth-century civil service, it is clear that nepotism continued to play a crucial role in the distribution of office. Robert van Niel argues that alliances among Indies families in the 1830s and 1840s actually "became more extensive and more intimately tied to various

of an intensified discourse on bourgeois respectability and sexual morality carried with it a new interest in the domestic milieu and scrutiny of the privatized habitus in which European bourgeois values could be cultivated and children raised. The third is that this assertion of European, rather than mestizo, supremacy was underscored by a more explicit discourse and set of policies that tied the self-disciplining of individual colonial Europeans to the survival of all Europeans in the tropics and thus to the biopolitics of racial rule. In short, the assertion of a bourgeois order and the membership criteria for which "full-blooded" Netherlanders pressed was never distinct from the changing definition of who was European. Cultural competencies and sexual practices signaled the lines of descent that secured racial identities and partitioned individuals among them.

While this truncated account appears to be consonant with Foucault's general argument, it is dissonant in other ways. Colonial regimes of the seventeenth and eighteenth centuries were never based on systems of alliance alone. Concubinary relations were a mainstay of colonizing settlement policy in sixteenth-century Mexico and as early as the seventeenth century elsewhere.[77] In the Indies, these relationships between subaltern European men and Asian women were not only sanctioned by the state, but encouraged by it. Local women were enlisted to provide the services that allowed civil servants and planters to maintain a European standard of living and "acclimatized" to the tropics at little cost. In Malaysia, Indochina, and parts of French- and British-ruled Africa, concubinage was the dominant domestic arrangement through the early twentieth century among subaltern Europeans, as well as many of the elite.[78]

Students of colonial history might think to interpret these illicit sexual practices as evidence of a regulative system that went awry, but this may be missing the point. This administrative economy of sex condoned arrangements that were neither conjugal, legal, nor necessarily reproductive of a ruling class. While well-placed families may have been solidifying their

---

aspects of government or private cultivations and assorted exporting arrangements." *Java under the Cultivation System* (Leiden: KITLV, 1992) 101.

77. See Asuncion Lavin "Sexuality in Colonial Mexico," *Sexuality and Marriage in Colonial Latin America* (Lincoln: U of Nebraska P, 1989) 57.

78. See John Butcher, *The British in Malaya, 1880–1914* (Kuala Lumpur: Oxford UP, 1979); Taylor, *Social World of Batavia*; George Fredrickson, *White Supremacy* 114, and my "Carnal Knowledge and Imperial Power."

prestige and power through marriage alliances, other forms of managed sexuality were proliferating. The sexual "disorders" of colonial society—venereal disease, prostitution, concubinage, illegitimate children, and a "wandering population of mixed-blood bastards" to which these illicit arrangements had allegedly given rise were sometimes subversions of the prevailing order of society—but as often expressions of it.[79] These were target problems, productive of a discourse that justified more invasive institutional control both of natives and of certain classes of Europeans. The point is that these deployments of alliance and sexuality were both part of the colonial order of things; at one moment competing, at other moments convergent venues through which distinctly gendered forms of racial and class power were ordered and displayed.

By the mid-nineteenth century, metissage ("racial mixing")—construed as the consequence of extra-marital alliances—was a focal point of political, legal, and social debate, conceived as a dangerous source of subversion, a threat to white prestige, the result of European degeneration and moral decay. Children—abandoned, illegitimate and of mixed-blood—had become the sign and embodiment of what needed fixing in this colonial society, giving force to the urgency for a more clearly defined bourgeois order based on white endogamy, attentive parenting, Dutch-language training, and surveillance of servants that might shore it up. These discourses on sexuality, as Foucault might have argued, were charged with instrumentality. They racialized the dangers of sex, by underscoring that illicit sex gave rise to bastard children, sexually precocious Indies youths, to daughters and sons of mixed unions predisposed to becoming prostitutes and patricides when they grew up. They needed to be watched with vigilant attention and to be subjected to state controls. Proposals to extend school hours in the Indies for the daughters of the Indo-European ("mixed-blood") poor were explicitly instituted not to improve their education, but to remove them from the immoral influence of their native kin and their mothers' native lovers.

These were not discourses designed to find a solution, as participants in these debates repeatedly professed. Instead, these concerns over racial and cultural hybridity fueled the administrative and practical fears of a heterogeneous European community that its boundaries needed policing in ever more intimate ways. Who was "dangerous" was as much those

79. See my "Carnal Knowledge and Imperial Power."

legally defined as European—that noxious "middle-race" inside the borders of this amorphous European community—as those clearly external to it.[80] These discourses provided liberal reformers with a constant reminder that colonialism was about not only incorporation, but also distinctions between the *echte* Dutch and those assimilated natives of "fabricated" European status, between citizens and subjects, between colonized and colonizer, and not least between different classes of Europeans.

Colonial law was no marginal player in these constructions of difference, as Foucault's account would suggest.[81] What Verena Martinez-Alier has noted for nineteenth-century Cuba holds for the Indies: legal codes and not norms alone determined a person's racial status "when his physical appearance was not an unambiguous guide."[82] Paradoxically, racial taxonomies in the Dutch East Indies were predicated on notions of fixity that were legally enforced, but these legal codes in turn depended on the identification of sexual and psychological essences that were ill-fixed and ill-defined. Similar to Spanish law, "the difference between being 'held to be white' and being 'truly white' was not one of physical colour."[83] In the Indies, the legal regulation of interracial marriage and the discourse that conferred specific sexual characteristics to social categories of persons did similar work. Together they structured and shaped inclusions in the category of European and its changing criteria of exclusions.

The Dutch case does not discredit Foucault's claims as much as it transforms them. It does suggest several issues to consider further. First, the tension between deployments of alliance and sexuality as distinct organizing principles of power may configure differently when the issue of racism is centrally posed. JanMohamed has rightly noted that racialized sexuality in U.S. slavery was not beyond the law, but constituted by it; by the legal designation of slaves as property and their children as the property of others.[84]

80. Fasseur, *De Indologen* 43.
81. In a carefully argued "counterexample" to Foucault's analysis of the relationship between discipline and law, see Laura Engelstein's "Combined Underdevelopment: Discipline and the Law in Imperial and Soviet Russia," *American Historical Review* 98.2 (April 1993): 338–363.
82. Verena Martinez-Alier, *Marriage, Class and Colour in Nineteenth-Century Cuba: A Study of Racial Attitudes and Sexual Values in a Slave Society* (London: Cambridge UP, 1974) 73.
83. Martinez-Alier 71.
84. Abdul JanMohamed specifically argues that "racialized sexuality replicates more features of the deployment of alliance than of bourgeois sexuality" . . . in that it is "tied not only to the

Second, in such colonial contexts as the Indies, discourses on libidinal desires were invariably shaped by how those desires were seen in
relationship to their reproductive consequences. The truth claims about
"peoples" were jointly contingent on the quantity and quality of their
sexual energy *and* on how much, how rapidly, with whom, and under
what conditions they could successfully reproduce. It was not just sexuality in which the truth was lodged, but in how productive that sexuality
was.[85] Part of the problem is one that Doris Sommer notes—Foucault's
virtual neglect of the "most obvious deployment of bourgeois sexuality,
the legitimate conjugal variety without which there could be no perverse
difference."[86] As we shall see in chapters 5 and 6, certain forms of racialized desire were animated in ways that buttressed bourgeois marriages,
sanctioning the colonial state's intervention in the sexual and marital arrangements among different classes of "Europeans."

In addition, Foucault's equation of social "homeostasis" with deployments of alliance and kinship makes little ethnographic or historical sense.
Jean Taylor's account evinces dynamic local interpretations of kin ties that
were far from homeostatic. What is striking when we review the colonial
policies of the Netherlands Indies, French Indochina, and parts of Latin
America is how much *selective* affirmations of kinship could cut through
the boundaries of privilege and race.

One of the more compelling examples of this sort of creative manipulation of kinship that scrambled racial categories was a phenomenon that
both French and Dutch colonial authorities identified as "fraudulent recognitions." These were cases in which children of "mixed-blood" or even
of "purely native origin" were acknowledged by European men who were
supposedly not their natural fathers. These claims to paternity, in which a
European man of modest or impoverished means would allegedly be paid
a fee by a native woman to recognize her child, could redefine who "by
descent" was European and who was not.[87] European status was a valuable

---

transmission and circulation of material wealth but to its very production" ("Sexuality on/of
the Racial Border" 113).

85. See Doris Sommer, *Foundational Fictions* (Berkeley: U of California P, 1991), 24, who makes this
point so well.

86. Sommer 33–34.

87. See J. F. Kohlbrugge, "Prostitutie in Nederlandsche-Indie," *Indisch Genootschap*, 19 February
1901: 26–28; (n.a.); "Ons Pauperisme," *Mededeelingen der Vereeniging "Soeria Soemirat"* 2 (1892). For a

commodity. Moreover, these were racial reorderings outside the state's control. In French Indochina, Madagascar, and the Indies in the late nineteenth century, the perceived danger of such false paternity claims was that they "both exposed the [European] element to being submerged by a flood of naturalized natives and introduced into their midst a questionable population."[88] The prevailing fear among colonial officials that fictive paternity could produce fictive Europeans suggests that some claims to alliance and descent subverted rather than substantiated racial taxonomies.

Race, Sexuality, and the Blood of the Bourgeoisie

It seems quite clear that the intimate hierarchies of colonialism prevailing in the slave, indentured, and wage labor regimes of Europe's "age of empire" would have produced a very different dynamic between alliance and sexuality than Foucault outlined for Europe. Nor undoubtedly would he have disagreed. His treatment of racism is focused on other issues and other sites; namely, on the shift in the eighteenth and nineteenth centuries from a "symbolics of blood" to an "analytics of sexuality." In societies in which systems of alliance, descent, and death were dominant, blood was a *"reality with a symbolic function"* (HS:147). In modern society on the other hand, the mechanisms of power are located elsewhere, "addressed to the body, to life, to what causes it to proliferate, to what reinforces the species, its stamina, its ability to dominate, or its capacity to be used" (HS:147). It is not the symbols of death that are charged, but sexuality as an "object and target" (HS:147). Lest we assume that a "substitution of sex for blood was by itself responsible for the transformation that marked the threshold of our modernity" Foucault refuses any such claim (HS:148). The new procedures of power "caused" our societies to shift from one to the other, but not without "overlappings, interactions, and echoes" (HS:148). A preoccupation with blood for nearly two centuries "haunted the administration of sexuality," and nowhere more clearly than with the rise of racism (HS:149). In one particularly clear passage, Foucault writes:

more detailed discussion of this "fraudulent recognitions" see my "Sexual Affronts and Racial Frontiers. . . ."

88. Raoul Abor, *Des Reconnaissance Frauduleuses d'Enfants Naturels en Indochine* (Hanoi: Imprimerie Tonkinoise, 1917) 41.

Beginning in the second half of the nineteenth century, the thematics of blood was sometimes called on to lend its entire historical
weight toward revitalizing the type of political power that was exercised through the devices of sexuality. Racism took shape at this point
(racism in its modern, "biologizing" statist form): it was then that
a whole politics of settlement (peuplement), family, marriage, education, social hierarchization, and property, accompanied by a long
series of permanent interventions at the level of the body, conduct,
health, and everyday life, received their color and their justification
from the mythical concern with protecting the purity of the blood
and ensuring the triumph of the race. (HS:149)

Indisputably, this was the case. Late nineteenth-century and early
twentieth-century discourses on miscegenation combined notions of
tainted, flawed, and pure blood with those of degeneration and racial
purity in countless ways.[89] Although French and Dutch liberal reformers often insisted that cultural "suitability" and not race was the basis on
which access to colonial educational opportunities and welfare entitlements rest, designation of those Europeans who were "full-blooded" and
"pur sang" was repeatedly invoked to identify how the lines between the de-
serving and undeserving poor were to be drawn. Thus Dutch and French
colonial commentators shared the notion that mixed-blood children, no
matter what their educational achievements, might always revert to their
native affiliations because of the "blood that flowed in their veins." A study
on child delinquency (published in the same year that removal of "the
racial criteria" from the Dutch East Indies constitution was being hotly
debated) notes that "by far the greatest percentage of European children
who perpetrated crimes were born in the Indies, children therefore with
more or less native blood," thereby absolving "pure-blooded" Europeans
from any association with crime.[90] Similarly, Virginia Dominguez's study of
racial classification in creole Louisiana powerfully illustrates how assumptions about the "properties of blood" determined racial identity and class

---

89. See, for example, J. M.Coetzee, "Blood, Flaw, Taint, Degeneration: The Case of Sarah
Gertrude Millin," *English Studies in Africa* 23.1 (1980): 41–58; Michael D. Biddis, *The Age of the Masses*
(London: Penguin, 1977).

90. A. de Braconier, *Kindercriminaliteit en de verzorging van misdadig aangelegde en verwaarloosde minderjarigen
in Nederlandsch-Indie* (Baarn: Hollandia, 1918) 11.

membership from the nineteenth through the mid-twentieth century.[91] The U.S. legal system of racial classification is still derived from the "one-drop" theory, a stipulation that a child with a single great-grandparent of African-American descent, is black.[92]

What is problematic in Foucault's argument is not his description of the reappearance of a "symbolics of blood" in the nineteenth century and its continued salience today, but rather the selective (northern) Europe-bound genealogy he draws for it. The myth of blood that pervades nineteenth-century racism may be traced, as Foucault does, from an aristocratic preoccupation with legitimacy, pure blood, and descent, but not through it alone. It was equally dependent on an imperial politics of exclusion that was worked out earlier and reworked later on colonial ground.[93] Boxer holds that the sixteenth-century Portuguese notion of "contaminated races" that pervaded colonial policy did more than distinquish the aristocracy from the poor and Christians from heathens; it was a color prejudice that underwrote the social hierarchies of Portuguese rule.[94] Deborah Root contends that the sixteenth-century Spanish state concern with "purity of blood" and the association of Moriscos with infection, vermin, and disease, were already part of the forging of a "cleansed" Spanish identity "that referred both to national unity and to the overseas empire."[95] Verena Stolcke argues that in colonial Latin America the notion of "purity of blood acquired new force as it lost any religious connotation, becoming

91. Virginia Dominquez, White by Definition: Social Classification in Creole Louisiana (New Brunswick, N.J.: Rutgers UP, 1986) 89.

92. See James David on the "one-drop rule" in Who is Black? One Nation's Definition (University Park: Pennsylvania State UP, 1991) 4–6 and an excellent piece on the persistence of that rule in debates over revisions being prepared for the 2000 U.S. census (Lawrence Wright, "One Drop of Blood" The New Yorker (July 25, 1994): 46–55.)

93. Verena Martinez-Alier in Marriage, Class and Colour in Nineteenth Century Cuba notes that "the concept of purity of blood, which had become largely discredited in Spain by the end of the eighteenth century . . . experienced a revival in Cuba" (1974: 75). Others have argued that official investigations of purity of blood in Spain itself lasted through the middle of the nineteenth century. See Charles Amiel's "La 'Pureté de sang' en Espagne" Etudes inter-ethniques 6 (1983): 27–45 on this point and on "the conjunction of religious, biological and classist racisms" that the Spanish state embraced (41).

94. C. R. Boxer, The Portuguese Seaborne Empire (New York: Alfred Knopf, 1969) 215–41.

95. See Deborah Root, "Speaking Christian: Orthodoxy and Difference in Sixteenth-Century Spain," Representations 23 (1988): 118–134.

a clearly racial notion" by the beginning of the eighteenth century.[96] I draw attention to these colonial contexts not to suggest that these racisms are the same, but to underscore the fact that the racial lexicons of the nineteenth century have complex colonial etymologies through which these aristocratic discourses on "purity of blood" were replayed and transformed.

When we turn to the nineteenth century anxieties around Eurasians, Indos, and mestizos, the colonial entailments of these discourses become clear. These were not only groups seen as "mixed" by blood. They were the "enemy within," those who might transgress the "interior frontiers" of the nation-state, who were the same but not quite, potentially more brazen in making their claims to an equality of rights with "true" Europeans, but always suspect patriots of colonial rule. Science and medicine may have fueled the re-emergence of the beliefs in blood, but so did nationalist discourse in which a folk theory of contamination based on cultural contagions, not biological taintings, distinguished true members of the body politic from those who were not. These folk theories of race were derived from how empire was experienced in Europe. They were disseminated through an imperial logic in which cultural hybridities were seen as subversive and subversion was contagious. In that imperial frame, native sensibilities and affiliations were the invisible bonds that could position those of "mixed-blood" as "world citizens" at the vanguard of revolt against those "full-blooded" Europeans who claimed the right to rule.[97]

Foucault's account may allow for such an understanding, but it does not provide one. He looked at "blood" as a body fluid, expressive of vitality, kinship and contamination, not at its part in defining the imperial body and its interior borders. For him, nineteenth-century racism was not about the symbolics of blood per se, but about how the meanings of blood worked through the technologies of sex in a power "organized around the management of life" (HS:147). Race is a theme of the text, but not the subject of analysis: "Through health, progeny, race, the future of the species, the vitality of the social body, power spoke of sexuality and to sexuality; the latter was not a mark or a symbol, it was an object and a target." His

96. Verena Stolcke, "Conquered Women," *Report on the Americas* XXIV.5 (1991): 25. Also see Magnus Morner, *Race Mixture in the History of Latin America* (Boston: Little, Brown, and Company, 1967), who notes that a "royal decree of 1805 declared that persons of "pure blood" had to ask permission of the viceroy or the audiencia in order to marry 'elements of Negro and Mulatto origin' " (39).
97. W. Horst, "Opvoeding en onderwijs van kinderen van Europeanen en Indo-Europeanen in Indie," *De Indische Gids* II (1900): 989.

focus is on the bourgeois body, an individual body menaced by heredity, a social body bent on affirming itself. As he tells us, it is more than a clever play of words to say that "the bourgeoisie's 'blood' was its sex" (HS:124). Within this equation, "sex" would come to define the distinction of the bourgeoisie, as blood had for the nobility; it would legitimate its moral highground, its claims to supremacy, and the healthy vigor of bourgeois rule. If the "special character" of the aristocratic body was hidden in the truth of its blood and not its wealth, then the uniqueness of the bourgeois body was to be lodged in the "truth" of its sex. Foucault writes: "This class must be seen . . . as being occupied, from the mid-eighteenth century on, with creating its own sexuality and forming a specific body based on it, a 'class' body with its health, hygiene, descent, and race . . ." (HS:124).

How does race figure in this equation, in this "transition from sanguinity to sexuality"? Foucault suggests that "the new concept of race tended to obliterate the aristocratic particularities of blood, retaining only the controllable effects of sex . . . (148). Within this new biopolitical regime, modern racism emerges out of the technologies of sex. For Foucault, race is a theme through which sexuality is discussed, modern racism follows from it. In his Europe-bound account, racism is a consequence of that "class body" in the making, but viewed in colonial perspective bourgeois bodies were constituted as racially and relationally coded from the outset. If race already makes up a part of that "grid of intelligibility" through which the bourgeoisie came to define themselves, then we need to locate its coordinates in a grid carved through the geographic distributions of 'unfreedoms' that imperial labor systems enforced. These were colonial regimes prior to and coterminous with Europe's liberal bourgeois order. As many have argued, the colonies have provided the allegorical and practical terrain against which European notions of liberty and its conceits about equality were forged.

Thus, from the vantage point of the 1990s, colonial historians may be drawn to Foucault's insights, but perplexed by the omissions and ultimately left cold. Can we understand these discourses of sexuality and race that fold into one another in eighteenth- and nineteenth-century Europe outside the wide sweep of empire in which biopolitics was registered and racial taxonomies were based? Is empire precluded by The History of Sexuality or subsumed by it? More pointedly, how central was race to this "class body" in the making? Was racism part of the formation of a modern, sexualized, bourgeois subject or a later elaboration of it? I take up these issues in chapter 4. Before doing so, I want to look closely at Foucault's 1976 Collège de France lectures. There, certain elements of *The History of Sexuality* come into sharper focus, while other silences remain pronounced. Foucault anticipated many of the challenges I have raised here in ways that render our queries more pressing and more relevant both to his project and to our pursuit of the colonial genealogies of racism more generally.

III

TOWARD A GENEALOGY OF RACISMS:

THE 1976 LECTURES AT THE COLLÈGE DE FRANCE

The reading I offered of Foucault's thinking on racism in the preceding chapter could be construed as a reasonable one, based on his schematic treatment of the subject in *The History of Sexuality*. But Foucault's effort to account for the fact of racism was not, as we know, confined to that volume alone. The Collège de France lectures, given in the winter of 1976 when volume 1 was in press, evince a more direct engagement, an effort to situate the discourse of race within a deeper genealogy, with attention to its changing form. What is significant for us, and what ties the lectures closely to *The History of Sexuality*, is Foucault's concluding argument that the emergence of biopower inscribed modern racism in the mechanisms of the normalizing state. If that was the central argument of the lectures, the task here would be relatively straightforward. But it is not.

Despite the fact that five of the eleven lectures center on the changing discourse of race from the seventeenth to the twentieth century, Foucault is emphatic that racism is neither his subject nor his primary concern. As he put it in the lecture of February 2nd

> For me, at this moment, it is not a question of writing a history of racism in the general or traditional sense of the term. I do not want to write a history of what in the Occident could be the consciousness of the appearance of a race, nor the history of the rituals and mechanisms by which one could exclude, disqualify, and physically destroy a race. The problem that I want to pose is another and does not concern either racism nor in the first instance the problem of races. It was, and for me still is, a matter of showing how in the West, a certain

critical, historical, and political analysis of the state, of its institutions, and its mechanisms of power appeared in binary terms.[1]

There are at least three significant points here. Foucault's focus is on the modern state and the emergence of state racism as a part of it. It is not racist *practice* that he tracks, but rather a new form of historical analysis, emerging in the seventeenth century that comes to conceive of social relations in binary terms. The subject is historical discourse as a strategic weapon of power, not the conjuncture of events, not a chronicle of racist confrontations, and not individual practice. The "grid of intelligibility" is not the discourse of sexuality as in volume 1, but rather an emergent discourse on the "war of races" in which state racism will appear as but one nineteenth-century "episode" within it.

On the face of it, Foucault's orientation seems to have dramatically shifted; the rupture with volume 1 seems remarkably clean. But this is not the case either. In fact, the last lecture of 1976 took up the precise themes that Foucault outlines in the final chapter of *The History of Sexuality*. What differs in the two texts—otherwise virtually identical in parts—is how he situates the issue of racism. While in that final chapter, Foucault's references to the relationship between racism and "biohistory" are tantalizingly brief, in the lectures that articulation is more centrally framed. In his own words, the final lecture on March 17, addressed "the birth of state racism," that historical moment when biopower transforms an earlier discourse into state racism and provides its unique form. As James Miller, in his biography on Foucault would note, the lectures were about "racism, class struggle, and the virulence of 'vital massacres' in recent history, deepening the analysis of bio-politics sketched in the last chapter of *The Will to Know*." [2]

But not everyone would agree. According to the editors of the pirated Italian edition that appeared in 1990, the lectures address the "theme of war as an instrument of analysis and a criteria of intelligibility of history and society." In attending "to the notion of a struggle of races," they were deemed "very up-to-date," highly relevant to contemporary religious and ethnic conflict.[3] According to Pasquale Pasquino, Foucault's close associate, friend, and translator—and the only scholar I know who has written on the lectures—they offer a political theory of war and peace, an excur-

1. *Difendere la società* (Florence: Ponte alle Grazie, 1990) 68.

2. James Miller, *The Passion of Michel Foucault* (New York: Simon and Schuster, 1993) 299.

3. *Difendere la società* (Florence: Ponte alle Grazie, 1990) 10.

sion into the "origins of the modern state."[4] Pasquino's interest was in Hobbes, and thus the issue of modern racism goes unmentioned.

The lectures are difficult to tackle on several counts. First, there is only one piece of commentary on them. Nor is this surprising given their relative unavailability to a wider audience. Only the first two lectures that focus more generally on "the insurrection of subjugated knowledges" have been published in English, and these make no reference to race.[5] The more or less complete transcription, published in Italian in 1990, was quickly taken off the market, as it appeared without permission of the Foucault estate.[6] In 1991, the final lecture on "the birth of state racism" was first published in French.[7] Pending resolution of a publication dispute between the French publishing house, Gallimard, and the guardians of Foucault's estate, a dispute that has been going on for some time, the complete lectures are still only available on scratchy cassette recordings at the Saulchoir library in Paris where Foucault worked during his final years.

And some might argue that they should be left there. Foucault was not only unwilling to have them published; as we know, he abruptly abandoned the project while on leave from the Collège the following year. The mystique that surrounds the fate of the lectures is stranger still. Few "Foucauldians" seem to know of the taped lectures, and even fewer have heard them. One scholar who initially offered to lend me the Italian transcript eventually declined to do so, fearing that if he were identified as my source, he would no longer be welcome at the Saulchoir library. But this was sheer fantasy since the very same Italian publication is available to the public in the library's open catalog. Finally, I learned upon my return to the U.S. that the last lecture that I had spent days deciphering had already been published three years earlier in Les Temps Modernes (albeit without in-

4. See Pasquale Pasquino, "Political Theory of War and Peace: Foucault and the History of Modern Political Theory," Economy and Society 22.1 1 (February 1993): 76–88.

5. These two lectures first appeared in Colin Gordon, ed., Power/Knowledge: Selected Interviews and other writings: 1972-1977 (New York: Pantheon Books, 1977) and have been recently reprinted in Nicholas B. Dirks, Geoff Eley, and Sherry B. Ortner, eds., Culture/Power/History: A Reader in Contemporary Social Theory (Princeton: Princeton UP, 1994) 200–222. I use the latter volume, hereafter referred to as CPH.

6. Difendere la società. In accordance with the instructions of the Foucault estate, I have not quoted from the cassettes. All quotes from the lectures, excluding the first, second and final ones, are derived from a translation of the Italian text, hereafter referred to as DS.

7. Michel Foucault, "Faire vivre et laisser mourir: la naissance du racisme," Les Temps Modernes 46 (535) (February 1991): 37–61, hereafter referred to as TM.

clusion of the audiences' questions). This was clearly my own oversight and no one else's fault, not least the Saulchoir library staff who graciously accommodated and facilitated my work. However, it does indicate some basic confusion and miscommunications about what is already in the public domain, what should be available, and what should not. For if three of the eleven lectures have been published, why not publish the eight others—particularly when the first two have appeared as free-standing essays, dissociated from the lectures on the discourses of race which they preface and with which they belong?

These logistical matters aside, the lectures are elusive and challenging in their own right: not least because, as in most of his work, Foucault sparingly footnoted other authors. There are obviously no footnotes for the lectures, but there are also no citations to anyone else's work on the subject. Even for Coke, Lilburne, Thierry, and Boulainvilliers, whose historical narratives provide the grist for his analysis, there is only rare mention of the specific texts to which he sometimes painstakingly attends.[8] To what extent Foucault drew on the quite extensive corpus on the historiography of French racism that already existed is difficult to tell. For example, just prior to the 1976 seminar, two major works had appeared on the subject. A study by André Devyver, published in 1973, entitled *The Purified Blood: Racial prejudices among the French nobility in the Ancien Régime, 1560–1720*—a six hundred page book—treated some similar themes and key historians of that period in far greater detail than could Foucault in a series of one-hour lectures. Another study by Arlette Jouanna, entitled *The Idea of Race in France in the 16th and the beginning of the 17th century (1498–1614)* is a fifteen-hundred-page thesis defended at the University of Paris in 1975.

Hannah Arendt's 1952 publication *The Origins of Totalitarianism* covered some similar ground. For Arendt, the metropolitan politics of race in Europe and the racial politics of imperialism both derived from the similar notion that the 'rights of man' were only inheritable by those deemed worthy of them. In her account, imperialism is central, in Foucault's it is not. While their readings differ on many other issues, both grappled with the same conversion of the idea of race from an aristocratic political weapon into its more pervasive bourgeois form.

---

8. Throughout this chapter, I have tried where possible to indicate those specific texts to which Foucault refers, as well as some of the well-known secondary commentaries upon them and their authors.

This is not to suggest that these were the only relevant texts on the basis of, or against which, Foucault might have worked. Coupled with the U.S. scholarship on race in the early 1970s, a bibliography on the history of racism from this period would be staggering. I cite these particular studies here because, similar to Foucault's lectures, they focus on seventeenth- and eighteenth-century racial discourse as a "defense" of the nobility against encroachments on its privilege and sources of wealth. The subtheme and historical terrain are similar, but not the conceptual framework or the analysis.

It would, however, be misleading to argue that racism is what these lectures are primarily about. In his *Résumé des cours*, those summaries published for all the prestigious Collège de France lectures, the chapter entitled "Il faut défendre la société" ("Society must be defended") makes only passing reference to race. Foucault was concerned with how war came to be an analytic tool of historical knowledge and of social relations at large. Moreover, the issue of racism in the lectures seems ancillary and oddly displaced. And if this is so, why bother with them?

This is not a prelude to an argument that we have all missed the "real" Foucault, and that the key to a genealogy of racism is waiting for us in his taped lectures rather than in published form. I am more interested in the productive tensions between *The History of Sexuality* and this subsequent project and in the ways they converge and precipitously diverge in linking biopower and race. More importantly, I am interested in what we might glean from his insights and where we might take them. Both texts are concerned with the emergence of an alternative discourse to that of sovereign right, to "a discourse of the war of races" that Foucault will identify as the first "*contre-histoire*" (counter-history) to a unitary conception of power represented in a historical discourse that served the sovereign state. In *The History of Sexuality*, racism emerges in the dramatic finale as one of several possible domains in which technologies of sexuality are worked out and displayed. In the lectures, state racism is not an *effect* but a *tactic* in the internal fission of society into binary oppositions, a means of creating "biologized" internal enemies, against whom society must defend itself. The shift between *The History of Sexuality* and the lectures is not in content, but in textual field and analytic emphasis.

On the issues of race and colonialism that concern us here, the lectures underscore several contradictory impulses in Foucault's work: a focus on racism and an elision of it, a historiography so locked in Europe and its discursive formations that colonial genocide and narratives about it could only be derivative of the internal dynamics of European states. The studied absence of the impact of colonial culture on Foucault's bourgeois order did more than constrain his mapping of the discourses of sexuality. In the end, Foucault confined his vision to a specific range of racisms, a range that students of colonial history who might choose to follow his genealogical methods would be prompted to reject.

Still, as always with Foucault, there are unexpected insights that compel our attention. His treatment of racism is prescient in other ways. It reads biopower as a crucial feature of racism, accounting for the proliferating presence of fascist, capitalist, and socialist state racisms and the discourses of purification that legitimate their violence. Here, colonization emerges as central to Foucault's analysis of racism, but not in the way we might expect. Racial discourse consolidates not because of Europe's imperial ventures in Asia, Africa and Latin America, but because of internal conquest and invasions within the borders of Europe itself. Racism is not based on the confrontation of alien races, but on the bifurcation within Europe's social fabric. This deep genealogy allows him to account for Nazism as well as the distinct nineteenth-century discourses of nation, race, and class, all as permutations of a seventeenth-century discourse on the permanency of social war.

But these lectures offer more. They bring into sharp relief some of the basic analytic quandaries that engaged Foucault and that tie the lectures to an unexpectedly broad range of his other projects. For one, in the lectures he clarifies the relationship between the archaeological and genealogical methods, not as a sequential methodological shift, but as organically dependent and *complementary* tools of analysis.[9] Two, it is here that the differences between disciplinary and regulatory power, alluded to at the end of *The History of Sexuality* are distinguished in a new sort of way; as forms of power that operate at *different levels* and that articulate in a "society of normalization," providing the required conditions for racisms of the state.

9. In the lecture of January 7th, he states, " 'archaeology' would be the appropriate methodology of th[e] analysis of local discursivities, and 'genealogy' would be the tactics whereby, on the basis of the descriptions of these local discursivities, the subjected knowledges which were thus released would be brought into play." CPH 205. See Dreyfus and Rabinow (1982: 105–6) who stress the similar point that with Foucault's turn to genealogy "archeology is still an important part of the enterprise. . . . [T]he presentation of genealogy must not be considered to encompass all of Foucault's methodological arsenal."

Three, we are privy to Foucault's grappling with what I take to be one of the hallmark features of his work: not only a search for the discontinuities of history as so many commentators have claimed, but a more challenging analytic concern with the tension between rupture and reinscription, between break and recuperation in discursive formations. This theme underwrites his analysis of the relationship between deployments of alliance and sexuality, between a "symbolics of blood" and an "analytics of sexuality" in *The History of Sexuality* and continues to guide his genealogy of modern racism in the lectures. What concerns him is not modern racism's break with earlier forms, but rather the discursive *bricolage* whereby an older discourse of race is "recovered," modified, "encased," and "encrusted" in new forms.

Moreover, this is an analytic project strikingly reminiscent of the project set out in *The Archaeology of Knowledge*, where he wrote:

> Should [the principles of the individualization of discourse] not be sought rather in the dispersion of the points of choice that the discourse leaves free? In the different possibilities that it opens of reanimating already existing themes, of arousing opposed strategies, of giving way to irreconcilable interests, of making it possible, with a particular set of concepts, to play different games?[10]

The discourse of race will play out these "different games" with "polyvalent mobility," at one moment seized in the seventeenth century by "levellers" in their struggle against British monarchy, in the eighteenth century by French aristocratic opponents to absolutism, and yet again in the nineteenth century in "reversal," as a primary weapon replayed through the genocidal technologies of racial states.

Fourth, then, it is the state and the nature of state power, to which Foucault turns with striking clarity. For those who have characterized his conception of power as one that wholly eschews its statist locations, these lectures encourage some reconsideration. Here, Foucault is riveted on the relationship between racism and the "statization" of biology, on the anatomy of modern state power and the murderous capacities within

10. *Archaeology of Knowledge.* (AR:36–37). The quote continues:
Rather than seeking the permanence of themes, images and opinions through time, rather than retracing the dialectic of their conflicts in order to individualize groups of statements, could one not rather mark out the dispersion of the points of choice, and define prior to any option, to any thematic preference, a field of strategic possibilities? (AR:37)

it. Finally, if any single theme informs the seminar, it is not a quest for political theory, but an appreciation of historiography as a political force, of history writing as a political act, of historical narrative as a tool of the state and as a subversive weapon against it.

In what follows, I examine some lectures in detail and others in a more cursory fashion, focusing on those that most directly address the discursive conditions for the emergence of state racism and its specific technologies. This is not an easy task, partly because Foucault's genealogy makes so much of the specific discursive transformation of social war that, for him, reconstituted the definition of historical knowledge itself. It is also difficult because his definition of "sovereignty" is idiosyncratic and often used only to refer to its French absolutist form. Moreover, his analysis seems to preclude the fact that state racism and European imperial expansion occurred together. Finally, my approach to the lectured texts are tentative and tempered by the fact that they were not intended to be published as is and perhaps were never meant to be published at all.

Given these constraints, I take up their content in three specific ways; to address those issues only programmatically stated in *The History of Sexuality* and to locate how his treatment here diverges from that project. Most importantly, I examine what the lectures say about the discursive production of unsuitable participants in the body politic, and how the maintenance of such internal exclusions were codified as necessary and noble pursuits to ensure the well-being and very survival of the social body by a protective state. While Foucault confined his field to internal divisions in European societies and to the discursive production of internal enemies within them, these issues are not as far removed from colonial concerns as one might imagine. In chapter 4, I suggest some of the ways in which his insights dovetail with the changing terrain of scholarship on empire, citizenship, and national identity more generally. Specifically, I re-view them in light of my own work on the cultivation of whiteness in French, British, and Dutch colonial settings and its relationship to the interior frontiers of these European nation-states.

Subjugated Knowledges: On the Discourse of Sovereigns and the War of Races

On January 7, 1976, Foucault opens his Collège de France seminar with a number of unsettling reflections on the value of his work. He characterizes his preceding five years of research as efforts that "had failed to develop into any continuous or coherent whole," and that in their repetition "perhaps says nothing" (CPH:200). But this rude disclaimer, expressed with such dismal force, signaled not a rejection of what he had pursued for so many years, but an analytic repositioning of it. Here Foucault sees these earlier projects as contributions to the "insurrection of subjugated knowledges," to oppositional histories that emerged out of the "historical knowledge of struggles," independent of "the approval of the established regimes of thought" (CPH:202–3). It is the "independence" of these "disqualified" knowledges that he challenges, querying how these oppositional histories resurface within the very unitary discourses they opposed:

> In fact, those unitary discourses which first disqualified and then ignored them when they made their appearance, are, it seems quite ready now to annex them, to take them back within the fold of their own discourse and to invest them with everything this implies in terms of their effects of knowledge and power. (CPH:206)

In this first lecture, Foucault poses the issue of recodification as a problem of the present, as a development of the "last fifteen years" (CPH:202). And the specific "subjugated knowledges" that he cites are what we might expect: those of "the psychiatric patient, of the ill person, of the nurse, of the doctor . . . , of the delinquent, etc." (CPH:203). But none of these specificities of time and person are what Foucault chooses to pursue in the lectures that follow. The processes of recodification and reinscription that he will trace are not of the last fifteen years, but of the last three centuries; nor is it the subjugated voices of the condemned, the mad, the deviant, the medicalized subaltern that he will track, but rather the subjugated knowledge and oppositional history embodied in seventeenth-century discourse on races.

In rejecting the notion of power as repression, Foucault reiterates a central theme of The History of Sexuality, but uses it toward a different end. Here power is not only productive, it is, inverting Clausewitz's aphorism, "war continued by other means." Politics "sanction[s] and uphold[s] the disequilibrium of forces that was displayed in war" (CPH:209). This, too, is not a new theme. In chapter 2 of The History of Sexuality, the same question is already posed: "should we . . . then . . . say that politics is war pursued by other means?" (HS:93). There, his analysis of the discourse of war is embedded in a broader discussion of power; in the lectures, the discourse of war is repositioned as the "grid of intelligibility" through which the discourse of race takes form.

In the second meeting of January 14th, Foucault turns back to what he sees as that quintessential unitary discourse that has shaped our understanding of power since the middle ages: namely the discourse of sovereignty in which the fact of domination is hidden in a language of legitimate rights. It is this "juridico-political theory of sovereignty" that he attacks in order to reject its usefulness for understanding the nature of power and to show how a new historical discourse of power emerged, "incompatible with the relations of sovereignty" and in contradistinction to them (CPH:218).

This new type of non-sovereign power is disciplinary power, "one of the great inventions of bourgeois society" (CPH:219). Again, it is not the rupture between sovereign and disciplinary power that concerns him and not the disappearance of sovereign power, but rather its superimposition "upon the mechanisms of discipline in such a way as to conceal its actual procedures, the element of domination inherent in its techniques" (CPH:219). At the same time, this discourse of discipline, "has nothing in common with that of law, rule or sovereign will. The disciplines may well be the carriers of a discourse that speaks of a rule, but a natural rule, a norm. The code they come to define is not that of law, but that of normalization" (CPH:220). It is within the technologies of power nurtured in this "society of normalization" that internal enemies will be constructed and that modern racism will be conceived. But this is to jump ahead of his argument; in the following lecture of January 21st, normalization is not yet mentioned and the war of races is only briefly discussed at its end. Nor is the distinction between sovereign and disciplinary power pursued. Instead, he first critiques a theory of sovereignty as one that assumes the subject and therefore cannot account for its manufacture. Dismissed as an inappropriate method for analyzing relations of power, Foucault asks, "who imagined that the civil order was an order of battle: who perceived war in the watermark of peace; who has sought the principle of intelligibility of order, of the state, of its institutions and its history in the outcry, in the confusion and in the mud of battles" (DS:45)? Paradoxically, it is with the development of states at the end of the Middle Ages, as "private wars" were cancelled and war was made the prerogative of states, as war proper moves to the margins of the social body, as society is "cleansed of war-like relations" that this "strange," "new" discourse emerged, one in which society itself was conceived as an entity saturated with the relations of war.

It is a new discourse in several ways: new because it is the first "historico-political discourse about society"; new because it differs from the juridical discourse that previously prevailed. It is a discourse of "double contestations—popular and aristocratic—of royal power" (DS:52). It appears clearly in the early seventeenth century around the English bourgeois revolution (in the texts of Sir Edward Coke and John Lilburne) and then again at the end of that century around the opposition of the French nobility to the absolutist monarchy (as in the historical accounts of the Counts de Boulainvilliers and d'Estaing). In both its bourgeois and aristocratic form, it is an instrument of political opposition and struggle against sovereign rule. It reappears in the revolutionary texts of the abbé Sieyes and Augustin Thierry and by the late nineteenth century it underwrites racist biology and eugenics.[11] These purveyors of erudite knowledge, however, are not its sole locutors (although these are the only texts that Foucault invokes). It is an ambiguous discourse harnessed to different political projects, a discourse combining erudite and subjugated knowledges, guaranteeing its broad dissemination and wide appeal. Interestingly, this combination of "learned" and "disqualified knowledges" is precisely what Foucault, in his initial lecture, has newly designated as the object of genealogical research and more generally as a "provisional definition" of the specific genealogies that he had explored over the last few years.[12]

This discourse no longer lays claim to a neutral subject. The one who speaks is "necessarily someone else's adversary." The "great pyramid description" of the social body is replaced by the notion that "there are always two groups, two categories of individuals, two armies confronting one another" (DS:45). It is a discourse that interrogates law and sees its formation as the consequence of massacres, conquests, and domination, not as the embodiment of natural rights. It is not, however, a discourse that detaches itself from the language of rights; on the contrary, its truth claims are made to specific rights and by specific holders of them; the rights of a family (to property), of a class (to privilege), of a race (to rule). Truth

11. The two major texts of Augustin Thierry are *Tales of the Franks: Episodes from Merovingian History*, trans. M. F. O. Jenkins (1840; The U of Alabama P, 1977), and *History of the Conquest of England by the Normans* (1825; London: J.M.Dent, 1907).
12. See CPH 203–4.

is tied to a particular, decentered perspective, confirming a "fundamental link between relations of force and relations of truth." No one is above the fray; in fact, it is those most immediately implicated whose accounts are elicited and those outspokenly partisan voices that are credible and heard.

In the seventeenth century, this idea of war as the "uninterrupted weft of history" appears in the specific form of a war of races, a binary conception of the social body that will provide the "matrix within which all the forms of social war will be sought afterwards" (DS:54). One wonders whether, *malgré lui*, this is not some sort of originary moment for Foucault in the genealogy of race; throughout the lectures, this discourse takes on the force of an almost cataclysmic creation. But here it is the subsequent forms of social war of the nineteenth century, represented in two distinct "transcriptions" that he will set out to explain. One is an "explicitly biological transcription," preceding Darwin, that will draw its concepts and vocabulary from "anatomo-physiology." Ambiguous like that discourse of the eighteenth century, it will articulate with nationalist movements in Europe against the state and underwrite the European politics of colonization.

The second "transcription" will also draw on this notion of social war, but in a different way, in a discourse that will "tend to erase all the traces of the conflict of races and redefine them as class struggle" (DS:54). Although Foucault will privilege the biological and not this class transcription, alluding to the latter only briefly in subsequent lectures, when we turn to the early racialization of bourgeois culture in the next chapter, it should become clearer why this prefiguring of the language of class in that of race is so important to his argument. Here, Foucault focuses on the development of an entirely new "biologico-social racism" predicated on the notion that, "the other race is neither one arrived from somewhere else, nor one which at a certain moment triumphed and dominated, but instead, one with a permanent presence, that incessantly infiltrates the social body—that reproduces itself uninterruptedly within and out of the social fabric" (DS:54). There is no confrontation of two alien races here, but the bifurcation of one into an "upper-race" and "lower-race," with the latter representing the "reappearance of its own past" (DS:54). Foucault explores how this "decentered" discourse of the seventeenth century struggle of races is "recentered" two hundred years later to become a discourse of normalizing and centralizing power:

It will become the discourse of a combat to be carried out not between two races, but between a race placed as the true and only one (that holds power and defines the norm) and one which constitutes various dangers for the biological patrimony. At this point, all those biologico-racist discourses on degeneration will appear as will all the institutions which function internal to the social body as principles of segregration, elimination and normalization of society. (DS:54)

In short the assertion that "we must defend ourselves against society" will be replaced by the inverted claim—providing the seminar's title—that "we must defend society against all the biological dangers of that other race, of that sub-race, of that counter-race that despite ourselves we are constituting" (DS:55). The key elements are still "society," "enemies," and "defense," but in new configuration. The speaking subject is different as is the epidemiology of danger. The theme of race will no longer serve one social group against another; it will become a "tool" of social conservatisms and of racisms of the state: "It is a racism that a society will practice against itself, against its own elements, against its own products; it is an internal racism—that of constant purification—which will be one of the fundamental dimensions of social normalization" (DS:55).

What then distinguishes Foucault's analysis of race? Does it, in fact, differ from the common "scapegoat theory" of racism, or merely reflect a more subtle variation, where the "enemy" is constructed, not outside the body politic, but organically within it? Certainly Foucault is not the first to seek the origins of racism in the political logic of the particular historians on whom he wrote. Francois Hotman in the sixteenth century, Boulainvilliers in the seventeenth century, Augustin Thierry in the early nineteenth century are familiar forbearers invoked in more conventional accounts.[13] Nor is his observation unique, as already noted, that the discourse of race was, among other things, of aristocratic origins. Others have commented at length on the internal bifurcations in seventeenth-century European society as the terrain on which notions of race were cast.[14]

13. Jacques Barzun, *The French Race: Theories of its Origins and their Social and Political Implications prior to the Revolution* (New York: Kennikat Press, 1932) deals with Hotman and Boulainvilliers at some length. On Boulainvilliers, see Hannah Arendt, *The Origins of Totalitarianism* (New York: Harcourt and Brace, 1948) 162–63.

14. See, for example, Devyver who, in a chapter entitled "A reflex of social defense," argues that the idea of a "purity of blood" emerged as a defense among an impoverished and re-

But Foucault's positioning of racism is distinctive and counter-intuitive in ways that are not mirrored elsewhere. For one, it is not based on the successive meanings of race as described, for example, by Michael Banton, for whom race changes sharply from a notion of lineage to that of typology between the seventeenth and nineteenth centuries.[15] Foucault's concern is not the changing meaning of race, but the particular discourses of power with which it articulates and in which it is reconceived. Two, the changing force of racial discourse is not understandable in terms of clean semantic breaks. Again, what occupies Foucault are the processes of recuperation, of the distillation of earlier discursive imprints, remodeled in new forms.

Three, racism in its nineteenth-century elaboration is not consolidated in biological science, but more directly in the biologizing power of the normalizing state. This is a crucial distinction. The biologizing of race is not a nineteenth-century invention (as he seemed to allude in The History of Sexuality), but part of an emergent biopower two centuries earlier. Nineteenth-century science may have legitimated racial classifications as many have claimed, but it does so by drawing on an earlier lexicon, on that of the struggle of races.

Four, while other scholars have certainly noted that the language of race prior to the nineteenth century was shared by those of varied political persuasions, Foucault makes very different analytic use of that observation. Race has not always been what we might assume, a discourse forged by those in power, but on the contrary, a counter-narrative, embraced

---

sentful nobility whose solvency was dependent on marriage alliances with an empowered and enriched bourgeoisie. The latter was deeply resented by the nobility because of the increasing number of titles conferred upon its members (8, 10). The "internal bifurcation" on which Devyver focuses is between the nobility and the bourgeoisie and only secondarily that between the nobility and commoners. Also see Jouanna, who argues that the idea of race emerged as a "system of defense" among the nobility against the "inundation" of "people without honor" (1270, 1272). A related but somewhat different argument is made by Albert Sicroff with respect to the Spanish debates that surrounded the statutes on purity of blood between the fifteenth and seventeenth centuries, namely, that "with the proclamation of the statutes, those nobles who could themselves be suspected of impure blood, as a defense, entirely dissociated themselves from people of the middle class" (Les controverses des statuts de pureté de sang en Espagne du XVe au XVIIe siècle [Paris: Didier, 1960] 129). In both cases it was the fragile distinctions of some nobility that were endangered and at issue.

15. Michael Banton, The Idea of Race (Boulder: Westview Press, 1977) 13–62, esp. 27–28.

by those contesting sovereign notions of power and right, by those un-masking the fiction of natural and legitimate rule.[16] While many histori-ans accept the premise that nineteenth-century racism drew on earlier "looser" notions of race, for Foucault, this polyvalent mobility does more than describe its etymology; it critically accounts for the nature of mod-ern racism and the sustained power invested in it. Racial discourses are not only righteous because they profess the common good; they are per-meated with resurrected subjugated knowledges, disqualified accounts by those contesting unitary power and by those partisan voices that speak for the defense of society. Others, such as George Mosse, Hannah Arendt, and Barbara Fields, have noted the "very broadness of racist claims" as well as the very broad political spectrum of participants that have embraced them. Foucault's genealogy organically joins the two.

In short, this is no scapegoat theory of race. Scapegoat theories posit that under economic and social duress, particular sub-populations are cor-doned off as intruders, invented to deflect anxieties, and conjured up pre-cisely to nail blame. For Foucault, racism is more than an ad hoc response to crisis; it is a manifestation of preserved possibilities, the expression of an underlying discourse of permanent social war, nurtured by the bio-political technologies of "incessant purification." Racism does not merely arise in moments of crisis, in sporadic cleansings. It is internal to the bio-political state, woven into the weft of the social body, threaded through its fabric.[17]

16. Foucault drew his examples solely from French and British history but equally compel-ling and applicable are those one could draw from the racial discourses of creole elites in Latin America's nineteenth-century nationalist movements. See Julie Skurski's subtle analysis of creole nationalism in Venezuelan ("The Ambiguities of Authenticity in Latin America: Dona Barbara and The Construction of National Identity," Poetics Today [Winter 1994] 15[4]:605–42)—and her powerful critique of Ben Anderson's fraternally based imagined communities—where she suggests how a privileging of whiteness and a coding of race were implicit in the claims to entitlement of creole elites against the Spanish crown. Also see Emilia Viotti da Costa's The Brazilian Empire: Myths and Histories (Chicago: Chicago UP, 1988) that examines the ambiguous role that a discourse of race and "whitening" played in the "myth of racial democracy" in nineteenth-century Brazil.

17. Foucault's argument that racial discourse emerged as a form of subjugated knowledge strik-ingly resonates with some of the more compelling historical analyses of racism today. In Wages of Whiteness (London: Verso, 1991), for example, David Roediger argues that a discourse on "whiteness" not only went hand and hand with working class formation in the nineteenth and twentieth-century U.S., but that working class "assertions of white freedom" and struggles

The War of Races as a Contre-Histoire

The fourth lecture on January 28th is where Foucault first justifies his use of the term "racism" and "racist discourse" exclusively for the nineteenth century. From *The History of Sexuality* we already know that he conceived of nineteenth-century racism as a specific kind, but offered no elaboration. Here, he reserves the term "racism" for a "particular localized episode . . . a phase . . . ," better yet, a "recovery" and "reversal" in sociobiological terms of this "old already secular discourse" on the war of races (DS:56).

His task here is a "eulogy" to the war of races, to that discourse that neither justified nor glorified sovereign power but loudly narrated opposition. Before chronicling its demise, he looks again at its "newness" in yet another way, as "a disruptive *prise de parole*" that told "a story in the shadows" that cut through the uninterrupted genealogies of power" (DS:59). The sovereign is no longer one with the city, the nation or the state and thus emerges "the possibility of a plurality of histories": "in short, the history of some is not the history of the others." The function of memory is also turned toward a different end; not to maintain the law and reinforce power, but to reveal its deceptions, to show that power is unjust because it is not "ours" (DS:57). As a discourse of binary distributions between the rich and the poor, the strong and the weak, it calls up new actors: the French, the Gauls, the Celts, the rulers and the ruled. This is not, he reiterates, only a discourse of the oppressed; rather one that "circulated," that enjoyed a capacity to metamorphize and serve different political projects—radical English thought in the seventeenth century, French aristocratic interests decades later, and by the early nineteenth century, "a popular post-revolutionary mobilization."[18] Colonialism outside Europe makes its appearance late in Foucault's historical frame; at the end of the nineteenth century, when that racial discourse was recouped yet again to deny a colonized "*sous-race*" the rights to autonomous rule.

---

against capitalist disciplinary were made in the language of race (49). It is not that the U.S. white working class conceived of itself as a race apart from those whites that ruled; rather, the struggle for rights required a psychological displacement, a projection onto Blacks of a "preindustrial past they scorned and missed" (97). While Foucault might have been sceptical of Roediger's Freudian explanation, in both accounts, the "watermark" of subaltern rights is indelibly etched in the discourse of race.

18. Whether this "popular post-revolutionary mobilization" refers to the German move against Napoleon is plausible but not clear.

But Foucault's interest is broader still; not only to register the disappearance of this counter-history, but to identify the political dynamics of historical narratives more generally. This counter-narrative does not represent the difference between an official discourse that produces knowledge and one that does not. On the contrary, it signals a paradigmatic shift in the function of European historical knowledge as an instrument of permanent war. And the very language and project of revolution is subsumed by it. It was Marx, Foucault recalls, who wrote to Engels in 1892: "but the war of classes, we know very well where to find it: among the French historians when they tell of the war of races" (DS:65). The early nineteenth-century discourse of war plays a "new game": at once "displaced" by a discourse of class and "converted" into the revolutionary discourse of class struggle. Displacement and conversion are not opposed; both are elements in the dynamic of this recuperative process. As Foucault somewhat cryptically writes, "racism is literally revolutionary discourse put in reverse" (DS:65). The project of revolution and the counter-history of race in the nineteenth century do not coexist par hasard; their etymologies are one and the same, derived from the recovery of an earlier discourse on the war of races.

The nineteenth century holds other conversions in store. Just as the seventeenth-century discourse of war entered the social body when war proper receded from it, in the mid-nineteenth century, the theme of a historic war will be converted into a discourse of war conceived in biological terms. "It is no longer battle in the warrior sense, but a biological battle of differentiation, stronger selection of the species, maintenance of the better adapted race" (DS:65). The "enemy" changes as does the role of the state. The theme of the unjust state will appear in reverse formula where "the state is and must be the protector of the integrity, the superiority, the purity of the race" (DS:66). Modern racism is born out of this conversion from a discourse on races in the plural to a discourse on race, in its singular form, from a discourse directed against the state, to one organized by it.

Foucault is not arguing for a racial discourse of generic form. Different racisms will be the product of that shift, exemplified by two "great transformations" of the early twentieth century: the Nazi state and Soviet state racism. The Nazi state both reinscribed the characteristics of late nineteenth-century racism (posing the state as biological protector) and "reimplanted" earlier themes drawn from the eighteenth-century discourse of social war: those of redeemed heros, of an ancestral war, and of the old legends of the war of races. The Soviet transformation did the inverse, not with the high drama displayed by the Nazi state, but in the form of a "surreptitious," "scientistic" transformation. These state racisms depend on a new sort of army, a medical police that "assure[s] the silent hygiene of an ordered society" (DS:66). The sick, the mad, and the deviant are designated as "class enemies" and targeted for elimination. Foucault writes, "On the one side, [you have] the Nazi reinscription of state racism in old legends of the war of races; [on the other side, you have] a Soviet reinscription of the class struggle in the mute mechanism of a state racism" (DS:67). The theme of social war articulated in biopower provides the overarching principle that subsumes both *la lutte des races* and *la lutte des classes*.

Several features of this account are worth underscoring. First, no one "theory of race" functioned as the particular thesis of one group against another. Foucault is concerned with a more general racial grammar, what he carefully labels as a racial "coding" ("*codage*") that provided an "instrumental space, at once discursive and political" in which each group could infuse a shared vocabulary with different political meaning (DS:77).

Second, he identifies not the end of one discourse and the emergence of another, but rather the refolded surfaces that join the two.[19] Third, a point made repeatedly in each lecture: race is a discourse of vacillations. It operates at different levels and moves not only between different political projects but seizes upon different elements of earlier discourses reworked for new political ends. Four, the discourses of class and revolution are not opposed to the discourse of social war but constituted by it. Thus, unlike Hannah Arendt, who identified the "economic struggle of classes" and the "natural fight of races" as the two prominent "ideologies" of the nineteenth century, for Foucault they are neither independently derived

---

19. Gilles Deleuze also uses this notion of a "fold" to capture what he refers to as Foucault's "fundamental idea . . . that of a dimension of subjectivity derived from power and knowledge without being dependent on them." See the chapter entitled "Foldings, or the Inside of Thought (Subjectivization) in Gilles Deleuze," *Michel Foucault* (Minneapolis: U of Minnesota P, 1986) 94–123. My notion of the fold is quite different. I use it to identify the recursive, recuperative power of discourse itself, in a way that highlights how new elements (new planes) in a prior discourse may surface and take on altered significance as they are repositioned in relation to a new discourse with which they mesh.

ideologies nor alternate "persuasive views"; their etymology is one and the same.[20]

The Politics of Historical Knowledge

The four subsequent lectures play out these vacillations in specific terms. They do so by interrogating the causes and consequences of this new historical knowledge. Since these lectures are not directly concerned with state racism, I explore them less fully than the others. They are not tangential, however, to the method by which Foucault eventually arrives at his analysis of biopower and nineteenth-century racism at the end of the 1976 course. They serve as a detailed substantiation of his general argument concerning the transformational grammar of racial discourse between the seventeenth and twentieth centuries.

In the first of these four lectures, Foucault draws on the sixteenth- and seventeenth-century histories of the Norman conquest of Saxon England to illustrate how a discourse on conquest and the war of races took over new political fields and was reframed by them.[21] He identifies it as the first historical discourse that both challenges absolutist rights and ties the "rights of the English people" to the expulsion of the Norman foreigners. But this discourse was also used toward other ends: seized on the one hand by a Norman aristocracy to claim that their "right of colonization"

20. Arendt, The Origins of Totalitarianism 159.

21. For some minimal help in situating those historians and political figures to whom Foucault refers (such as Adam Blackwood, Sir Edward Coke and John Lilburne) see Christopher Hill, "The Norman Yoke," Puritanism and Revolution (New York: Schocken, 1958) 50–123. Hill's interpretation of the myth of the Norman conquest and its political uses resonates with Foucault's in at least one striking way: both noted its "polyvalent mobility." Hill saw this theory of conquest, that originally justified absolutism, "turned against its inventors" to become a "rudimentary class theory of politics," historically significant because it was among the first popular opposition theories that was not religious but secular (57). But also see J. G. A. Pocock who disagreed with Hill, arguing that absolutist monarchy never legitimated itself "on the theoretical basis of a conqueror's right." The Ancient Constitution and the Feudal Law: A Study of English Historical Thought in the Seventeenth Century (Cambridge: Cambridge UP, 1957) 54. However, note too Pocock's contention (again in line with Foucault's) that historians have wrongly assumed a continuity in use of the myth of the Norman conquest by the early common lawyers such as Coke and the later Levellers such as Lilburne. He argues that their deployment of the myth was to very different ends (125–126).

provided them with the right to rule and on the other hand, by parliamentarians opposed to the unchecked power of the Stuart monarchs.[22]

According to Banton (and Foucault), the popular version of the myth of the Norman yoke as retold in Sir Walter Scott's *Ivanhoe* (1820) portrayed the "opposition between Saxon and Norman . . . as a struggle between two races." Banton counts the term "race" used fifty-seven times in the novel.[23] Both hold that the discourse of races (but not yet that of "race") was already evident in the seventeenth century, in a form that allowed it continually to be turned toward different ends. Foucault focuses on its strategic mobility, on its "series of elements" that could allow the "coding" of fundamental social conflicts "in the historical form of conquest and the domination of one race over another." That coding neither confers uniformity on the function of the discourse nor implies a commonality in the classes that will embrace it. The importance for Foucault is that this discourse on the war of races anticipates the notion of "two nations" inside a society that will conceive of itself in binary terms.[24]

One particular part of Foucault's treatment of sixteenth century historiography should draw our attention. A text he attributes to Adam Blackwood contains what he calls a "very strange and important analogy"; namely, how the Norman conquest of England and the European conquest of the Americas were discursively constructed as similarly legitimized events, both confirming that early Normans and the contemporary English shared a right of colonization and a right to rule.[25] While the issue of colonization is broached in earlier lectures, here for the first and only time, Foucault explicitly ties the discourse of internal colonialism within

22. According to Michal Banton, the parliamentarians claimed that "Englishmen are descended of German race" thereby allying themselves with a tradition in which "the authority of the kings is not unlimited." See Banton, *The Idea of Race* 16–17.

23. Banton, *The Idea of Race* 20.

24. Nearly half of this lecture is devoted to a discussion of Hobbes. Because it is less directly concerned with the discourse of races, I do not deal with it here. Foucault dispells any "false affinity" that might be found in his approach with that of Hobbes, and discusses at some length why their notions of social war are not the same. He argues that Hobbes' analysis was not based on the notion of a society made up of inequitable power, in perpetual civil war with itself, as often assumed, but on a fundamental notion of "insufficient difference," a war of equality, a "sort of infinite diplomacy of rivalries that are naturally equalitarian." According to Foucault's reading, Hobbes never attacked the structure of power, but held fast to a discourse of contract, of sovereignty, and thus remained within a discourse of the state.

25. The text in question is "Apologia pro regibus," dated 1581.

Europe to the fact of its external expansion—in a way unanticipated by any of his previous accounts:

> I think at this end of the sixteenth century one sees a return effect [effet de retour] on the juridico-political structures of the West, but it is a return of colonial practice. It should not be forgotten that colonization with its techniques and juridical and political weapons transported European models to other continents, but that this same colonization had a return effect on the mechanisms of power in the Occident, on the institutional apparatuses and techniques of power. There had been a whole series of colonial models that had been brought back to the Occident and that made it so that the Occident could traffic in something like a colonization, an internal colonialism. (DS:78)

This is an extraordinary passage on several counts. Here Foucault clearly identifies a process that has become central to contemporary colonial studies and European history more generally: namely, the observation that external colonialism provided a template for conceptualizing social inequities in Europe and not solely the other way around. As a growing corpus of new colonial history has shown, and as Mary Louise Pratt specifically argues, "Europe's aggressive colonial and imperial ventures" served as "models, inspirations and testing grounds" for Europe's eighteenth-century bourgeois order.[26] While we cannot credit Foucault with demonstrating the link between the sixteenth-century discourse on foreign conquest and the disciplinary strategies of Europe's bourgeois world, the "return effect" he identifies is a piece of that process scholars are only beginning to follow, part of the discursive work that external colonialism has played in ordering social oppositions 'back home'. Unfortunately, this is the beginning and end of his story; Foucault neither pursued this connection nor elaborated further.

The following lecture of February 11th covers some similar ground but introduces another theme, as well. Foucault retells a familiar set of narratives from the Middle Ages to the Renaissance on the origins of England and France.[27] While many others have combed these accounts for their later political appropriations, Foucault re-examines the specific Trojan and Germanic myths of France's origins to substantiate two specific claims:

---

26. Mary Louise Pratt, *Imperial Eyes: Travel Writing and Transculturation* (London: Routledge, 1992) 36.
27. For a detailed account of these, see Jacques Barzun, *The French Race*.

one, already made, that the seventeenth century witnessed the emergence of a discourse that challenged "the uninterrupted character of the genealogy of kings and their power." In both France and England it was, he argues, the sixteenth-century theme of the invasion, of "two foreign nations inside a state" that provided the basis for these later accounts (DS:84).

The second claim pushes his specifications of this new historiography further. This discourse of aristocratic historians represents more than a new conception of power, but a new kind of historical knowledge forged by a nobility whose claims to privilege and property were eroding fast. What Boulainvilliers, then Buat-Nancy and Montlosier, attack is not only the legitimacy of sovereign power but "the knowledge-power mechanism that tied the administrative apparatus to the absolutism of the state" (DS:93). What this impoverished and marginalized nobility sought to "reconquer" was historical knowledge, to deploy it as a political weapon in its own interests, to narrate a history with another object and with another speaking subject than that constituted by the state. For Foucault, this new subject is the nation: "hence the fundamental concepts of nineteenth century nationalism will be born; hence will emerge the notion of race: hence will appear the notion of class" (DS:93). The subject of this new kind of historical knowledge will be those social antagonisms below, outside and against the state. No wonder, Foucault argues, that states would attempt to regain control of it. Beginning in the late eighteenth century, state institutions would be created to recolonize, centralize and relocate historical knowledge for the state's own ends. It is out of this aristocratic narration of the nation and its later bourgeois variant that two discourses would emerge: the struggle of race and the struggle of class. In short, the new subject of history is invented by the nobility not the bourgeoisie. Historical knowledge is no longer reserved for the state's historians who narrated its glory, but seized by historians of a nation pitted against the state, a nation that "considers itself as the object of its own historical narrative" (DS:97).

In the third lecture, Foucault again takes up Boulainvilliers whose writings exemplify an aristocratic version of history as a war waged on two fronts: one positioned against the third estate, legitimating the naturally endowed rights of the nobility that followed from invasion and the other against the unchecked power of the king. In this notion of history as a "calculus of forces," the grid of intelligibility for society is the theme of permanent war. Such histories, Foucault argues, contested received notions of power, confronting the dynamics of political force: "The aristocracy invented history because it was decaying, above all because it was waging its war and could consider its own war as an object of analysis" (DS:112).

The lecture of February 25th pursues this theme further. The battle is not between knowledge and ignorance as most accounts of the Enlightenment would have it, but rather over which forms of knowledge could lay claims to truth-values about the contemporary social order (DS:119). Here, the project of The History of Sexuality and the lectures converge again. The Will to Knowledge and Foucault's analysis of the truth claims of historical knowledge share a similar concern. In both, he explores the state's part in that process. In the lectures, the state intervenes in this struggle in four ways; by disqualifying some knowledges and valorizing others, by normalizing the communication between them, by establishing a hierarchy of knowledges, "a sort of chinese box," in which the material and the particular are subordinate knowledges, encased by the more general and abstract knowledges at the top, and finally, by a centralization of knowledge that makes state control possible (DS:120).

Up to this point, Foucault has concentrated on historical knowledge as an instrument of war for the nobility at one moment and for bourgeois and popular politics at another. In the lecture of March 3rd he reframes that question: how did this historical-political discourse become a "tactical instrument that could be employed in strategies that were completely different from those pursued by the nobility" (DS:125)? Other historians such as André Devyver and Hannah Arendt would interpret seventeenth-century racial discourse as the weapon of a beleaguered nobility threatened by bourgeois incursions on the one side, by the absolutist monarch on the other. But Foucault will make a different sort of argument, identifying the French revolution as the moment when this discourse that once served the nobility was generalized and confiscated by society at large:

> [Historical discourse] must not be considered as either an ideological product nor as the effect of the nobility's class position, but as a discursive tactic, of a technology of power-knowledge that precisely because it was a tactic could be transferred and could become both the law governing the formation of knowledge and the critical form of all political battles. (DS:125)

Foucault describes the specificity of that moment in this way: during the French revolution, historical knowledge was deployed in three different directions, "corresponding to three different battles, that in turn produced three different tactics": a battle over the nation, over social classes, and over race. Each was tied to a specific form of knowledge: philology, political economy, and biology: "to speak, to work, to live" (DS:125). Focusing on the tactical generalization of historical knowledge, he draws on Boulainvilliers again to show how and why this instrument of the nobility could become a general instrument in the political struggles of the eighteenth century. It was Boulainvilliers who turned "national dualism" into the principle of intelligibility of history by finding the initial conflict from which all others would derive, by identifying the carriers of domination and destroyers of civilization as the "barbarian" within Europe itself.[28] He explains his long digression on Boulainvilliers in these terms:

> I believe it is possible to specify quite easily the way in which, beginning with Boulainvilliers, an historical and political discourse was constituted whose range of objects, whose criteria of relevance, whose concepts, and whose methods of analysis, all turn out to be quite close to one another. That is, in the course of the eighteenth century an historical discourse formed that was common to an entire series of historians, who nonetheless find themselves in strong opposition to one another regarding their theses, their hypotheses, and their political dreams . . . It would be possible to pass very easily from one of these histories to another, identifying nothing more than some simple transformations in the fundamental propositions. (DS:136)[29]

28. On Boulainvilliers' historical account of the origins and history of the French nation (compared to the same events but in a different story told by the "democrat" Mably) see Francois Furet and Mona Ozouf, "Deux légitimations historiques de la société française au XVIII siècle: Mably et Boulainvilliers," L'Atelier de l'historie, Francois Furet (Paris: Flammarion, 1982) 165–183.

29. Foucault was not alone in looking to Boulainvilliers as emblematic of a particular kind of history. Lévi-Strauss used the term "Boulainvilliers transformation" to describe the relationship between different levels of historical analyses and why each history produces "anti-histoires." In the final chapter of The Savage Mind, he writes:

> Each history is thus accompanied by an indeterminate number of anti-histories, each complementary to the others: to a history of grade I there corresponds a history of grade 2, etc. The progress of knowledge and the creation of new sciences take place through the generation of anti-histories which show that a certain order which is possible only on one plane ceases to be so on another. (1966:261)

See Devyver (1973:111) who concurs with Levi-Strauss as to how that principle worked in the case of Gobineau. Foucault's notion of a "contre-histoire" obviously bears some semblance to Levi-Strauss' "anti-histoire," but Foucault uses it to elaborate a different set of properties be-

What he calls the "tight epistemic weave" of this discourse "does not mean that everyone is thinking in the same way" (DS:137). On the contrary, he identifies something like Adorno's "force-field" for a discourse that is at once powerful and shifting, without reducing to a "generative principle."[30]

> The condition for being able to not think in the same way is the same condition which makes it possible to think in a different mode and which makes this difference politically relevant . . . in other words, the reversibility of the discourse is a direct function of the homogeneity of its rules of function. It is the regularity of the epistemic field, it is the homogeneity in the manner of discourse formation which renders it usable within struggles . . . [that] are extra-discursive. (DS:137)

Given Foucault's frequent reiterations throughout the seminar, one might have expected a restatement of what made up the "regularity" of this "tight epistemic weave"; more so, since this is the first time that he would refer to epistemology at all. Neither issue is pursued further. Instead, the lecture concludes on the subject of the bourgeoisie, on the "anti-historical" and "anti-historicist" stance of it. As in the preceding lectures, there is a sense that, despite the telegraphic treatment, his audience should clearly see by now this bourgeois connection, but again the bourgeois order and its relationship to historical knowledge remains elliptical and only partially explained.

In yet a subsequent lecture, some of these vagaries are resolved. Foucault turns away from the aristocratic origins of eighteenth-century history to the early nineteenth-century embourgeoisment of it. As the bourgeoisie appropriated national discourse, it transformed the notion of war from a "condition of existence" to a "condition of survival," positing internal war as a defense of society against itself, against the "dangers that are born in its own body" (DS:142). Foucault examines the late eighteenth- and early nineteenth-century texts of the abbé Sieyes whose redefining of the nation positioned the Third Estate, not the nobility, at its essential core.

---

cause he has a specific genealogy of historiography in mind. Nevertheless, both are concerned with the sorts of counter/anti-histories that emerge when particular narratives resurface and are recontextualized for different political ends.

30. On Adorno's use of the notion of a "force-field" to "signify a juxtaposed rather than integrated cluster of changing elements that resist reduction to a common denominator, essential core, or generative principle" see Martin Jay, *Adorno* (Cambridge: Harvard UP, 1984) 14–15 as well as Martin Jay, *Force-Fields: Between Intellectual History and Cultural Critique* (London: Routledge, 1993).

With Sieyes, the task of the nation was recast, no longer designed to dominate others, but "to administer itself, to direct, to govern, to assure itself"
(DS:146). Unlike the aristocratic discourse that attacked the unitary state,
this narrative refocuses history on another sort of battle, on the inherent
"national duality" of French society at war with itself, at once challenging
the universality that had been reserved for the sovereign state and reclaim-
ing universality for the popular nation. It is not the past that holds the
truth of society, as it was for the aristocracy; universal truths are located in
the present. The discourse of history is curtailed in this process, "delimited, colonized, implanted, redivided and up to a certain point pacified"
(DS:141).

This discussion of historical knowledge might seem to bring us away
from the subject of racism, but for Foucault, such new forms of knowledge are at its core—and perhaps in more ways than he imagined. In
Sieyes' case, as Bill Sewell has shown, a racial grammar slips into Sieyes'
ruminations about citizenship, class and nation.[31] While Foucault presents
the nineteenth-century bourgeois appropriation of national discourse as a
pacification of the historical discourse of social war, it is not one that signaled the latter's demise. On the contrary, the final lecture explores "how
the theme of race comes, not to disappear, but to be recovered in an entirely other thing which is state racism" (TM:37). And it is "the birth of
state racism" that he talks about on the seminar's last meeting, in fact the
last day that he will write and lecture so explicitly about racism at all.[32]

On Biopower, Normalization, and the Birth of State Racism

Foucault's final lecture in Spring 1976 is a departure from those that preceded it in a number of important ways. First of all, it alone specifically
dovetails with The History of Sexuality, overlapping significantly with the final
chapter of volume 1. Secondly, it is the only one devoted to the nineteenth-
and twentieth-century racisms of the state; here, the sometimes cryptic
and cumbersome rehearsal of the discourse on the war of races is put
aside. Thirdly, it shifts temporal and analytic terrain. This lecture is about
modern racism and the biopolitical state. The term biopower has not ap-

31. See William Sewell, A Rhetoric of Bourgeois Revolution: Abbé Sieyes and "What Is the Third Estate?"
(Durham: Duke UP, 1994).
32. Foucault's 1978 lectures at the Collège on "the birth of biopolitics" discuss Nazism but not
genealogies of racial discourse in the detailed fashion elaborated here.

peared before, despite the fact that by Foucault's dating, its emergence coincides precisely with that of the discourse on social war. With the demise of sovereign power and rise of disciplinary regimes, the political technology of biopower begins to take shape. Invested in the management of life not the jurisdiction over death, this technology will convert a discourse of races into a discourse of race, investing the state as protector of social purifications. These connections are clarified, as Foucault turns to the reinscription of specific elements of sovereign power in the racist state.

The "statisation of the biological" (TM:37–38) was a "fundamental phenomenon of the nineteenth century," and it is within the biologized state that modern racism flourishes and rests. Once again, Foucault turns back to the classical theory of sovereignty where "the right over life and death was one of the fundamental attributes of sovereign rule." This right "to take life and let live," however, is a strange one that operated in asymmetric fashion. The sovereign could only intrude on life at the moment when he could take it away, by exercising the "right of the blade." Foucault captures its critical transformation in the nineteenth century with an agile turn of phrase that first appeared in The History of Sexuality and that he will use again here: the sovereign right "to kill and let live" (faire mourir et laisser vivre) will become the right "to make live and let die" (faire vivre et laisser mourir) (TM:38).

> [It] consisted not exactly in a substitution, but in a completion of this old right of sovereignty—to kill and let live—by another new right, that would not efface the first, but would penetrate it, cut across it, modify it and which would be a right, or rather a power that was precisely the inverse: the power to make live and let die. (TM:39)

This is not a new formulation. In The History of Sexuality, biopower was defined in similar terms, as a power "organized around the management of life," where wars were "no longer waged in the name of a sovereign who must be defended," but

> on behalf of the existence of everyone; entire populations are mobilized for the purpose of wholesale slaughter in the name of the life necessity: massacres have become vital. It is as managers of life and survival, of bodies and the race, that so many regimes have been able to wage so many wars, causing so many men [sic] to be killed . . .

at stake is the biological existence of a population. If genocide is indeed the dream of modern powers, this is not because of a recent return of the ancient right to kill; it is because power is situated and exercised at the level of life, the species, the race, and the large-scale phenomena of the population. (HS:137)

Foucault traces this emergent form of biopower in the seventeenth and eighteenth century through those "techniques of power that were essentially centered on . . . the individual body" (TM:39). These are the disciplinary technologies familiar to us from *Discipline and Punish* and to a lesser extent from *The History of Sexuality*. But here Foucault draws a distinction not made in his earlier work: namely, the development of a new technology of biopower in the mid-eighteenth century, that of regularization. This is not a variant form of discipline (as it appeared in *Discipline and Punish*); it occupies a different social and political space:

A technology of power that would not exclude the first, but that would encase it, integrate it, partially modify it and that would most of all come to utilize it by way of a sort of implanting of itself in it and by effectively encrusting itself, owing to this prior disciplinary technique. This new technology does not cancel out the disciplinary technique because it is at another level, it is at another rung . . . (TM:40)

Addressed not to the individual body, but to the life of the species and its "global mass," it presides over the processes of birth, death, production, and illness. It is not individualizing, but what he calls "globalizing" ("*massifiante*"). It acts not on the human body, but on the human species. Not a variation of the eighteenth-century anatomo-politics of the body, this biopower is a new thing. It does not concern itself with fecundity alone, nor with the morbidity caused by sporadic epidemics. Its focus is on the "*endemic*," those "permanent factors" that cut into the time for work, that lower energies, that diminish and weaken life itself (TM:42). Its primary instrument is not the disciplinary technology of individual dressage, but *regularization*, a "technology of security," a "bio-regulation by the state" of its internal dangers (TM:47).[33]

33. This attention to "the technology of security" anticipates a theme that will become central to Foucault in his 1978 Collège de France lectures on governmentality as he turns away from the issue of racism per se and focuses on "the apparatuses of security," what Colin Gordon

Power is no longer lodged in the sovereign right "to kill and let live" but rather in "the reverse of the right of the social body to ensure, maintain, or develop its life" (HS:136). It is "the right to intervene in the making of life, in the manner of living, in 'how' to live" (TM:46). This is, for Foucault, the ultimate bourgeois project. In The History of Sexuality, he has already described this "how to live" as central to the cultivation of the bourgeois self. It is through the technologies of sexuality that the bourgeoisie will claim its hegemony, its privileged position, its certified knowledge and jurisdiction over the manner of living, over the governing of children, over the civilities, conduct and competencies that prescribe "how to live."

No surprise then that Foucault turns back (for the first time in the lectures) to the strategic importance of sexuality as the "crossroads" where that power over, and invested in, individual bodies and populations would converge, in technologies of discipline and regularization (TM:50). Thus he explains the medical valorization of sexuality in the nineteenth century and the dangers that sexuality was deemed to hold in store. When undisciplined and irregular, sexuality could have two catastrophic effects at the level of the individual and the population. His example is the discourse on masturbating children, sketched in The Will to Knowledge and in the first of the lectures. The masturbating child would not only risk illness all of his (sic) life, but perpetuate a degeneracy that would be carried from generation to generation (TM:50). Medicine would become a technique of knowledge/power, serving both as a "scientific seizure on biological and organic processes" and a "political technique of intervention" (TM:50–51).

What Foucault is after is something more than the technology of power residing in medicine. That is only one site of a more general process of normalization that Pasquino rightly argues is a common theme of Discipline and Punish and The History of Sexuality.[34] What interests him rather is the norm that circulates between the processes of disciplining and regularization and that articulates the individual and the population:

---

has called a "specific principle of political method and practice" that joins the governing of the social body to "proper conduct" of the individual, to the governing of one's self. See Colin Gordon, ed., The Foucault Effect: Studies in Governmentality (Chicago: Chicago UP, 1991) esp. 1–52 and 87–104.

34. Pasquale Pasquino, "Michel Foucault (1926–84): The Will to Knowledge," Economy and Society 15.1 (1986): 98.

The society of normalization is not then, under these conditions, a sort of generalized disciplinary society in which disciplinary institutions swarm all over and eventually take over. This, I think is only a first insufficient interpretation. . . . The society of normalization is a society where the norm of discipline and the norm of regularization intersect . . . To say that power in the nineteenth century . . . has taken life in charge, is to say that it was able to cover the entire surface that stretched from the organic to the biological, from the body to the population, by a double play of technologies of discipline on the one hand, of technologies of regulation on the other. (TM:51)

Within this modern biopolitical state, the sovereign right to kill appears in new form; as an "excess" of biopower that does away with life in the name of securing it (TM:52). The death penalty serves as his example in The History of Sexuality (HS:137–138) and the atom bomb in the lectures (TM:51–52). From both, Foucault returns to the problem of racism and to a basic paradox of a biopolitical state: how does this disciplinary and regulatory power over life permit the right to kill, if this is a power invested in augmenting life and the quality of it? How is it possible for this political power "to kill, to give the order to kill, to expose to death not only its enemies but even its own citizens? How to exercise the power of death in a political system centered on biopower" (TM:52)?

For Foucault, this is the point where racism intervenes. It is not that all racisms are invented at this moment. Racisms have existed in other forms at other times: Now, "what inscribes racism in the mechanisms of the state is the emergence of biopower. . . . racism inscribes itself as a fundamental mechanism of power that exercises itself in modern states" (TM:53). What does racist discourse do? For one, it is a "means of introducing . . . a fundamental division between those who must live and those who must die" (TM: 53). It fragments the biological field, it establishes a break (césure) inside the biological continuum of human beings by defining a hierarchy of races, a set of subdivisions in which certain races are classified as "good," fit, and superior.

More importantly, it establishes a *positive* relation between the right to kill and the assurance of life. It posits that "the more you kill [and] . . . let die, the more you will live." It is neither racism nor the state that invented this connection, but the permanency of war-like relations inside the social body. Racism now activates this discourse in a novel way, establishing a biological confrontation between "my life and the death of others" (TM:53). It gives credence to the claim that the more "degenerates" and "abnormals" are eliminated, the lives of those who speak will be stronger, more vigorous, and improved. The enemies are not political adversaries, but those identified as external and internal threats to the population. "Racism is the condition that makes it acceptable to put [certain people] to death in a society of normalization" (TM:54). The murderous function of the biopolitical state can only be assured by racism which is "indispensable" to it (TM:54).

Several crucial phenomena follow from this. One is evident in the knot that binds nineteenth-century biological theory and the discourse of power:

> Basically, evolutionism understood in the broad sense, that is not so much Darwin's theory itself but the ensemble of [its] notions, has become . . . in the nineteenth century, not only a way of transcribing political discourse in biological terms, . . . of hiding political discourse in scientific dress, but a way of thinking the relations of colonization, the necessity of war, criminality, the phenomena of madness and mental illness . . . (TM:55).

In addition, racism will develop in modern societies where biopower is prevalent and particularly at certain "privileged points" where the right to kill is required, "primo with colonization, with colonizing genocide." How else, Foucault rhetorically asks, could a biopolitical state kill "peoples, a population, civilizations" if not by activating the "themes of evolutionism" and racism (TM:55). Colonialism is only mentioned in passing because what really concerns him is not racism's legitimating function to kill "others," but its part in justifying the "exposure of one's own citizens" to death and war. In modern racist discourse, war does more than reinforce one's own kind by eliminating a racial adversary; it "regenerates" one's own race (TM:56).

In conditions of war proper, the right to kill and the affirmation of life productively converge. But, he argues, one could also see criminality, madness, and various anomalies in a similar way, thereby resituating the subjects of his earlier projects (on madness, prisons, and sexuality) as expressions of the murderous qualities of the normalizing state, as subthemes in a genealogy of racism in which the exclusion and/or elimination of some assures the protection of others (TM:56). Here discourse has concrete effects; its practices are prescribed and motivated by the biological taxonomies of the racist state:

> You see that we are very far from a racism that would be, as tradi-
> tionally, a simple disdain or hate of some races for others. We are also
> very far from a racism that would be a sort of ideological operation
> by which the State or a class would attempt to divert those hostilities
> towards a mythical adversary . . . I think it is much more profound
> than an old tradition . . . than a new ideology, it is something else. The
> specificity of modern racism . . . is not tied to mentalities, ideologies,
> to the deceits of power. It is linked to the technology of power . . .
> to that which places us far from the war of races and this intelligi-
> bility of history: to a mechanism that permits biopower to exercise
> itself. Racism is tied to the functioning of a State that is compelled to
> use race, the elimination of races and the purification of the race to
> exercise its sovereign power. (TM:56–57)

Not surprisingly an explanation of the Nazi state underwrites his argument. As a state that combined the tightest regimes of discipline and
regulation, it expressed the "paroxysms of a new mechanism of power"
culled from the eighteenth century" (TM:57). At once disciplinary and
universally assuring ("assurancielle"), insuring, and regulatory, the Nazi state
generalized both biopower and the right to kill in a form that was "racist,
murderous, and suicidal" (TM:59).

Foucault ends his final lecture here on a prescient and ominous note.
While the deadly play between a power based on the sovereign right to
kill and the biopolitical management of life are exemplified in the Nazi
state, it is not housed there alone. His argument is broader still, namely
that this play between the two appears in *all* modern states, be they fascist,
capitalist or socialist;

> I think that the socialist State, socialism, is also marked by racism . . .
> social racism does not await the formation of socialist states to ap-
> pear . . . It is difficult for me to speak about this. . . . But one thing
> is certain: that the theme of biopower . . . was not just criticized by
> socialism, but, in fact, embraced by it, developed, reimplanted, modi-
> fied on certain points, but absolutely not reexamined in its founda-
> tions and in its modes of functioning. (TM:59–60)

Invoking nineteenth-century popular mobilizations revered by the French left, Blanquism, the Communards, and the Anarchists, Foucault contended that their notions of society and the state (or whatever authoritarian institutions might substitute for it) were predicated on the strongly racist principle that a collective body should manage life, take life in charge, and compensate for its aleatory events. In so doing, such forms of socialism exercised the right to kill and to disqualify its own members. Whether this should rightly be labelled a "racist principle" or be understood as a particular effect of biopolitical technologies more generally is open to question. Foucault justifies his designation in these terms: "Each time that socialism has had to insist on the problem of the struggle, of the struggle against the enemy, of the elimination of the adversary inside capitalist society . . . racism has revived . . . a racism that is not really ethnic but biological" (TM:60).

If this was difficult for Foucault to speak about, it appeared even more difficult for his audience to hear. Although no questions from the audience appear in the Italian or French transcriptions, a barrage was fired at him as he uttered his last sentence—striking in the context of the staid Collège de France format where challenging questions are still frowned upon and where even general ones are rarely posed. One member of the audience asked about the relationship between the Paris communards and racism. Another pressed him to specify the difference between capitalist and socialist states. Foucault's answers were both direct and evasive. He refused to take the bait. Instead, he merely alluded to a point made in earlier lectures that under socialism, class and racial enemies were often conflated and confused, embodied in the anti-semitism of the Paris commune, where financiers were first of all conceived as Jews. Apologizing for explaining himself badly, he repeated his contention that the same mechanisms of biopower and sovereign right were indistinguishable in socialist and capitalist states.

James Miller is convinced that Foucault's attack on nineteenth-century socialist strategies had a much more recent target, directed at the violent tactics of the French left in the wake of 1968.[35] One might also conclude that he was registering his view of Stalin's (biopolitical) purgings that prompted him to leave the Communist party two decades earlier. It cer-

---

35. Miller, *Passion of Michel Foucault* 291.

tainly resonates with his more recent indictment of Soviet prison camps, evident in one striking interview he gave to *Nouvel Observateur* in February 1976 where he condemned Soviet "mechanisms of power, systems of control, surveillance, and punishment" as similar in form to those by which the bourgeoisie had asserted their domination at another time.[36] In contemporary perspective, Foucault's analysis has an almost eerie quality. It speaks to, and even seems to anticipate, the conditions for "ethnic cleansing" in Eastern Europe's fractured states.

If these lectures did not work as effective history, it is not because Foucault did not try. As a history of the present, the lectures are disturbingly relevant today, and given the questions raised by those in the Collège de France audience, they were disturbing at the time. His attack on socialism certainly caught the attention of those who attended, but no one took up his more pessimistic indictment; namely that racism was intrinsic to the nature of all modern, normalizing states and their biopolitical technologies. Nor was he called upon to account for those varying intensities of racist practice ranging from social exclusions to mass murder. The state looms so large in his account, but the critical differences between state formations that discursively *threaten* expulsion and extermination as opposed to those that *carry it out* went unaddressed. On this unsettling note, he ended an extraordinary seminar.

Bourgeois Racism, Empire and Biopower in Light of the Lectures

I do not think it necessary to rehearse the broad analytic openings that these lectures provide. Those I outlined at the beginning of this chapter should be more than apparent now. Foucault's sustained concern with the nature of the state, with the distinction between disciplinary and regulatory power, and with changing forms of biopower emerge with force if not always with clarity. Moreover, they make new sense of the two initial lectures on subjugated knowledges that have been available in English for some time. Here I am more interested in looking at how the seminar informs our thinking about racism, *The History of Sexuality*, and our colonial reading of it.

To my mind, one of the seminar's most striking contributions is the ten-

---

36. See *Dits et ecrits* III:74.

sion that underwrites Foucault's historical analysis: namely, that between rupture and reinscription in the discourse of history and the implications it carries for the practices predicated on it. Using a substitutable set of terms (reinscription, recuperation, recovery, reimplantation, encasement), he identifies how racial discourse underwent micro- and macro-transformations: from a discourse on war proper to a discourse on war conceived in biological terms; from a power based on discipline to one transfigured into normalization; from a discourse that opposed the state to one annexed by it; from an ancient sovereign right to kill converted into a deadly principle in the modern state's biopolitical management of life; from racial discourse as the nobility's defense against the state into a discourse in which the state intervenes to defend society against itself. At each of these moments of conversion Foucault broaches what appears discursively continuous and what does not. What remains unclear, however, are the dynamics of that transformation, the discursive and non-discursive mechanisms that account for the selective recuperations of some elements and not others. What his analysis does do is unseat the conventional coupling of a discourse with a *specific* political ideology, alert us to discursive vacillations and to what this "polyvalent mobility" can mean.

The analytic and political tension between rupture and recuperation has strong contemporary relevance. It underscores what I would identify as one of the most striking features of racism and the historiography about it; namely, that racism always appears *renewed* and *new* at the same time. How else could we account for the fact that historians have come up with such an enormously different range of datings to track its emergence, have identified so many different crucial conjunctural moments to pinpoint its consolidation, have disagreed so fundamentally about its origins in place and time? Why is there such disagreement over whether there is a "new," "everyday" racism today? Why does Winthrop Jordan offer one date and Edmund Morgan another for the emergence of racism in the U.S.? Why is LePen's racism viewed by some as a new cultural racism and by others as a reformulation of tried and true forms? One could make two counterarguments: first, that a common definition of racism is not shared by many scholars, that they are not necessarily talking about the same thing. For some, it is defined by evidence of prejudice, while others mark racism by its structural, institutional edifice and its practical consequences. Thus one could argue that the datings differ because the phenomena in question are not the same. Alternately, one might invoke the work of Stuart Hall, or Michael Omi and Howard Winant who hold that racial formations are shaped by specific relations of power and therefore have different histories and etymologies, a point with which Foucault would have likely agreed.[37] Foucault might have been equally intrigued by Lawrence Hirschfeld's distinction between a commonly shared theory of race—what we might call an underlying grammar—and the distinct and varied systems of racial referencing and categorization adduced from it.[38]

Neither of these counter arguments, however, address a fundamental paradox of racial discourse. Namely, that such discourse invariably draws on a cultural density of prior representations that are recast in new form; that racism appears at once as a return to the past as it harnesses itself to progressive projects;[39] that scholars can never decide among themselves whether they are witness to a legacy of the past or the emergence of a new phenomena all together. Foucault's analysis suggests that these scholarly discrepancies are irresolvable precisely because they mirror what is intrinsic to the paradoxical power of racist discourse itself; namely, that it is, as George Mosse once noted, a "scavenger" discourse or as Barbara Fields writes, a "promiscuous critter," but not in unpatterned ways. Racial discourse is not opposed to emancipatory claims; on the contrary, it effectively appropriates them. Nor does it always cast itself as the voice of the state: it can speak as articulately for a beleaguered nobility against the state, for a creole elite opposed to the crown, and for the "silent majority." [40]

A genealogy of racisms would not entail the search for some culturally consistent originary moment from which racism derives; it would rather attempt to locate, as Foucault does for sexuality, why certain truth claims are banked on it; why racism, as Etienne Balibar notes, "embodies a very

37. Stuart Hall, "Race, Articulation and Societies Structured in Dominance," *Sociological Theories: Race and Colonialism* (Paris: UNESCO, 1980) 305–346; Michael Omi and Howard Winant, *Racial Formation in the United States: From the 1960s to the 1990s* (London: Routledge, 1994).

38. Lawrence Hirschfeld "Do Children have a Theory of Race?" *Cognition* 54 (1995): 209–252.

39. See André Taguieff's compelling analysis of Le Pen's racial discourse where he shows how Le Pen substantiates the necessity of stringent racist policies vis-à-vis immigrants in the name of a demand for a "real French revolution" and a more just "direct democracy." "The Doctrine of the National Front in France (1972–1989): A 'Revolutionary' Programme? Ideological Aspects of a National-Populist Mobilization," *New Political Science* 16–17 (Fall/Winter 1989): 29–70.

40. Whether this facility of appropriation is more true of the discourse of race than of any other number of powerful discourses—of, for example, class and gender—is not entertained.

insistent *desire for knowledge*," about the articulation of psychic/somatic features of individuals and about what is inherent in the dispositions of particular social groups.[41] Racisms provide truth claims about how the social world once was, why social inequities do or should persist, and the social distinctions on which the future should rest.

This is in no way to credit Foucault with having worked out a complete genealogy of racisms or even to suggest that his own criteria for genealogical research that might trace racism's "numberless beginnings, . . . minute deviations, . . . complete reversals . . . and false calculations" were carefully followed or adequately mapped.[42] On the contrary, the lectures confirm, even more strongly than *The History of Sexuality*, that Foucault's selective genealogical attention to the dynamics of internal colonialism within Europe by and large positioned the racial formations of Europe's imperial world outside his epistemic field and off his analytic map. Because Foucault's account of racial discourse is so endemically detached from the patterned shifts in world-wide imperial labor regimes of which those discourses were a part, we are diverted from the gritty historical specificities of what racial discourse did both to confirm the efficacy of slavery and to capture new populations in the transition to wage-labor.[43] Our task then would not be to follow his genealogy of racism with exegetical care, but rather to explore how his insights might inform our own.

The lectures, thus, are clearly of interest in their own right, but they also allow us to read *The History of Sexuality* in a somewhat different light. First of all, they obviously put to rest any question as to whether Foucault was concerned with the issue of race. Second, they make sense of the somewhat bizarre dating he offered for the emergence of "racism," by providing a clearer analysis of that specific form of "state racism" for which he reserved that term. Third, the lectures contextualize what many commentators have viewed as the somewhat "enigmatic" final chapter,

41. Etienne Balibar, "Racism as Universalism," *Masses, Classes, Ideas* (London: Routledge, 1994) 200.

42. See Foucault's "Nietzsche, Genealogy, History," *Language, Counter-Memory, Practice: Selected Essays and Interviews*, ed. Donald Bouchard (Ithaca: Cornell UP, 1977) 139–164.

43. See Brion Davis Brion's classic work on this subject, *The Problem of Slavery in the Age of Revolution, 1770–1823* (Ithaca: Cornell UP, 1975). Also see Tom Holt's excellent study of this process in *The Problem of Freedom: Race, Labor and Politics in Jamaica and Britain, 1832–1938* (Baltimore: Johns Hopkins UP, 1992).

and why the issue of sovereign right and particularly the articulation of the "right to kill" and the "management of life" were so central to it.

Not least, the lectures read along with The History of Sexuality resituate the nineteenth-century discourse of sexuality and the discourse of the biological war of race within a common frame as productive sites in a broader process of normalization.[44] One of the more riveting themes of the lectures, on the production of "internal enemies" within the body politic, alters our reading of The History of Sexuality in yet another way. Foucault's finer tracing in the lectures of a "racism that a society will practice against itself" provides a strong rationale for two of his claims: that the biopolitical management of life was a critical bourgeois project and that the management of sexuality was crucial to it. His contention in The History of Sexuality that the affirmation of the bourgeois self was secured through specific technologies centered on sexuality emerges in the lectures as part of a specific set of strategies not only of self-affirmation (as argued in volume 1) but self-defense of a bourgeois society against the internal dangers it has produced. What is at issue in the discourse of sexuality is not only the unproblematic cultivation of a bourgeois self already formed, but as we shall see in the following chapter, a more basic set of uncertainties about what it means to be bourgeois, about the permeability of its distinctions, and what constituted its vulnerabilities.

Despite some of the clarifications that the lectures provide, a number of critical lapses and ellipses remain: the most obvious being the connection between the normalizing bourgeois project in which racisms have developed and the imperial context of them.[45] There is no place made in

44. Note the striking similarity between Foucault's analysis of the relationship between racism and normalization and that of Partha Chatterjee's in The Nation and Its Fragments (Princeton: Princeton UP, 1993). Strongly influenced by Foucault but unfamiliar with these lectures Chatterjee writes:

> Indeed, the more the logic of a modern regime of power pushed the processes of government in the direction of a rationalization of administration and the normalization of the objects of rule, the more insistently did the issue of race come up to emphasize the specifically colonial character of British dominance in India. (19)

45. For an example resonant with Foucault's analysis of how the discourses on disease and those on defense of society fed off one another see Reynaldo Ileto's "Cholera and the Origins of the American Sanitary Order in the Philippines" (Imperial Medicine and Indigenous Societies, David Arnold, ed. [Manchester: Manchester UP, 1988] 125–48), where he comments on the relationship between the discourse of germ theory in which "a foreign agent must be excised from the

Foucault's account for the fact that the discourse that surrounded the fear of "internal enemies" was one that was played out over and over again in nineteenth-century imperial contexts in specific ways: where those who were "white but not quite"—mixed-blood children, European-educated colonized elites, and even déclassé European colonials themselves—contested the terms of that biopolitical discourse and found themselves as the new targets for "internal purification."

Part of the problem here derives from Foucault's cursory treatment in the 1976 lectures of the relationship between nation, citizenship, and race. While he may have rightly derived the discourse of the nation from a more basic discourse on the war of races, the full consequences of that common derivation are not explored. For the discourse of the nation, as much recent work has shown, did not obliterate the binary conception of society, but rather replaced it with a finer set of gradated exclusions in which cultural competencies continued to distinguish those who were *echte* Dutch, pure-blood French, and truly English. The discourse of race was not on parallel track with the discourse of the nation but part of it; the latter was saturated with a hierarchy of moralities, prescriptions for conduct and bourgeois civilities that kept a racial politics of exclusion at its core. Racism has not only derived from an "excess" of biopower as Foucault claimed, but, as Balibar argues, from an "excess" of nationalism.[46]

Finally, the most glaring omission from Foucault's analysis is its non-gendered quality. Just as feminists have long questioned how Foucault could write a history of sexuality without gender or for that matter women, we could query a genealogy of racism and a history of normalizing biopolitical states that fail to account for the formative work that gender divisions have played in them. State racism has never been gender-neutral in the management of sexuality; gender prescriptions for motherhood and manliness, as well as gendered assessments of perversion and subversion are part of the scaffolding on which the intimate technologies of racist policies rest. The following chapter on bourgeois identity and colonial

---

healthy parts of society" (135) and the Philippine-American war of 1899–1902. Ileto writes: "It can be argued . . . that the war was simply transposed from the battlefields to the towns, that the struggle continued over the control, no longer of territorial sovereignty, but of people's bodies, beliefs and social practices" (131).

46. Balibar, *Masses, Classes, Ideas* 203.

projects in the nineteenth-century Dutch East Indies should allow us to re-engage Foucault on a number of these fundamental questions. In looking to the sexual politics of race and the racial derivation of the language of class on imperial terrain, we are better positioned to interrogate the racial underpinnings of Europe's bourgeois order. We are in the felicitous position to draw on Foucault's insights and go beyond them.

IV

CULTIVATING BOURGEOIS BODIES AND RACIAL SELVES

The emphasis on the body should undoubtedly be linked to the process of growth and establishment of bourgeois hegemony; not, however, because of the market value assumed by labor capacity, but because of what the 'cultivation' of its own body could represent politically, economically, and historically for the present and the future of the bourgeoisie. Its dominance was in part dependent on that cultivation . . . (HS:125).

In the two preceding chapters, I closely followed Foucault's treatments of modern racism in *The History of Sexuality* and the lectures, as he traced its emergence through a discourse of sexuality, normalizing power, and the technologies of the biopolitical state. In *The History of Sexuality*, modern racism is a late effect in the biohistory of bourgeois hegemony; in the lectures that genealogy is more nuanced, more complicated, and in some ways more blurred. There, a discourse of races (if not modern racism itself) antedates nineteenth-century social taxonomies, appearing not as a result of bourgeois orderings, but as constitutive of them. It is to this shift in analytic weight and to incumbent colonial implications that I turn here. I want to suggest that by drawing on Foucault's deeper genealogy of racial discourse in the lectures, we can re-examine his history of bourgeois sexuality to enrich that account in ways more consonant with what we are beginning to understand about the work of race and the place of empire in the making of Europe's bourgeois world.

Thus, I want to keep two sorts of issues in focus: how we can use Foucault to think about a specific range of colonial issues, and, in turn, what these colonial contexts afford us for rethinking how European bourgeois culture recounted the distinctions of its sexuality. Two themes of the lectures are of interest here: one is Foucault's attention to racism as part of a state's "indispensable" defense of society against itself. This resonant and recurrent theme in the racial discourses of colony and metropole was critical to how European colonial communities expressed the "defense" of its privileged members. I look here at how the regulatory mechanisms of the colonial state were directed not only at the colonized, but as forcefully at "internal enemies" within the heterogeneous population that comprised the category of Europeans themselves. What is compelling in Foucault's analysis is less its novelty than its anticipation and confirmation of some of the very directions that studies of nationalism and colonialism are now taking.

On the other hand, Foucault by no means prefigured nor anticipated all these new directions. While he insisted on the primacy of a discourse on social war within Europe's eighteenth-century borders, giving only marginal attention to France's simultaneous colonial ventures that were under way, students of colonialism have made tentative efforts to sort out that connection. Lisa Lowe, for example, has drawn on eighteenth-century French travel literature to show how that literature became "the means through which internal domestic challenges to social order could be figured and emplotted as foreign challenges."[1] While Foucault plotted the rise of modern racism out of these domestic tensions, Lowe, like Ben Anderson, turns that same observation of noble and popular attacks on monarchical sovereignty to a different end to show how critical this early period of colonial expansion was in "registering and regulating" Europe's domestic conflicts.[2] If empire already figured in the class politics of eighteenth-century Europe, as Lowe, Pratt and others suggest, then surely it becomes harder to imagine a nineteenth-century bourgeois order that excludes empire from it.

Still, other insights of Foucault's, particularly his identification of a nineteenth-century shift in the tactic of power away from discipline to a "technology of security," dovetail with new directions in colonial studies in important ways. Key to this "technology of security"—like biopower more generally—was its joining of the governing of a population to new interventions in the governing of the self. While this form of power emerged around 1800 (as signaled in Discipline and Punish), in the course of the nineteenth century it comes to legitimate increasing intervention in

1. Lisa Lowe, Critical Terrains: French and British Orientalisms (Ithaca: Cornell UP, 1991) 54.
2. Lowe 54.

the ethics of conduct, geared to the management of "how to live" (TM:46). In the late colonial order, such interventions operated on European colonials in gendered forms that were class-specific and racially coded. Management and knowledge of home environments, childrearing practices, and sexual arrangements of European colonials were based on the notion that the domestic domain harbored potential threats both to the "defense of society" and to the future "security" of the [European] population and the [colonial] state.

In short, these colonial variants confirm some of Foucault's claims, but not others. I want to focus not on the *affirmation* of bourgeois bodies as Foucault does in *The History of Sexuality*, but on the uncertainties and porous boundaries that surrounded them. I am concerned with the ways in which racial discourse reverberated between metropole and colony to secure the tenuous distinctions of bourgeois rule; how in this "management of [bourgeois] life," middle-class distinctions were made not only in contrast to a European-based working class, but through a racialized notion of civility that brought the colonial convergence of—and conflict between—class and racial membership in sharp relief. My starting point is not the hegemony of imperial systems of control, but their precarious vulnerabilities.

While convinced that an understanding of the relationship between bourgeois biopower and colonial taxonomies entails tracing discourses on morality and sexuality through empire and back to the making of the interior frontiers of European nation-states, I only suggest some of those trajectories here. This task demands a reassessment of the anthropology of empire as well as of Foucault's selective Europe-bound genealogies. As a first step, I treat bourgeois sexuality and racialized sexuality not as distinct kinds, as does JanMohamed, but as dependent constructs in a unified field. Not least, my account confirms those challenges levelled at a European historiographic tradition in which the "age of empire" and this "century of bourgeois liberalism" have been bracketed more often than treated as parts of a whole.[3] In drawing on this emergent scholarship that

3. For one of the earlier and still definitive statements on this connection see Eric Stokes, *The English Utilitarians and India* (Oxford: Clarendon Press, 1959) and, of course, James Mill himself, *The History of British India*, 6th ed., 6 vols. (London: James Madden, 1858). For one specific effort to draw these linkages for the late nineteenth century, see David Johnson, "Aspects of a Liberal Education: Late Nineteenth-Century Attitudes to Race, from Cambridge to the Cape Colony," *History Workshop Journal* 36 (1993): 162–182. Also see Javed Maheed, *Ungoverned Imaginings: James Mill's*

attempts to span metropolitan and colonial social histories, I pursue those questions we are just beginning to ask, and suggest why we have not asked them until now.[4]

Rethinking Colonialism as a Bourgeois Project

It is beyond the fifty degree longitude that one starts to become conscious of what it means to be European.[5]

It may be the case that Foucault's work speaks less to the making of colonized subjects than to how European colonials constructed themselves, that his insights address, as Gayatri Spivak notes, more the "constitution of the colonizer."[6] Despite her allusion to Foucault's possible applicability to the normalizing contexts in which European colonials lived, Spivak never pursues this particular venture, dismissing it as a dangerous project. But even if we were to apply Foucault's story of the making of bourgeois distinctions to the ruling technologies of colonizing agents, that story and our treatment of it comes up against some serious problems. Some are Foucault's, and some our own.

Much of the anthropology of colonialism, as I have argued for some time, has taken the categories of "colonizer" and "colonized" as givens, rather than as constructions that need to be explained.[7] Scholars have

---

The History of British India and Orientalism (Oxford: Clarendon Press, 1992), who argues that the colonies were more than a "testing ground" for bourgeois liberal philosophy but the means through which European society "fashioned a critique of itself" (128). Also see Linda Colley ("Britishness and Otherness: an Argument." Journal of British Studies 331 [October 1992]: 309–329) who argues that for nineteenth century Britons "empire did serve as a powerful distraction and cause in common" (325).

4. On the problematic bracketing of national from imperial history in Britain and a well-argued plea for a rethinking of it, see Shula Marks, "History, the Nation and Empire: Sniping from the Periphery," History Workshop Journal 29 (1990): 111–119.

5. Louis Malleret, L'exotisme indochinois dans la littérature française (Paris: Larose, 1936) 51.

6. The quote in full reads: "what remains useful in Foucault is the mechanics of disciplinarization and institutionalization, the constitution, as it were, of the colonizer. Foucault does not relate it to any version, early or late, proto- or post-, of imperialism. They are of great usefulness to intellectuals concerned with the decay of the West. Their seduction for them, and fearfulness for us, is that they might allow the complicity of the investigating subject (male or female professional) to disguise itself in transparency" (Marxism and the Interpretation of Culture 294).

7. See my "Rethinking Colonial Categories: European Communities and the Boundaries of Rule," Comparative Studies in Society and History 31.1 (January 1989): 134–161.

focused more on colonizers' accounts of indigenous colonized societies than on how Europeans imagined themselves in the colonies and cultivated their distinctions from those to be ruled. In short, there may be so few colonial readings of The History of Sexuality because questions of what constituted European identities in the colonies and the problematic political semantics of "whiteness" have only recently come squarely within the scope of our analysis.[8]

The ellipses deriving from that constricted vision are more than apparent now as students of African, Asian, and Latin American colonial contexts have come to dismantle the received notion of colonialism as a unified bourgeois project. We have boldly and deftly undone its hegemonic conceits in some domains, but still skirt others. We know more than ever about the legitimating rhetoric of European civility and its gendered construals, but less about the class tensions that competing notions of "civility" engendered.[9] We are just beginning to identify how bourgeois sensibilities have been coded by race and, in turn, how finer scales measuring cultural competency and "suitability" often replaced explicit racial criteria to define access to privilege in imperial ventures.[10]

We still need to turn away from a founding premise. Colonialism was not a secure bourgeois project. It was not only about the importation of middle-class sensibilities to the colonies, but about the making of them. This is not to suggest that middle-class European prescriptions were invented out of whole cloth in the outposts of empire and only then brought

8. On the variable meanings of "whiteness" see, for example, my "Carnal Knowledge and Imperial Power . . ."; Catherine Hall's "Gender and Ethnicity in the 1830s and 1840s," White, Male and Middle-Class: Explorations in Feminism and History (London: Polity Press, 1992) 205–253.

9. For recent work on the gendered tensions of colonial projects, in addition to works already cited, see: Nupur Chaudhuri and Margaret Strobel, eds., Western Women and Imperialism: Complicity and Resistance (Bloomington: Indiana UP, 1992); Claudia Knapman, White Women in Fiji, 1835–1930: The Ruin of Empire? (Boston: Allen and Unwin, 1986); Patricia Grimshaw, Paths of Duty: American Missionary Wives in Nineteenth-Century Hawaii (Honolulu: U of Hawaii P, 1989); Nancy Paxton, "Mobilizing Chivalry: Rape in British Novels about the Indian Uprising of 1857," Victorian Studies (Fall 1992): 5–30; Frances Gouda, "The Gendered Rhetoric of Colonialism and Anti-colonialism in Twentieth Century Indonesia," Indonesia 55 (April 1993): 1–22. For a critique of some of this literature see Margaret Jolly, "Colonizing Women: The Maternal Body and Empire," Feminism and the Politics of Difference, eds. Sneja Gunew and Anna Yeatman (Boulder: Westview Press, 1993).

10. On the substitution of a discourse of cultural competency for an explicitly racial discourse see my "Sexual Affronts and Racial Frontiers. . . ." Comparative Studies in Society and History 34, 3 (July 1992): 514–51.

home. I want to underscore another observation: that the philanthropic moralizing mission that defined bourgeois culture in the nineteenth century cast a wide imperial net; that the distinctions defining bourgeois sexuality were played out against not only the bodies of an immoral European working class and native Other, but against those of destitute whites in the colonies and in dubious contrast to an ambiguous population of mixed-blood origin. If we accept that "whiteness" was part of the moral rearmament of bourgeois society, then we need to investigate the nature of that contingent relationship between European racial and class anxieties in the colonies and bourgeois cultivations of self in England, Holland, and France.

This issue of "contingency" is not easy to unpack in part because scholars have taken such different phenomena as evidence and have relied on such varied sources. The very range of questions we have started to pose reflect that breadth of approach and perspective. Should evidence of that contingency be the submerged presence of racially charged colonial images in the European bourgeois novel or the studied absence of them?[11] Were European bourgeois norms developed in contrast to a phantom colonized Other, and can we talk about common European bourgeois imaginings of empire at all? Was it the experience of empire that produced these linkages as Malleret's quote above suggests, or was it the metropolitan imaginings of what that experience was? Were the racial politics of colonialism the dominant backdrop against which European bourgeois sexuality was defined or did the eroticization of the exotic play more indirectly into how Dutch, French, and British middle classes garnered their moral authority over metropolitan working-classes, using representations culled from colonial contexts to define themselves?[12] Or was the language of class itself racialized in such a way that to subscribe to bourgeois respectability entailed dispositions and sentiments coded by race? Finally,

11. On the processes of imperialism consolidating within that "sanitized" realm of Europe's "unchanging intellectual monuments" in education, literature, and the visual and muscial arts, see Edward Said, *Culture and Imperialism* (New York: Knopf, 1993). Fredric Jameson argues that imperialism did more than leave "palpable traces on the *content* of metropolitan literary works," but on how modernism resolved the fact that there was always necessarily "something missing" and outside metropolitan experience in an imperial world. ("Modernism and Imperialism," *Nationalism, Colonialism and Literature*. Minneapolis: U of Minnesota P, 1990: 44, 51).

12. See Sharon Tiffany and Kathleen Adams, *Wild Woman: Inquiry into the Anthropology of an Idea* (Cambridge: Schenkman, 1985).

if this relationship between the affirmation of bourgeois hegemony and colonial practices was contingent, should we assume that the latter was *necessary* to the former's "cultivation" or merely supportive of it?

This chapter broaches some of these questions more fully than others, but they should *all* be kept in mind. I pose them here to underscore how much recent efforts to identify these tensions of empire remain dependent on different assessments of what those connections were. Even a partial untangling should allow us a more analytically and historically nuanced story of what part colonialism has played in the construction of Europe's bourgeois order and some minimal agreement about what we might take to be a substantiation of it. In that effort, I turn first to the class tensions around racial membership in the Indies and then back to the work of race in fixing bourgeois distinctions in Europe itself.

Colonial Oxymorons: On Bourgeois Civility
and Racial Categories

If there is anything shared among historians about the nature of French, Dutch, and British colonial communities in the nineteenth century, it is the assumed fact that they were largely peopled by what Ben Anderson has called a "bourgeois aristocracy"; those of petty bourgeois and bourgeois origins, who saw their privileges and profits as racially bestowed.[13] But this picture of European colonial communities is deeply flawed and not only for certain missionary groups, as Thomas Beidelman, John Comaroff and

---

13. At least one plausible accounting for this perspective is that it was extrapolated, as Victor Kiernan does, from "the run of officials" who populated the British civil service in India. Thus Kiernan writes:

> [they] belong to the type of the *gentleman* who was evolving in Victorian England. An amalgam of the less flighty qualities of the nobility with the more stodgy of middle-class virtues, he had a special relevance to the empire, and indeed was partly called into existence by its requirements, made to measure for it by England's extraordinary public-school education."
> *The Lords of Human Kind* (London: Wiedenfeld and Nicolson, 1969) 37.

But even in India, this knighted bourgeoisie was not in the majority. David Arnold calculated that "nearly half the European population [living in India by the end of the nineteenth century] could be called poor whites" (104). "European Orphans and Vagrants in India in the Nineteenth-Century," *The Journal of Imperial and Commonwealth History* 7.2 (January 1979): 104–127. Also see Hugh Ridley's detailed and subtle analysis of the myth of an "aristocratic democracy" of whites in German, French, and British colonies in *Images of Imperial Rule* (London: St. Martin's Press, 1983) esp. 124–145.

Catherine Hall have so rightly pointed out.[14] In the nineteenth century Indies, it is impossible to talk about a European bourgeois order that was not racially problematic at the outset.

What is striking is both how self-evident *and* tentative the joinings of middle-class respectabilities and membership in European colonial communities actually were. If colonial enterprises were such secure bourgeois ventures, then why were European colonials so often viewed disparagingly from the metropole as *parvenus*, cultural incompetents, morally suspect, and indeed "fictive" Europeans, somehow distinct from the real thing? While many historians would agree that colonized European-educated intellectuals and those of mixed-racial origin were seen as "white but not quite," this was also true of a large segment of those classified as "fully" European.[15] If colonialism was indeed a class levelling project that produced a clear consensus about European superiority—a consoling narrative that novels, newspapers, and official documents were wont to rehearse—we are still left to explain the pervasive anxiety about white degeneration in the colonies, the insistent policing of those Europeans who fell from middle-class grace, the vast compendium of health manuals and housekeeping guides that threatened ill-health, ruin, and even death, if certain moral prescriptions and modes of conduct were not met.

The question is whether those who made up these European colonial communities in fact saw themselves as part of a firmly entrenched ruling class, and if so on what basis? Eric Hobsbawm's definition of Europe's nineteenth-century bourgeoisie offers a useful contrast:

14. See John Comaroff, "Images of Empire, Contests of Conscience: Models of Colonial Domination in South Africa," *American Ethnologist* 16.4 (1989): 661–685, who demonstrates the colonial effects of a nonconformist missionary movement in Africa whose members "were caught uneasily between a displaced peasantry, an expanding proletariat, and the lower reaches of the rising British bourgeoisie" (663). Also see T. O. Beidelman, *Colonial Evangelism* (Bloomington: Indiana UP, 1982).

15. Homi Bhabha's provocative analysis of a difference that is "almost the same but not quite" ("Of Mimicry and Man: The Ambivalence of Colonial Discourse," *The Location of Culture* [London: Routledge, 1994]) has spawned a profusion of studies that examine the inherent ambivalence of specific colonial institutions that at once incorporated and distinguished colonized populations without collapsing the critical difference between ruler and ruled. My point is that this sort of colonial ambivalence was also a national one, directed at a much broader population whose class differences literally colored their perceived and proper racial membership as designated by colonial authorities.

[It was] . . . a body of persons of power and influence, independent of the power and influence of traditional birth and status. To belong to it a man had to be 'someone'; a person who counted as an individual, because of his wealth, his capacity to command other men, or otherwise to influence them.[16]

Some European colonial men would have numbered themselves within that class but not others. Some may have characterized themselves as having "power and influence" over the native population, but not over other Europeans. Still others, as George Orwell's subdistrict officer in "Shooting an Elephant" attests, were only too well aware of their dubious command over "the natives," and their limited mastery over themselves.[17] While the colonial right to command was allegedly independent of "traditional birth and status," the rosters of high government officials in India and the Indies suggest otherwise. In the nineteenth century, these positions were increasingly delimited to those who could afford to send their sons to law school in Leiden or to an Oxbridge public school, to those of the "cultivated classes," and to those of "full-blooded" Dutch or British birth. If "everyone [European] in India was, more or less, somebody" as the British novelist Maud Diver professed in 1916, how do we explain the sustained presence of a subterranean colonial discourse that anxiously debated who was truly European and whether those who were both poor and white should be included among them?[18] Contra Diver's claim, we know from a range of colonial contexts that class distinctions within these European colonial communities were not increasingly attenuated but sharpened over time, lending credence to Robert Hughes's contention for another colonial context that "the question of class was all pervasive and pathological."[19]

In fact, it is not clear how many "Europeans" in the colonies ever en-

16. Eric Hobsbawm, The Age of Capital: 1845–1878 (New York: Scribner, 1975) 244.

17. See Michael Taussig's "Culture of Terror—Space of Death," Comparative Studies in Society and History 26 (1984): 467–97 and my "In Cold Blood: Hierarchies of Credibility and the Politics of Colonial Narratives," Representations 37 (Winter 1992): 151–89 that both broach the "epistemic murk," the incomplete sorts of knowledge, and the terror of rumor through which many colonial officials operated.

18. Divers quoted in Hugh Ridley, Images of Imperial Rule (London: St. Martin's Press, 1983) 129.

19. George Woodcock, The British in the Far East (New York: Atheneum, 1969) 163; Robert Hughes, The Fatal Shore (New York: Knopf, 1987) 323.

joyed the privileges of belonging to a "bourgeois aristocracy" at all.[20] This is not to suggest that there was not a large segment of the European population that made up a social and economic elite. Those of the Indies' stolid *burgerstand* (middle-class/bourgeois citizenry) recruited from Holland included plantation and trading company management, upper-level civil servants, professional personnel in the fields of education, health, and agriculture. But while colonial sources bespeak a European colonial elite comprised of those from "good" families, birth in the Indies could exclude well-heeled creole families from membership. In 1856, W. Ritter observed:

> We count as European all those with white faces, who are *not* born in the Indies, all Dutch, English, French, Germans . . . even North Americans. Our readers will repeat: A European is a European and will remain so wherever he finds himself. . . . We know him well. But you are greatly mistaken, Readers, for a European . . . in the Indies is an entirely different being than in his country. . . . There, he identifies himself so much with all that surrounds him that he no longer can be considered as a European, at least for the duration of his stay in the Indies, but rather as belonging to a specific caste of the Indische population . . . whose morals, customs and habits are certainly worthy of close examination.[21]

While Ritter's exclusion of all those born in the Indies from the category "European" was unusual, it belies an anxiety that was much more widely shared: that even for the European-born, the Indies was transformative of cultural essence, social disposition, and personhood itself. His Lamarckian distinction was rarely so explicitly expressed; namely, that "Europeanness" was not a fixed attribute, but one altered by environment, class contingent, and not secured by birth.[22] Thus the Dutch doctor Kohl-

---

20. Benedict Anderson, *Imagined Communities* (London: Verso, 1983).

21. W. L. Ritter, *De Europeanen in Nederlandsche Indie* (Leyden: Sythoff, 1856) 6.

22. These categories were further complicated by the fact that the Indies was never wholly a Dutch-populated colony and certainly not from its beginning when many of its European inhabitants spoke no Dutch, were unfamiliar with Dutch cultural conventions, and were not Dutch by birth. In the seventeenth century, Portuguese served as the lingua franca "on the streets, in the markets, in church and in the households where European men kept Asian mistresses." Jean Taylor, *The Social World of Batavia* (Madison: U of Wisconsin P, 1983) 18–19. In the nineteenth and twentieth centuries, the colonial enclave was an international community made

brugge would write fifty years later that Europeans born and bred in the Indies lived in surroundings that stripped them of their European sensibilities to such an extent that they "could easily . . . metamorphize into Javanese."[23] What is at issue here is not a shared conviction of the fixity of European identity but the protean nature of it. In both cases, as we shall see, what sustained racial membership was a middle-class morality, nationalist sentiments, bourgeois sensibilities, normalized sexuality, and a carefully circumscribed "milieu" in school and home.

Ritter counted three major divisions among Europeans in the Indies: the military, civil servants and merchants for whom the lines of class distinction [were] "not clearly drawn." By his account, the Indies had no "so-called lower [European] classes."[24] But such lower classes did exist and in increasing numbers throughout the nineteenth century as a burgeoning archive of government investigations on the problem of destitute Europeans in the Indies can attest. For the category "European" also included an ill-defined population of poor whites, subaltern soldiers, minor clerks, abandoned children of European men and Asian women, as well as creole Europeans whose economic and social circumstances made their ties to metropolitan bourgeois civilities often tenuous at best.[25] At later moments it was to include Japanese, Africans and Chinese.[26] Being "European" was supposed to be self-evident but was also a quality that only the qualified were equipped to define.

Complicated local folk taxonomies registered these internal distinctions. Thus, the term indischen menschen might refer, as did Ritter, to those hybrid offspring of Dutch men and native women "whose blood was not

---

up of temporary and permanent expatriates who used Malay more easily than Dutch and many of whom had never been to Holland.

23. J. Kohlbrugge, "Het Indische kind en zijne karaktervorming," Blikken in het zielenleven van den Javaan en zijner overheerschers (Leiden: Brill, 1907).

24. W. L. Ritter, De Europeanen in Nederlandsche Indie (Leyden: Sythoff, 1856) 30.

25. See Charles van Onselen, "Race and Class in the South African Countryside: Cultural Osmosis and Social Relations in the Sharecropping Economy of the South-Western Transvaal, 1900–1950," American Historical Review 95 (1990): 99–123 who argues for a more complex view of South African racial history that challenges prevailing assumptions about the homogeneity of race relations by attending to the divergent alliances and interests of a broader class spectrum of subaltern whites.

26. A. Van Marle, "De group der Europeanen in Nederlands-Indie," Indonesia 5.2 (1952): 77–121; 5.3 (1952): 314–341; 5.5 (1952): 481–507.

unmixed European," but it could also connote those with lasting ties in the Indies, marking cultural and not biological affiliations. Creole whites born in the Indies were distinguished from those who were not. Those who came from and returned to Holland when their contracts expired (*trekkers*) were distinguished from those for whom the Indies was a permanent residence for generations (*blijvers*). "Pure-blooded (*zuiver*) Dutch were distinguished from those *mestizen*, "Indo-European," *métis*, of mixed-blood origin.

But perhaps the most telling term in this racial grammar was that which prevailed throughout the nineteenth century for those who were white but impoverished, and usually, but not always, of mixed-blood origin. Firmly dissociated from the European born, the term *inlandsche kinderen* neither referred to "natives" nor "children" as a literal translation might lead us to expect. It identified an ambiguous, hybrid population of those who were neither native nor endowed with the class background nor cultural accoutrements that could count them as truly European and fit to rule (accounting perhaps for Ritter's categorical exclusion of them). In the 1860s, some officials estimated thousands of such impoverished whites in the Indies; by the turn of the century, others calculated as many as sixty thousand.[27]

The enormous administrative energy levelled at the destitute living conditions of the *inlandsche kinderen* and proposals for their amelioration joined the policing of individuals with the defense of Dutch rule in specific ways. It was this group that confused the equation of whiteness and middle-class sensibilities in a discourse that legitimated the state's interventions in how all Europeans raised their children and managed their domestic and sexual arrangements. The discourse on destitute and degenerate whites whose "Dutchness" was suspect underscored what could happen to European colonials who did not know "how to live." Debates about the moral degradation of the *inlandsche kinderen* did more than produce narratives about maternal vigilance, child rearing, and appropriate milieu. It prompted new institutional initiatives and government policies that made claims to racial superiority *dependent* on middle-class respectability for the entire European population. It made linguistic competence in Dutch the marker of cultural "suitability" for European middle-class norms. It im-

27. Algemene Rijksarchief, Verbaal 9 July 1860. Governor-General's summary report to the Minister of Colonies concerning the establishment of a technical/craft school in Surabaya; J. H. F. van de Wall, "Het Indoisme," *De Reflector* 39 (1916): 953.

plicitly tied the quality of maternal sentiment and parental care to racial affiliation and nationality.

Architects of colonial policy worked off a set of contradictory premises. If the legitimation of European privilege and profit rested on a social taxonomy that equated Europeanness and bourgeois civilities, were those legally classified Europeans who fell short of these economic and cultural standards to be pulled back into these communities or banished from them? Was being poor and white politically untenable, a veritable colonial oxymoron? Were the unacknowledged children of European men and their native concubines to be reclaimed and redeemed by the state as Dutch, French, and British citizens or categorically barred?

These questions of racial identity and class distinction pervaded the colonial discourses in the Dutch East Indies, French Indochina, British Malaya, and India in the nineteenth and early twentieth centuries at different moments but in patterned ways. Mixed bloods were seen as one problem, poor whites as another, but in practice these persons were often treated as indistinguishable, one and the same. In each of these contexts, it called into question the very criteria by which Europeanness could be identified, how citizenship would be accorded and nationality assigned. In the Indies, the problem of "European pauperism," debated and scrutinized in government commissions throughout the late second half of the nineteenth century, was about indigent whites and their mixed-blood progeny, mixed-blood European men and their native wives whose life styles indicated not always a failed effort to live up to the standards of bourgeois civility but sometimes an outright rejection of them.[28]

But subaltern and economically marginal whites were not the only challenge to the taxonomic colonial state. The equation of middle-class dispositions and European membership were threatened by creole Europeans as well, not by those impoverished but as strongly by the well-heeled and well-to-do. Thus, it was this group of respectable "city fathers" of creole origin who petitioned the Dutch authorities in 1848 for the establishment of equivalent schools of higher education in the Indies and protested policies requiring their sons be sent for training to Holland to meet civil service entry requirements. It was their children who conversed more easily in Malay than Dutch, whose fatherland was more the Indies than the

---

28. This point is detailed in Chapter 5 of *Carnal Knowledge and Imperial Power* (Berkeley: U of California P, forthcoming).

Netherlands, who were feared to see themselves as "world citizens," not faithful partisans of continued Dutch rule.[29]

It is striking, for example, that in the 1850s Indo-Europeans born in the Indies were barred from posts in the civil service that would put them in direct contact with the native population at precisely the time when new administrative attention was focused on the inadequate training in native languages displayed by the Indies' colonial civil servants. At issue was obviously not whether civil servants knew local languages, but how those languages were learned and used and whether that knowledge was appropriately classified and controlled. While enormous funds were dispensed on teaching Javanese at the Delft Academy in Holland to students with a proper "Dutch rearing," those inlandsche kinderen who already new Javanese or Malay but lacked the proprieties and cultural knowledge that a Dutch rearing provided, were categorically barred. What was being taught to future officers in the colonial civil service at Delft was not only language but a more general set of disciplines that included distancing postures of comportment and imperious forms of address to inferiors that were crucial to appropriate language use.[30] Given the emphasis placed on "character" and conduct, the sustained attention of the colonial state to the importance of home environments is not surprising. The increasing attention given to a moral "upbringing" (opvoeding) as a prerequisite for the proper use of a formal education (onderwijs) turned on a basic assumption: that it was in the domestic domain, not the public sphere, where essential dispositions of manliness, bourgeois morality, and racial attribute could be dangerously undone or securely made.

While we could read these debates on the "so-called inlandsche kinderen" and the philanthropic moralizing impulses directed toward them as discourses prompted by threats to white prestige, these discourses spoke to other concerns as well. The "civilizing mission" of the nineteenth century was a bourgeois impulse directed not only at the colonized as often as-

29. On the fact that a "European upbringing" was considered "necessary to cultivate love for the fatherland and to strengthen the ties binding the colony to the motherland" see Algemeen Rijksarchief, Kol. 1848 geheim, no. 493, and the additional reports cited therein where this discourse on subversion, national security and upbringing is explicitly expressed.

30. See Fasseur who, while not taking note of this paradox, does provide evidence of the rationales for barring "inlandse kinderen" and the simultaneous emphasis placed on native language acquisition in the Indies colonial civil service (De Indologen 112–129).

sumed, but at recalcitrant and ambiguous participants in imperial culture at home and abroad.[31] But these bourgeois initiatives were as strongly directed at "reform of themselves."[32] As a new generation of Dutch social historians now argue, the "civilizing offensive" was not only about the "poor and their needs, but the rich and their motives."[33] In Indies perspective, the validity of these observations is well borne out. To abide by *burgerlijk* values was crucial to the racial rhetoric of rule, but that rhetoric often diverged from the messier realities of culturally hybrid urban wards where persons of varied class origin, in a range of domestic and sexual arrangements lived side by side—where the moral highground of middle-class prescripts was seen under threat in how the "European village population" (*Europeesche kampongbevolking*) lived—on colonial ground.[34] As we shall see in the next chapter, the charged discourse on the sexual precocity of Indies youths was not only a discourse about native contaminations but about the education of bourgeois desire, about alienations of affection in the homes of the most stolid *burgerlijk* colonial families themselves. As Nancy Armstrong has so convincingly argued for eighteenth- and nineteenth-century Britain, "programs for cultivating the heart . . . constituted a new and more effective method of policing" those who were to embody "the triumph of middle-class culture."[35]

Taking our cue from Armstrong's contention that British conduct books and novels during this period antedated the bourgeois way of life they represented, we might read the colonial guides to European survival in the tropics in a similar light: as prescriptive texts of how a *burgerlijk* colonial life style was suppose to look, not *a posteriori* affirmations or distillations of what colonial ventures had secured and already become. These were not reflections of a commonly shared knowledge, but creative sites of a new kind of knowledge that tied personal conduct to racial survival, child neglect to racial degeneracy, the ill-management of servants to disastrous

31. Hans Rigart, "Moraliseringoffensief in Nederland in de periode 1850–1880," *Vijf Eeuwen van Gezinsleven* ed. H. Peeters, et. al. (Nijmegen: SUN, 1986) 194–208.

32. Stuurman, 1993 360.

33. Ali de Regt, *Arbeidersgezinnen en beschavingsarbeid* [Workingclass families and the civilizing mission] (Boom: Amsterdam, 1984) 151.

34. On the living conditions of village-based Europeans as compared to the housing of the poor in Amsterdam see H.C.H. Gunning, "Het Woningvraagstuk," *Koloniale Studien* 2 (1918): 109–126.

35. Nancy Armstrong, *Desire and Domestic Fiction: A Political History of the Novel* (London: Oxford, 1987) 15.

consequences for the character of rule. They register how much a lack of self-discipline was a risk to the body politic. But, most importantly, in prescribing the medical and moral care of adult and children's bodies, the requirements for a *gezellig* (cozy) and well-protected European home, and the attributes of a "modern white mother" whose native servants were kept in check, they tied bourgeois domesticity to European identities and thus racial orderings to bourgeois rule.

Recasting Foucault's frame, this micro-management of domestic life might be seen less as an affirmation of bourgeois hegemony than as a contested and transgressive site of it. For if one definition of the nineteenth-century middle class in Europe was its "servant-holding status," in the Indies (as in Europe) it was precisely those who served the needs of the *middenstand* who were viewed as subversive contagions in those carefully managed colonial homes. It is only as historians have turned to these other domains of imperial culture where the meanings of "whiteness" were far less veiled that the "vigor" of European bodies shows itself as precariously secured through these racialized prescriptions and practices.

Our blindspots in colonial studies derive from certain assumptions, Foucault's from others. His story of what sexuality meant to the eighteenth-century bourgeoisie refuses an account that explains the management of sexuality in any class relational terms, i.e. as a strategy to harness the energies of the working class. For Foucault, the technologies of sex were first designed to affirm the bourgeois self. He writes:

> The primary concern was not the repression of the sex of the classes to be exploited, but rather the body, vigor, longevity, progeniture, and descent of the classes that 'ruled'. This was the purpose for which the deployement of sexuality was first established, as a new distribution of pleasures, discourses, truths, and powers; *it has to be seen as the self-affirmation of one class rather than the enslavement of another;* a defense, a protection, a strengthening, and an exhaltation that were *eventually extended to others*—at the cost of different transformations—as a means of social control and political subjugation . . . What was formed was a political ordering of life, *not through an enslavement of others,* but through an affirmation of self . . . it provided itself with a body to be cared for, protected, cultivated, and preserved from the many dangers and contacts, to be isolated from others so that it would retain its differential

value; and this, by equipping itself with—among other resources—a technology of sex. [my emphasis] (HS:123)

Here sexuality is about middle-class affirmations, not working-class exploitation; the term "enslavement" is used only in its metaphorical sense. Foucault's economy of sex produces power, truths, and pleasures. It contrasts the sort of repressive model of sex implied in an analysis of political economy where the energies expended on sex are viewed as detractions from the energies expended on work and where labor power is exchanged. But in substituting an economy of sex for an economy of labor does Foucault let the discourse of bourgeois sexuality stand in for the sociology of it? Even if we were to accept his bourgeois emphasis, we cannot help but notice the awkward syntax that absents key actors from his account. For even within his frame, these bourgeois bodies were never in fact isolated, but defined by intimate relationships and daily contacts of a special kind.

We are just beginning to explore some of the quotidian ways in which European bourgeois bodies were produced in practices, but these were never contingent on the will to self-affirmation alone. The cultivation of the European bourgeois self in the colonies, that "body to be cared for, protected, cultivated, and preserved from the many dangers and contacts . . ." required other bodies that would perform those nurturing services, provide the leisure for such self-absorbed administerings and self-bolstering acts. It was a gendered body and a *dependent* one, on an intimate set of exploitative sexual and service relations between European men and native women, between European women and native men, shaped by the sexual politics of class and race. Those native women who served as concubines, servants, nursemaids and wives in European colonial households not only defined what distinguished bourgeois life: they threatened that "differential value" of adult and children's bourgeois bodies they were there to protect and affirm. Others did so as well. Young European women of modest rural means who served as governesses to European colonial children were part of that "large supporting cast of houseboys, grooms, gardeners, cooks, amahs, maids, [and] washerwomen" whose tendings invaded these well-guarded homes.[36] This 'cast of characters' were not only there as ritual objects, symbolically affirming the hierarchies of Dutch au-

36. Anderson, *Imagined Communities* 137.

thority; through them Europeans could conjure a typology of natives that legitimated the structured subordinations of rule.

The self-affirmation of white, middle-class colonials thus embodied a set of fundamental tensions between a culture of whiteness that cordoned itself off from the native world and a set of domestic arrangements and class distinctions among Europeans that produced cultural hybridities and sympathies that repeatedly transgressed these distinctions. The family, as Foucault warns us, should not be seen as a haven from the sexualities of a dangerous outside world, but as the site of their production. Colonial authorities knew it only too well. They were obsessed with moral, sexual, and racial affronts to European identity in Indische households, but also in "full-blooded" Dutch homes. Housekeeping guides, medical manuals, and pedagogic journals produced in the nineteenth-century Indies and the Netherlands reiterated such dangers in many forms. Nor should it be surprising that this barrage of advice on contaminations intensifies as germ theory develops and biomedicine begins its triumphs.[37]

These prescriptive texts repeatedly urged that mixed-blood children in poor white households needed to be salvaged from the "damaging domestic milieu," severed from their native mothers and social environments. As late as the 1930s, the Indies civil service and police were congratulating themselves for "isolating" the daughters of European men and Javanese women from the "fatal, disastrous surroundings" and nefarious influences to which they were subject when "abandoned" to their mother's village homes.[38] European children of the well-to-do were equally at risk of degeneration, of "metamorphosing into Javanese," if the proper habitus was not assured and certain social protocols were not met; if they played in the streets with Indo-European children, if they attended Indies schools that could not instill a proper Dutch "spirit," and most perniciously, if they enjoyed too much indulgence from their native nursemaids, and in general had too much intimacy with and knowledge of things Javanese. I

37. This is not to suggest that biomedicine, and germ theory in particular, were merely colonial ideologies, but rather to understand how the technologies of colonial rule and the construction of certain kinds of scientific knowledge were, as Jean and John Comaroff convincingly argue, "cut from the same cultural cloth." "Medicine, Colonialism and the Black Body," *Ethnography and the Historical Imagination* (Boulder: Westview Press, 1992) 216. Also see Paul Rabinow's perceptive discussion of the central roles that the "concept of milieu in biology and conditions de vie or modes de vie in geography" played at this time. *French Modern* (Cambridge: MIT Press, 1989) 126–167.

38. Mr. C. T. Bertling, "De zorg voor het adatlooze kind," *Koloniale Studien* 15 (1931): 790–844.

have explored these quotidian technologies of self-affirmation elsewhere and turn in more detail to the specific discourse on native nursemaids in the following chapter.[39] Here, however, there are several distinctive features in this making of a bourgeois habitus in the colonies that I want to underscore.

First of all, Foucault assumes a middle-class culture sure of what it needed to defend and sure of how to do it. It is not clear this was the case in Europe or in the U.S.; in the colonies it was certainly not.[40] These strategies of identity-making and self-affirmation were unstable and in flux. European identities in the colonies were affirmed by a cultural repertoire of competencies and sexual prescriptions that altered with the strategies for profit and the stability of rule. Thus, concubinage was still seen to uphold a European middle-class standard in the 1880s, but seen to undermine it two decades later.[41] Adoptions of Javanese dress by European-born Dutch colonials were only permissible at leisure, as other more hardfast cultural distinctions between European and native were drawn. Early nineteenth century warnings against the performance of manual labor for whites in the tropics were reassessed by its end, when the Indies-born Netherlanders became associated with indulgent and ostentatious life-styles, contrasting the work ethic prescribed for the self-disciplined European-born Dutch. In short, while the vocabulary of European moral superiority was constant, that was neither true of the criteria used to measure that superiority nor of the specific sub-population of "Europeans" deemed morally worthy of inclusion in that select category.

Moreover, the logic that made being *echte* Dutch contingent on being middle-class frequently came up against the changing demands of the

39. See my "Sexual Affronts and Racial Frontiers: European Identities and the Cultural Politics of Exclusion in Colonial Southeast Asia," *Comparative Studies in Society and History* 34.2 (1992): 514–51, and "A Sentimental Education . . ." in *Fantasizing the Feminine.* L. Sears, ed. Durham: Duke UP, 1995.
40. On the emergent bourgeoisie's efforts to "impose order on the chaos that surrounded them" in the U.S. see Carroll Smith-Rosenberg, *Disorderly Conduct: Visions of Gender in Victorian America* (New York: Oxford, 1985) esp. 86–87. Also see Dorinda Outram's discussion of Alan Cobban and Francois Furet's similar characterizations of the French revolutionary period and its aftermath as a "competition for legitimacy among various sections of the French middle class through the appropriation of a validating political discourse and its embodiment" in *The Body and the French Revolution: Sex, Class and Political Culture* (New Haven: Yale UP, 1989) 29.
41. See my "Carnal Knowledge and Imperial Power" (1991) for a discussion of the different timings of this shift in British Malaya and the Dutch East Indies.

Indies' economy. As new demands for skilled technical labor emerged in the nineteenth century, the *inlandsche kinderen* were promoted as suitable candidates to fill such positions in naval shipyards, arms ateliers, and the expanding plantation industry. Various proposals designed to provide "scientific" as well as "practical" training to the Indies' European underclass were quickly defeated: others were never tried. Efforts, as early as 1835, to train Indies-born children of European descent to become "an industrious *burgerstand*" met with little success, prompting officials twenty years later to question whether they should be "made into a self-supporting *burgerlijk* class or a skilled working class differentiated from the natives."[42] By 1874 some authorities considered the notion of creating an independent *middenstand* a "total fiasco" on the argument that the *inlandsche kinderen* lacked both the "inclination" and the "suitability" for manual work of any kind, even skilled artisanal labor. In a revised vision, the state's task was reconceived as one that would turn them not into "imitation" or "defective Europeans" but into "perfected natives."[43]

At the heart of these debates were competing visions of what constituted a European "critical mass," and whether the "quality" and "character" of European residents was less important than the sheer quantity of them; whether the rash passions of subaltern soldiers and other lower-class men could reflect the nineteenth-century image of the "stolid and dispassionate" (*bezagigd*) Dutch nation and not undermine the moral tenets of Dutch rule.[44] Thus it was not only the mixed-blood *inlandsche kinderen* whose moral and intellectual attributes were under attack. Some observers in fact claimed that those workers imported directly from Holland were so utterly dissipated, so lacking in "vitality" (*levenskracht*) and zest for work (*werklust*) that the notion of making them into a *burgerklasse* was absurd.[45] Others claimed that the problem in the Indies was of a different order. As J. van de Waal put it in 1916:

---

42. Algemeen Rijksarchief. Considerations and advice of the directors of the naval establishment and factory in Soerabaja, 24 November 1858.

43. Algemeen Rijksarchief, KV 28 Maart 1874, 47. Also see *Het Pauperisme onder de Europeanen in Nederlandsch-Indie. Deerde Gedeelte.Kleine Landbouw* (Batavia: Landsdrukkerij, 1901).

44. On a similar note Hugh Ridley makes the point that a racial difference in British India was predicated on the notion that "sentiment" was "a European experience" while "sheer passion" was Indian (*Images of Imperial Rule* [New York: St. Martin's Press, 1983] 74).

45. Algemeen Rijksarchief, Verbaal 9 July 1860, 13, 24 November 1958.

The descendants of Europeans who are "unfit" for European nationality because of a lack of intellectual development and a high moral
conscience and who were brought up in pure native, and largely immoral, surroundings form a troubling part of society in the Indies that
does not show itself, as in Europe, in reckless anarchism or disso-
lute bestiality but that works in secret, nearly invisibly as a corroding
cancer gnawing at the sexual strength (steunkracht) of our society.[46]

Note here that this "biopolitical" discourse targets internal dangers and
excesses within the Dutch polity, weak biological links within its ranks
and not external, native contaminations.

Europeanness was not only class-specific but gender coded. A European
man could live with or marry an Asian woman without necessarily losing
rank, but this was never true for a European woman who might make a
similar choice to live or marry a non-European. Thus, in the legal debates
on mixed-marriage in 1887, a European woman who married a native man
was dismissively accorded native legal status on the grounds that her very
choice of sexual and conjugal partner showed that she had "already sunk
so deep socially and morally that it does not result in ruin . . . [but rather]
serves to consolidate her situation."[47] Foucault was undoubtedly right that
the affirmation of the body was "one of the primordial forms of class consciousness," but bourgeois "class bodies" defined their "healthy sexuality"
with a consciousness of civilities and social hygiene always measured in
racial terms (HS:126). Sexual promiscuity or restraint were not abstract
characteristics attached to any persons who exhibited those behaviors, but
as often post-hoc interpretations contingent on the racialized class and
gender categories to which individuals were already assigned.[48] Being a less
well-to-do woman and of mixed descent coded a range of social relations
as erotically driven, sensually charged, and sexually precocious by definition. Such assessments valorized that bourgeois health was pur sang and
European, governed by a logic in which moderation showed self-mastery
and "productive sexuality" defined what was morally acceptable and what
would improve the race.

46. J. H. F. van de Waal, "Het Indoisme," De Reflector 39 (1916): 953.

47. Taco Henny, Verslag van het Verhandelde in de Bijeenkomsten der Nederlandsch-Indische Juristen-Vereeniging
(Batavia, 1887) 39.

48. In a process similar to that described by Ian Hacking in "The Looping Effects of Human
Kinds," Foundation Fyssen Conference, Paris, 7–11 January 1993.

Questions about the shifting, visual signs of middle-class rearing were indices of what was invisible and harder to test—namely, what defined the essence of being European and whether creole and mestizen affinities for things Javanese were a threat to it. Thus the Indies 1884 law that specified the requirements for acquiring European equivalent status listed "complete suitability for European society" and/or indisputable evidence that the concerned party was "brought up in European surroundings as a European."[49] Although Dutch language use, attire, schooling, and church membership matched burgerlijk values to European status, that was rarely enough. As van de Waal observed children clothed in modest frocks and shoes when attending the government schools, enjoyed such a shortlived and insufficient education that these efforts at "Europeanism" were of little avail; "native dishes as always were awaiting them" when they returned to their village homes.[50] The powerful force of "environment" in this discourse slipped back and forth between two principle referents: the geography of the tropics and the architecture of sensibilities cultivated in the home. In constantly posing the question as to whether natives and inlandsche kinderen could be transformed, social reformers in metropole and colony could not help but ask the same question of themselves. But their answers were not the same. A basic disquieting asymmetry underwrote their racial grammar: for while an Indo child could not be shorn of its native sensibilities because of the "native blood that flowed in its veins," that logic—as we have seen and contra the stories colonial elites sometimes told themselves—did not work the other way around.

Bourgeois Insecurities, Racial Selves and the "Stolid" Dutch Nation

These colonial contexts make clear that bourgeois culture was in question on its social and geographic outposts, among those working out its changing standards. But there is also good evidence that it was not securely hegemonic even at its ostensible core.[51] Although Dutch historians

49. W. F. Prins, "De Bevolkingsgroepen in het Nederlandsch-Indische Recht," Koloniale Studien 17 (1933): 677.
50. Van de Waal 1918, 953.
51. For a succinct review of the debate on the hegemony vs. the "failure" of the British middle-class to "stamp its authority on the whole social order" see Janet Wolff and John Seed, eds., The Culture of Capital: Art, Power, and the 19th Century Middle-Class (New York: St. Martin's Press,

have long held that Dutch national character was clarified and fixed in the Golden Age of the seventeenth century, recent scholarship casts increasing doubt on that claim. Even Simon Schama who otherwise insists that "the essential traits of Dutch nationhood" endured major shifts in its governing institutions," concedes that the Dutch "conventional self-image" in the early nineteenth century underwent fundamental change.[52] With convincing argument, the Dutch historian Siep Stuurman notes that although the nineteenth century commonly has been referred to as the "century of the middle-class citizenry" (burgerij), that was only a partial truth.[53] His study of nineteenth-century liberalism contends that the "burgers who at this time were not called the middle-classes for no reason" had to wage a "continuous and tenacious struggle to acquire a dominant position next to the old ruling elite."[54] During the first half of the nineteenth century (from the French interregnum between 1795–1813 through the establishment of the Dutch monarchy and rise of constitutional democracy in 1848), there is little indication that state institutions were in the bourgeoisie's control.[55] By Stuurman's account, bourgeois hegemony in the Netherlands emerges at the end of the nineteenth century, not at its beginning. Liberalism was not the product of "a bourgeoisie that already dominated state

---

1988) esp. 1–44. My argument is not contingent upon proving the existence of bourgeois hegemony in the nineteenth century but, if anything, on its opposite—on its precarious ascendancy and its deployment of a biopolitical technology of power in which racial discourse played a pivotal role.

52. Simon Schama, *Patriots and Liberators: Revolution in the Netherlands, 1780–1813* (New York: Vintage, 1977).

53. Stuurman 14. Dictionary definitions of the term burgerij differ markedly. In some its first meaning is "commoners," in others "citizenry," and in others the "middle-class." On the different uses of the term "burgerlijk" and its similarities and differences with the term "bourgeois" in Dutch historiography and national politics see Henk te Velde's "How High Did the Dutch Fly? Remarks on Stereotypes of Burger Mentality," *Images of the Nation: Different Meanings of Dutchness, 1870–1940* eds. A. Galema, B. Henkes, and H. te Velde (Amsterdam: Rodopi, 1993) 59–80.

54. Siep Stuurman, *Wacht op onze daden: Het liberalisme en de vernieuwing van de Nederlandse Staat* (Amsterdam: Bert Bakker, 1992) 13–14.

55. In addition to those cited above see Lenders, *De Burgers en de Volksschool: Culturele en mentale achtergronden van een onderwijshervorming, Nederland 1780–1850* (Den Haag: SUN, 1988) 31. On the political struggles leading up to the establishment of the Dutch monarchy and the restoration of the House of Orange in 1813 see Simon Schama's magisterial account in *Patriots and Liberators: Revolution in the Netherlands 1780–1813* (New York: Random House, 1977). On the importance of the year 1813 to the subsequent development of a specifically Dutch form of liberalism see C. H. E. de Wit, *De strijd tussen Aristocratie and Democratie in Nederland, 1780–1848* (Heerlen: Winants, 1965).

and society," but one whose power was in the making.[56] In a related vein, the Dutch historian, Ali de Regt, argues that the mid-nineteenth century "civilizing offensive" that targeted the immoral living conditions of the working class as its object of reform was designed less to "uplift" the latter than to distinguish a burger class whose boundaries of privileges were not clearly drawn.[57]

These rethinkings of Dutch social history raise issues that go beyond domestic politics alone. If *burgerlijk* identity was less self-evident than many Dutch historians have claimed, then the sustained efforts to define who could belong to the *burgerstand* and who was really Dutch in the nineteenth-century Indies may take on a different valence. They may signal more than the reactions of a beleaguered colonial minority in a vast sea of colonized as often assumed, but rather a dynamic—even productive—tension between the making of Dutch bourgeois identity at home in the Netherlands and abroad.

Whether the Indies was central to the construction of nineteenth-century Dutch bourgeois culture is still difficult to affirm given the compartmentalization of Dutch historiography. Ritter's observation in 1856 that "the Indies is nowhere less known than in the country to which it belongs" may no longer be true, but the discrete treatment of the social history of the Indies and the Netherlands remains true today.[58] The question itself places these Indies-based debates about what it meant to be Dutch, *burgerlijk*, and sexually moral in a different light. These were sites where the moral authority of bourgeois values were played out, where the tension between desire and decorum, opulence and thrift were in uneasy display. The Indies discourse about Dutch bourgeois virtues infused the vocabulary of social reform and nationalist priorities with racial meaning.

This is not to suggest that these debates about "moral milieu" had their originary moment in colonial settings. Numerous studies of the late eigh-

---

56. Stuurman, *Wacht op onze daden* 14.

57. Ali de Regt 246–247. Others have interpreted the "*burgerlijk* civilizing offensive" as the direct expression of a "deep angst" about paupers, a disciplining gesture in which the valorization of "virtue" (*deugdzame*) would denote the forces of popular discontent. See Hans Righart, "Moraliseringsoffensief in Nederland in de periode 1850–1880," *Vijf Eeuwen gezinsleven*, eds. H. Peeters, et. al. (Nijmegen: SUN, 1986) 205, and Bernard Kruithof, "De deugdzame natie: het burgerlijk beschavingsoffensief van de Maatschappij tot Nut van 't Algemeen tussen 1784 en 1860," *Symposion* II/I (1980): 22–37.

58. W. L. Ritter, *De Europeanen in Nederlandsche Inde* (Leyden: Sythoff, 1856) 17.

teenth century show that new directives for education and the domestic environment of children represented pointed attacks by a *burgerlijke middenklasse* on the social hierarchies of France and the Netherlands' ancien regimes, that such reforms were part of the identity formation of the middle class itself.[59] The Dutch campaign for popular education was framed as a reform of an "orderless" morally corrupt society, where "ignorance, immorality, and savagery" were the enemies of the natural order. Reform rested on the instillment of "personal self-discipline" as well as collective moral control.[60]

But the nineteenth-century discourse, in which these internal enemies were identified and targeted, circulated in a racially inflected imperial field. Metropolitan debates over the critical importance of well-guided mothercare (*moederzorg*) for the alleviation of poverty, in the Indies fixated on whether mixed-blood and creole women specifically could provide the sort of *moederzorg* that would obviate assistance from the state (*staatszorg*). Similarly, European debates about whether men should be held responsible for their illegitimate children, in the Indies took on an explicitly racialized form: there, the question was whether European men should be charged with the care of their mixed-blood offspring and whether this would lead to an unhealthy expansion of a population of "fabricated Europeans."[61] Such parallel debates situate the moral contortions of Dutch colonials as part of the inherent contradictions within the liberal rhetoric of nineteenth-century bourgeois culture, rather than as marginal embellishments of it.

We have ample evidence that representations of racial ambiguity served to define the parameters of Dutch colonial communities in important ways. Racialized others of mixed-blood and creole origin and the suspect sexual moralities, ostentatious life-styles, and cultural hybrid affiliations attributed to them were productive of a discourse on who was appropriate to rule. But this traffic in charged representations may have reflected deeper concerns still; not only the vulnerabilities of Dutch hegemony in the colonies, but uncertainties about what constituted the inclusionary

59. See Jan Lenders, *De Burger en de Volksschool: Culturele en mentale acthergrondern van een onderwijshervorming, Nederland 1780–1850* (Nijmegen: SUN, 1988) 21, 52.
60. Lenders 63.
61. Cf. Selma Sevenhuijsen's nuanced discussion of the contradictions around the discourse on paternal responsibility and women's rights in the Netherlands (*De orde van het vaderschap* [Amsterdam: Stichting Beheer IISG, 1987]).

distinctions of bourgeois culture in the Netherlands where the very term "burgerlijk" could ambiguously refer to that which was at once exclusively middle class and that which was much more inclusively identified with the "civic," the "civil," the "citizen."[62]

Curiously, that tangled field that encompasses the cultivation of bourgeois bodies and the cultivation of *homo Europeaus* is one that few Dutch social historians have sought to entertain. While Stuurman and others have rightly noted how the Protestant nineteenth century *burgerij* rewrote the past in their own image, using the myth of a calvinist nation of "civilized morals" (*beschaafde zeden*) to program the future, their attention has focused more on the warped accounts of domestic social history than on the systematic and sustained omission of the East Indies from it.

Take the case of nineteenth-century Dutch liberalism and the history of social reform. The coincidence of dates that mark the *burgerlijk* "civilizing mission" in the Netherlands and the Indies is striking. By virtually all accounts, 1848 marked the emergence of a liberal-parliamentary state, identified with philanthropic bourgeois interventions to uplift the home environments of the domestic working class.[63] In the very same year, racial dualism in the Dutch East Indies was "legally anchored" in explicit terms.[64] One could argue that there is nothing incompatible about this. As Stuurman notes, although Dutch "liberals" spoke for the nation and the people, no pretense of universal representation was really implied: the "democratic element" of the mid-nineteenth century was confined to the virtuous and industrious middle class alone.[65] Citizenship (*burgerrecht*) categorically excluded "all women, minors, madpersons, beggars, prisoners, the dishonored . . . and all persons who did not have full use of their

---

62. For an effort to explore the contingency between colonial racism and its metropolitan variant in a later period, see Willem Wertheim's "Netherlands Indies Colonial Racism and Dutch Home Racism" in Jan Breman, ed. *Imperial Monkey Business: Racial Supremacy in Social Darwinist Theory and Colonial Practice* (Amsterdam: VU UP, 1990) 71–88.

63. Ali de Regt, "Arbeiders, burgers and boeren: gezinsleven in de negentiende eeuw," *Familie, Huwelijk en Gezin in West-Europa*, ed. Ton Swaan (Boom: Open Universiteit, 1993) 193–218. Also see Frances Gouda's well-documented comparative study of the nineteenth-century discourses on poverty, pauperism, and state-sponsored welfare in the Netherlands and France (*Poverty and Political Culture* [Lanham, MD.: Rowen and Littlefield, 1995]).

64. C. Fasseur, "Cornerstone and Stumbling Block: Racial Classification and the Late Colonial State in Indonesia," *The Late Colonial State in Indonesia: Political and Economic Foundations of the Netherlands Indies, 1880-1942*, ed. Robert Cribb (Leiden: KITLV, 1994) 31–56.

65. Stuurman 134.

freedom, their minds, or their possessions."[66] While those excluded from citizenship in the Netherlands made up the population that was the object of state intervention, in the Indies race structured the parameters of dependence and excluded many of those same categories not only from citizenship, but even from assistance and/or the opportunity to benefit from social reform.

Simultaneous with the enormous expansion of juvenile reformatories, orphanages, and agrarian colonies that targeted Holland's urban poor were a concomitant set of similar Indies institutions that repeatedly faltered on whether their potential recipients should include the illegitimate children of mixed-blood origin. Even those supporters of expanded European orphanages in the Indies never forgot to distinguish the mixed-blood children of lower-class Dutch soldiers from the orphans of deceased civilians who had, in their lifetime been well-to-do. Similarly the debates over poor relief, widows pensions, and improved medical care were implemented in ways that not only excluded those classed as "native," but those Europeans of suspect origin, either because they were deemed culturally "nativized" and lived in a fashion that required no such benefits or because some were seen as natives in disguise—only "fictive" Europeans. State reforms to set up public schools for "all Europeans and their legal equivalents" in the mid-nineteenth century, promptly designated special schools (armen-scholen, literally schools for the poor) for the children of subaltern whites, for those abandoned to the streets, for those destitute and of "mixed" origin.[67] Even some of the practitioners of these policies were sometimes the same. Johannes van de Bosch who founded the Maatschappij van Weldadigheid (Benevolent Society) in the Netherlands in 1818, was the same van de Bosch who, as the Indies' Governor-General some years later, introduced the oppressive cultivation system on Java that liberals in Holland were

66. Quoted in Stuurman 120.

67. See Izaak Johannes Brugmans, Gescheidenis van het Onderwijs in Nederlandsch-Indie (Groningen: J.B. Wolters, 1938), who notes that in 1875 many of the children attending an armenschool in Soerbaja ("even of parents who were pure European") came to school in a "neglected state, shabbily clothed, timid, speaking and understanding nothing but Malay even at the age of eleven or twelve" (269).

Note that the term "mixed" is virtually always racially inflected but discursively labelled in national terms. I have rarely seen it used to refer, for example, to children of "mixed" French and Dutch origin. It is most commonly used only for children of "mixed" racial descent, African fathers and Asian mothers, European and Chinese, etc.

soon to attack. It was also he who argued that the *inlandsche kinderen* were the colonial state's responsibility and its alone.[68]

The Froebel kindergarten movement that swept through Germany, England, Holland, and France in the mid-nineteenth century, that quintessential laboratory of liberal experiment, in the Indies was heralded not only as hothouse for nurturing Dutch middle-class sensibilities of morality, self-discipline, and thrift, but as a strategic method of removing [European] children from the immoral clutches of native nursemaids, native playmates and most importantly native mothers.[69] One might be tempted to argue that reformist gestures in the colonies produced these exclusionary, racialized reactions from a more conservative constituency. But this was not the case. These were proposals crafted by the most ardent social reformers whose visions were racially specific, highly class conscious, and exclusionary by definition.

Even such critically persuasive historians as Stuurman, who argues that "liberal-burgerlijke culture" was in the making in the nineteenth-century Netherlands, makes only passing reference to the Indies context where the exclusionary principles of liberalism were in such sharp relief. Ali de Regt's observation that the civilizing offensive in the Netherlands was never aimed at embourgeoisment resonates in the Indies in virtually every field of social reform. Plans to set up artisanal and industrial schools for impoverished whites and those of mixed-origin foundered on whether such a population could and should be shaped into an "industrious *burgerstand*" or not.[70] In debunking the myth of the "stolid" Dutch nation as the culture of a "self-sufficient middle-class," Stuurman prompts us to ask just those questions that Dutch historians have not sought to pose, questions

---

68. See Frances Gouda, *Poverty and Political Culture*, 1995, 115–116.

69. See Ann Tylor Allen, "Gardens of Children: Gardens of God: Kindergartens and Daycare Centers in 19th century Germany," *Journal of Social History* 19 (1986): 433–450 and Michael Shapiro, *Child's Garden: The Kindergarten Movement from Froebel to Dewey* (University Park: The Pennsylvania State UP, 1983). In the Indies, the first nursery school set up in Batavia in 1850 was designed to keep children from the ages of two to seven "out of the harmful environment of native servants" (Brugmans 276). See my "A Sentimental Education: European Children and Native Servants in the Netherlands Indies," *Fantasizing the Feminine in Indonesia* ed. Laurie J. Sears (Durham: Duke UP, 1996), where I discuss the Dutch colonial administration's interest in European nurseries at much more length.

70. *Algemene Onderwijs Verslag 1846–1849*, 55, quoted in Brugmans, *Gescheidenis van het Onderwijs in Nederlandsch-Indie* 87.

about the relationship between bourgeois projects and imperial ventures that are being asked by students of colonialism for Germany, the U.S., Britain, and France.[71] While this relationship was certainly tighter and more explicit in some places than in others, we cannot begin to contrast them unless we sort out whether national variations of emphasis and absence in historiography reflect national variations in lived history as well.

Discourses of Race/Languages of Class

One might argue that racialized notions of the bourgeois self were idiosyncratic to the colonies and applicable there alone. But a repertoire of racial and imperial metaphors were deployed to clarify class distinctions in Europe at a very early date. While social historians generally have assumed that racial logics drew on the ready-made cultural disparagements honed to distinguish between middle-class virtues and the immorality of the poor, as well as between the "undeserving" and the "respectable" poor among themselves, it may well be that such social etymologies make just as much sense reversed. The racial lexicon of empire and the sexualized images of it, in some cases, may have provided for a European language of class as often as the other way around. In a study of race and politics in Jamaica and Britain, Tom Holt cautiously notes that "this language of class [may have] provided a vocabulary for thinking about race, or vice-versa. It hardly matters; what is important is the symmetry of the discourse. . . ."[72] For my reading of Foucault, however, these racial etymologies of the language of class matter very much. They place the making of racial discourse, and a discourse on slavery in particular, as formative in the making of

---

71. Stuurman 23, 25. I have in mind a growing field of interdisciplinary scholarship that includes the recent work of Catherine Hall (in her collected essays entitled *White, Male and Middle-Class: Explorations in Feminism and History*). See the contributions of Lora Wildenthal and Susan Thorne in Frederick Cooper and Ann Laura Stoler, *Tensions of Empire: Colonial Cultures in a Bourgeois World*, forthcoming. A new generation with dissertations on these subjects include Laura Bear on Anglo-Indians, railways and modernity, Elizabeth Beuttner on British children and colonial South Asia, John Stiles on culture and citizenship in France and Martinique, and Laurent Dubois on questions of race and citizenship in the Antilles during the French Revolution. See Chris Schmidt-Nowara, "Hispano-Antillean Antislavery: Race, Labor and Nation in Spain, Cuba, and Puerto Rico, 1833–1886," diss., U of Michigan, 1995. All the above are, or have been, doctoral students in history and/or anthropology at the U of Michigan.

72. Tom Holt, *The Problem of Freedom* (Baltimore: Johns Hopkins P, 1992) 308.

a middle-class identity rather than as a late nineteenth-century addition to it.

Certainly, Foucault's contention that the language of class grew out of the discourse of races would support such a claim. From Montaigne to Mayhew to Balzac, in Britain, the Netherlands, and France, imperial images of the colonized native American, African, and Asian as eroticized savage or barbarian saturated the discourses of class. In an intriguing analysis similar to Foucault's, Hayden White argues that the "race fetishism" surrounding the eighteenth-century notion of the "noble savage" was "soon transformed . . . into another, and more virulent form: the fetishism of class."[73] But, unlike for Foucault, the template is not only an earlier racial discourse directed at internal enemies within Europe, but one prompted by imperial expansion. White writes:

> Like the "wild men" of the New World, the "dangerous classes" of the Old World define the limitations of the general notion of "humanity" which informed and justified the Europeans' spoliation of any human group standing in the way of their expansion, and their need to destroy that which they could not consume.[74]

The opening chapter of Eugene Weber's Peasants into Frenchmen, entitled "A country of savages," is emblematic of the confused ways in which these social categories were seen to converge. Quoting a mid-nineteenth-century Parisian traveller in rural Burgundy who opines that "you don't need to go to America to see savages," Weber argues that the theme of the French peasant as the "hardly civilized," rural savage "of another race" was axiomatic in a discourse that "sometimes compared them unfavorably with other colonized peoples in North Africa and the New World."[75] Nor do we have to wait for the nineteenth century to find those convergences between class and racial disparagements sharply drawn. The abbé Sieyes, that late-eighteenth-century Frenchman so renowned for his egali-

73. See Hayden White's analysis of the entanglements of class and racial categories in "The Noble Savage Theme as Fetish," The Tropics of Discourse: Essays in Cultural Criticism (Baltimore: Johns Hopkins Press, 1978) 183–196. Drawing on Louis Chevalier's Laboring Classes and Dangerous Classes in Paris During the First Half of the Nineteenth Century, he, like Foucault, finds the nineteenth-century language of class rooted in an earlier discourse of race and also in the bourgeoisie's efforts to undermine "the nobility's claim to a special human status" (194).

74. White, "The Noble Savage" 193.

75. Eugene Weber, Peasants into Frenchmen (Stanford: Stanford UP, 1976) 3, 6, 7.

tarian treatise that redefined the French nation in terms of its Third Estate, produced other visions of a just society that reveal profound contradictions in his argument.[76] Although Sieyes professed an identity between participation in work and citizenship, in a prerevolutionary note he invoked the notion of a hierarchy of races, and a definition of citizens that would exclude the real producers and include only the "heads of production" who "would be the whites." Sieyes' language of class and nation drew on a racial lexicon as well.

Edmund Morgan notes for seventeenth-century Britain that the poor were "the vile and brutish part of mankind . . . in the eyes of unpoor Englishmen, [they] bore many of the marks of an alien race."[77] Certainly this was true of British images of the Irish, who as early as the seventeenth century saw the Irish as "racially distinct."[78] Strong parallels were made between the immoral lives of the British underclass, Irish peasants, and "primitive Africans" by the eighteenth century, crescendoing in the early nineteenth century when the "influx of Irish amounted to an urban invasion."[79] Punch ran articles in mid-nineteenth century suggesting that the Irish were "the missing link between the gorilla and the Negro."[80]

Thus, for the nineteenth century the case is stronger still. Reformers such as Mayhew pursued their projects with a moral authority that rested on comparing the moral degradation of the British urban poor, with "many savage tribes" (1851:43). Such colonial historians as Victor Kiernan were well aware of the connection:

> In innumerable ways his [the European gentleman's] attitude to his own 'lower orders' was identical with that of Europe to the 'lesser breeds.' Discontented native in the colonies, labour agitator in the mills, were the same serpent in alternate disguise. Much of the talk about the barbarism or darkness of the outer world, which it was

76. See William Sewell, *A Rhetoric of Bourgeois Revolution: The Abbé Sieyes and 'What is the Third Estate'?* (Durham: Duke UP, 1994).

77. Edmund Morgan, *American Slavery, American Freedom* (New York: Norton, 1975) 325–326.

78. Richard Lebow, *White Britain and Black Ireland* (Philadelphia: Institute for the Study of Human Issues, 1976) 41.

79. See Lebow and Lynn Hollen Lees, *Exiles of Erin: Irish Migrants in Victorian London* (Ithaca: Cornell UP, 1979) 15.

80. Quoted in Lebow, *White Britain* 40.

Europe's mission to rout, was a transmuted fear of the masses at home.[81]

Jean and John Comaroff note that efforts to shore up British bourgeois domesticity drew on resonant parallels between the "dangerous classes" at home and abroad, a "coupling [of] the pauper and the primitive in a common destiny," in ways that implicated African domesticity in the making of modern English society.[82] Susan Thorne, in a study of missionary imperialism, argues that racial metaphors were pervasive in the religious discourse that shaped the language of class in early industrial England.[83] Edward Said synthesizes another strand of that story by looking at the canonical texts of British fiction in which colonial landscapes provided the backdrop against which British middle-class culture was set in relief. Catherine Hall explores the pervasive presence of a racialized Other in the repertoire of visual, verbal, and written images that set off the distinctions of bourgeois sensibilities and the virtues of the bourgeois home.[84] As Eric Hobsbawm once put it, "the bourgeois was, if not a different species, then at least the member of a superior race, a higher stage in human evolution, distinct from the lower orders who remained in the historical or cultural equivalent of childhood or adolescence. From master to master-race was thus only a short-step."[85]

There is something strikingly similar in most of these accounts; namely, that the invocation of race is interpreted as a rhetorical political strategy. Race serves as a charged metaphor with allegorical weight. It emphasizes the deep differences between working class and bourgeois culture, naturalizing the inherent strengths or weaknesses that these collectivities allegedly shared. In short, as Elaine Showalter notes, "metaphors of race were . . . used to describe class relationships."[86] But is metaphor and alle-

---

81. V. G. Kiernan, *The Lords of Human Kind* (1969; New York: Columbia, 1986): 316 .

82. Jean and John Comaroff, "Home-Made Hegemony: Modernity, Domesticity, and Colonialism in South Africa," *African Encounters with Domesticity*, ed. Karen Hansen (New Brunswick: Rutgers UP, 1992) 37–74.

83. Susan Thorne, "The Conversion of England and the Converserion of the World Inseparable: Missionary Imperialism and the Language of Class, 1750–1850," *Tensions of Empire: Colonial Cultures in a Bourgeois World*, Frederick Cooper and Ann Laura Stoler, forthcoming.

84. See Catherine Hall, *White, Male and Middle-Class: Explorations in Feminism and History* (London: Polity Press, 1988) esp. chapter 9, 205–53.

85. Hobsbawm, *Age of Capital* 247–248.

86. Elaine Showalter, *Sexual Anarchy: Gender and Culture at the Fin de Siecle* (London: Penguin, 1990) 5.

gory all that this relationship is about? I think not. For it assumes first of all that "class" and "race" occupied distinct spaces in the folk social taxonomies of Europe, that they were discursively and practically discrete social categories. We might question whether this was the case, particularly for the eighteenth century when notions of "race" and "class" had both looser and richer meanings and when the hardened distinctions inherited from the nineteenth century were not yet so clearly drawn.[87]

The point is an important one because if these were indeed not only "symmetrical discourses" as Tom Holt has argued but at once overlapping and interchangeable ones, then some notion of race must figure much more organically in the making of bourgeois distinctions than we have assumed.[88] Such an argument would not rest on the assumption that the social categories of "race" and "class" were always substitutable or that the meanings of "race" in the seventeenth, eighteenth, and nineteenth centuries were the same. Nor would Foucault's reverse genealogy in which the language of class *always* emerges out of an earlier discourse of race necessarily be the case. On the contrary, both "race" and "class" in their early usage marked a more fluid environmentally conditioned Lamarckian set of somatic differences, differences in ways of being and living, differences in psychological and moral essence—differences in human kind. When Douglas Lorimer argues that "English racism . . . rested upon established attitudes toward distinctions of class," and that mid-Victorians "perceived race relations abroad in the light of class relations at home," his own evidence belies a more fluid semantic field.[89] For he also writes that the white London poor were considered "a race" apart, that servants were also not a "distinct class but . . . a separate race." [90] Those features that confirmed the Irish as a separate race—"chronic self-indulgence, indolence and laxity of purpose" were invoked to distinguish the urban and rural laboring classes throughout Europe, both mixed-bloods and subaltern whites throughout the colonies. It captured in one sustained image internal threats to the health and well-being of a social body where those deemed a threat lacked an ethics of "how to live" and thus the ability to govern themselves. When

87. On the changing meanings of "class" see Raymond Williams, *Keywords* (London: Croom Helm, 1976) 51–58.
88. On the "interchangeability" of class and racial discrimination see Hugh Ridley, *Images of Imperial Rule* (London: St. Martin's Press, 1983) 140.
89. Douglas Lorimer, *Colour, Class and the Victorians* (Leicester: Leicester UP, 1978) 93.
90. Lorimer 105.

Mayhew wrote that "hearth and rootedness," those "sacred symbols to all civilized races" (Mayhew 1851:43), were lacking in London's poor, he was not only claiming that the unmanaged mobility of society's subalterns was a threat to colonial and metropolitan authority. He was identifying what was distinctively part of the bourgeoisie's conception of itself: one that embraced property ownership, rootedness, and an orderly family life as attributes that at once distinguished the middle class and explained why they were inherently and socially superior.

While Foucault may be right that the discourse of races was immanent in the language of class, I would still question his limited tracing of its varied meanings. If racial discourse is polyvalent, as he would argue, it also has multiple etymologies as I have suggested in chapters 2 and 3. In its varied nineteenth-century forms, it came loaded with a barrage of colonial representations of savagery, licentiousness, and basic truths about human nature that joined early visions of the "others" of empire with the "others" within Europe itself.

Nowhere is this colonial imprint clearer than in how bourgeois bodies were evinced to be sexually distinctive and in how their self-cultivation was conceived. Sharon Tiffany and Kathleen Adams argue that the sexual model of the promiscuous working-class woman in nineteenth-century, industrializing England construed her as a "primitive relic of an earlier evolutionary period," a myth of the "wild woman" who stood in contrast to "the moral model of . . . middle-class sexual restraint and civility."[91] Sander Gilman similarly shows how the iconography of prostitutes in nineteenth-century France was modeled on the "lascivious sexuality" and exaggerated genital physiogomy of Hottentot women of South Africa, on depictions that naturalized and *explained* the pathological, unrestrained, atavistic, and diseased bodies of both.[92] In both cases, bourgeois bodies were both race and class-specific, based on distinctions of quality and human kind.

Of course, they were also heavily gendered. If there is any discourse that joins the triumph of rational bourgeois man in colony and metropole,

91. Tiffany and Adams, *The Wild Woman* 12–17.

92. Sander Gilman, "Black Bodies, White Bodies," *Race, Writing and Difference*, ed. Henry L. Gates, Jr. (Chicago: U of Chicago P, 1986). For a discussion of empire as one of the domains in which European middle-class "conflicts of reason and emotion, of desire and duty, and of competition and harmony could be resolved" see Joanna de Groot's " 'Sex' and 'Race': the Construction of Language and Image in the Nineteenth Century," *Sexuality and Subordination*, ed. Susan Mendus and Jane Rendall (London: Routledge, 1989) 108.

it was that which collapsed non-Europeans and women into an undifferentiated field, one in which passion and not reason reigned.[93] Empire provided the fertile terrain on which bourgeois notions of manliness and virility could be honed and put to patriotic test. Passion was unseemly, but compassion was as well. As Hugh Ridley has argued, it was in the colonies that "indifference to suffering was a sign of national strength, an essential condition of manhood," proving as the French colonial novelist Henry Daguerches writes, "the strength of my blood and the strength of my race."[94]

But colonial conditions also highlighted conflicting interpretations of manliness and its vulnerabilities. If George Hardy's warning in 1926 that "a man remains a man as long as he remains under the watchful gaze of a woman of his race" was held to be a truth, then an enormous number of European men would have had little claim to a secure European manhood at all.[95] In the Indies, more than half of the European male population were cohabiting out of wedlock with native women in the late nineteenth century. Among subaltern soldiers, concubinage was the "necessary evil" that would ward off venereal disease and, more importantly, homosexuality within the lower ranks.[96]

93. See Jean and John Comaroff's identification of this shackling of women and non-Europeans to their sexual natures in *Of Revelation and Revolution* (Chicago: U of Chicago P, 1991) esp. 105–108. For an excellent more general discussion see Nancy Leys Stepan's "Race and Gender: The Role of Analogy in Science," *The Anatomy of Racism*, ed. David Goldberg (Minneapolis: U of Minnesota P, 1990).

94. Ridley, *Images of Imperial Rule* 142.

95. George Hardy quoted in C. Chivas-Baron, *La Femme Française aux colonies* (Paris: Larose, 1929) 103.

96. See Hanneke Ming, "Barracks-Concubinage in the Indies, 1887–1920," *Indonesia* 35 (1983): 65–93. The absent presence of the dangers of homosexuality in these debates is striking. What is more, in the Dutch archives, the threat of homosexual desire among stolid Dutch agents of empire, of the colonial *middenstand*, is rarely if ever mentioned. When homosexuality is broached, it is always in the form of a *deflected* discourse, one about sodomizing Chinese plantation coolies, about degenerate subaltern European soldiers, never about respectable Dutch men.

My silence on this issue and the prominent place I give to heterosexuality reflects my long-term and failed efforts to identify any sources that do more than assume or obliquely allude to this "evil," thereby making the other "lesser" evils of concubinage and prostitution acceptable. Hyam seems to have come up with many more accusations if not explicit accounts. As such, my colonial treatment of Foucault's fourth "strategic unity," constituting the "perverse adult" is only minimally explored. Ronald Hyam, *Empire and Sexuality: The British Experience* (Manchester: U of Manchester P, 1990).

Hardy's warning underscores that good reason and "character"—that common euphemism for class breeding—were not all that imperial security was about. It required managed passions, self-discipline over unruly drives and the education of sentiment and desire as well. As Tom Holt argues, the liberal democratic presumption that all men shared certain inherent traits and values also assumed that "the boon of freedom—the right to govern oneself—should be granted only to those who had assimilated certain internal controls. For liberals and conservatives alike, work-discipline was both the source and the test of [it]."[97] In the case of those descendants of Europeans labelled *inlandsche kinderen*, this axiom was precisely what classified them as "children of the Indies," not Europeans. They allegedly lacked the "inclination" to skilled work, the "suitability" for it, the self-discipline, sexual morals, and economic independence that would count them among a citizenry fit to rule. But whether it was their "class location" or racial attributes that were maligned is difficult to tell, for here was a scrambled social category that made the distinctions between racial and class discriminations blurred and problematic.

To see the struggle of classes as economic and "the natural fight of races" as biological (as Hannah Arendt and others do) may be not only misleading and ahistoric but anachronistic. For if Foucault's biohistory of the discourses of race and class is correct, that both emerged out of an earlier binary conception of the social body as part of the defense of society against itself, out of a shared vision of a deeper biologized "internal enemy" within, then racism emerges not as the ideological reaction of those threatened by the universalistic principles of the modern liberal state, but as a foundational fiction within it. This is precisely where recent studies of liberalism and nationalism have taken us. We could look specifically to those who have attempted to explain the racialized "interior frontiers" that nationalisms create, not as excesses of a nationalism out of hand, but as social divisions crucial to the exclusionary principles of nation-states.

Sexuality, Race, and the Bourgeois Politics of Exclusion

Empire figured in the bourgeois politics of liberalism and nationalism in ways we have only begun to explore. Uday Mehta makes the strong

97. Holt, *Problem of Freedom* 308.

case that eighteenth-century liberalism, that quintessential inclusionary philosophy of the European bourgeoisie, had written into it a politics of exclusion based on race. The most basic universalistic notions of "human nature" and "individual liberty," elaborated by Locke and Mill, rested on combined notions of breeding and the learning of "naturalized" habits that set off those who exhibited such a "nature" and could exercise such liberty from the racially inferior—and in their cases—South Asian colonized world.[98] David Goldberg makes a similar argument, more generally:

> the primary principles of our moral tradition—virtue, sin, autonomy, and equality, utility and rights—are delimited in various ways by the concept of race . . . liberalism's commitment to principles of universality is practically sustained only by the reinvented and rationalized exclusions of racial particularity."[99]

Edmund Morgan has argued that racism was "an essential ingredient of a republican ideology" devoted to equality and liberty and that racism in colonial Virginia was crucial to disciplining the poor.[100] Etienne Balibar makes the stronger claim, not only that universalistic principles were used to "cover and implement racist policies," but reminds us how many historians and philosophers have argued that the very concept of universalism was gendered—as Carole Pateman has shown—and racially inflected.[101]

If liberalism was implicitly exclusionary, most nineteenth-century nationalisms were explicitly so by definition. Throughout Europe, the nationalizing of education designated radically different learning strategies and environments for the middle-classes versus the "undeserving poor." Dutch liberal proposals for an extension of the franchise specified the exclusion of "all men who had been on poor relief at any time during the three years prior to elections."[102] Citizenship in a national polity, as feminist historians have demonstrated, made the rights of women and children solely dependent on their sexual and conjugal contracts with men. Women were seen as crucial to civil society not as participatory citizens in the public sphere, but as those who would insure that marriage, sexual morality,

98. Uday Mehta, "Liberal Strategies of Exclusion," *Politics and Society* 18.4 (1990): 427–54.
99. Goldberg, *Racist Culture* 39.
100. Morgan, *American Slavery, American Freedom* 386.
101. Balibar, *Masses, Classes, Ideas* 195.
102. Siep Stuurman, "John Bright and Samuel van Houten: Radical Liberalism and the Working Classes in Britain and the Netherlands, 1860–1880," *History of European Ideas* II (1989): 595.

and family provided the natural foundations for civil life.[103] Many have argued that women's rights were restricted by the argument that motherhood was a "national service."[104] It was also a heavily racialized one; as much as a rhetoric of a master race in peril forced middle-class women in Britain to accept limits put on their civil rights, this same rhetoric of racial superiority served British women in India, American women in the Philippines, and Dutch women in the Indies, all of whom sought new ways to clarify their selfhood and assert their independence.[105]

While these discourses around citizenship and national identity were centered on the constituents of European polities, the very principles of national belonging implicated race in many of these distinctions. The charged debate in the late nineteenth century on nationality and citizenship rights for women prompted by the emigration of thousands of women overseas devolved into one about their needed protection against "white slavery" on the argument that European women would never "willingly submit to sexual commerce with foreign, racially varied men."[106] Dutch de-

103. Pateman, The Sexual Contract 177.

104. See the articles in Seth Koven and Sonya Michel, eds., Mothers of a New World: Maternalist Politics and the Origins of Welfare States (London: Routledge, 1993) and in Gisela Bock and Pat Thane, eds., Maternity and Gender Policies: Women and the Rise of the European Welfare States 1880s–1950s (London: Routledge, 1991). Two important pieces not included in the above are Susan Pedersen, "Gender, Welfare, and Citizenship in Britain during the Great War," American Historical Review 95.4 (1990): 983–1006, 1006 and Nancy Fraser and Linda Gordon's "Key Words of the Welfare State," Signs 19 (1994): 309–36.

105. See Rosemary George, "Homes in the Empire, Empires in the Home," Cultural Critique (Winter 1993–94): 95–127 and Vicente Rafael's careful attention to the "phantasmagoria of domesticity" for American women in the Philippines and at "home" ("Colonial Domesticity: White Women and United States Rule in the Philippines," unpublished manuscript). For the Indies see Frances Gouda, "The Gendered Rhetoric of Colonialism and Anti-Colonialism," Indonesia (1992). For a telling tale of the ways in which British women in England deployed campaigns for indigenous women's rights to their own ends see Susan Pederson "National bodies, Unspeakable Acts: The Sexual Politics of Colonial Policymaking," Journal of Modern History 95.4 (1990): 983–1006.

106. This issue of white slavery comes up in a wide-range of colonial contexts. See Donna J. Guy, " 'White Slavery,' Citizenship and Nationality in Argentina," Nationalisms and Sexualities, eds. Andrew Parker, Mary Russo, Doris Sommer and Patricia Yaeger (New York: Routledge) 203, and Cecile Swaisland, Servants and Gentlewomen to the Golden Land: The Emigration of Single Women from Britain to Southern Africa, 1820–1939 (Oxford: The U of Natal P, 1993) esp. 24–25. An earlier racial inflection on the need for national and cross-national regulations of prostitution focused on the fact that in the late nineteenth century the alleged traffic in women was organized by New York and Johannesburg-based Jewish men. See van Onselen, "Prostitutes and Proletarians, 1886–

bates over the citizenship rights of European women in mixed-marriages in the Indies were less concerned with the civil status of women than with another consequence: the conferral of Dutch citizenship on their native husbands and mixed-blood sons. It was the clarity of racial membership, among other things, that jurists and policymakers had in mind.

In this age of empire, the question of who would be a "subject" and who a "citizen" converged on the sexual politics of race. Whether a child was born out of prostitution, concubinage, cohabitation, or marriage and whether that child was acknowledged by a European father partially sealed his or her fate. It is not coincidental that the same colonial lawyers who wrote the Indies mixed-marriage laws were those with a strong voice in the changing Dutch nationality laws of the same period. French and Dutch authorities strongly debated whether métis and Indos displayed inherent dispositions that were more native than European and whether education could deeply transform them.

Concerns for such ambiguously positioned interstitial groups in the national body preoccupied colonial authorities, but also resonated from colony to core. In a study of French antisemitism, Stephen Wilson argues that late nineteenth-century nationalist (and antisemitic) rhetoric in France was "modelled" on the violent cultural racism against Jews who straddled the colonial divide in French Algeria decades earlier.[107] The naturalization of Algerian Jews under the Cremieux decree of 1870 that preceded the Dreyfus affair heightened anxieties in the metropole that Jews were an internal enemy, morally, and sexually distinct from those who were of "pure French blood."[108] This is not to argue that European antisemitism derived from colonial tensions across the board, but rather that the dangers of cultural and racial hybridity were deeply embedded in popular and scientific discourses whose cast of characters could include subversive Indo-Europeans at one moment and perverse Jews at another.

Discourses of sexuality, racial thinking, and rhetorics of nationalism have several things in common. All hinge on visual markers of distinc-

---

1914," *Studies in the Social and Economic History of the Witwatersrand. Volume I: New Babylon* (New York: Longman, 1982) 109–11, 137, 138.

107. Stephen Wilson, *Ideology and Experience: Antisemitism in France at the Time of the Dreyfus Affair* (London: Associated University Presses, 1982) see esp. chapters 9 and 12.

108. Elizabeth Friedman, *Colonialism and After: An Algerian Jewish Community* (South Hadley, MA.: Bergin and Garvey, 1988) 25.

tion that profess to—but only poorly index—the internal traits, psychological dispositions, and moral essence on which these theories of difference and social membership are based. The strength and weakness of such social taxonomies is that they are malleable, their criteria opaque and ill-defined.[109] Balibar touches on those anxieties when he notes, "that the 'false' are too visible, will never guarantee that the true are visible enough."[110] The German philosopher Fichte saw eighteenth-century German society as based on "invisible ties," a moral attitude, and "interior frontiers" that bounded both the nation and the constitution of individual subjects within it.[111] In the nineteenth century, nationalist discourses about who was echte Dutch or "truly French" were replete with such ambiguous evaluations of breeding, cultivation, and moral essence. In the Dutch East Indies, it was no longer jus soli (right by birth) and jus sanguinis (right by descent) that could provide the criteria of nationality, but rather what the colonial lawyer Nederburgh defined in 1898, echoing Fichte, as shared "morals, culture, and perceptions, feelings that unite us without one being able to say what they are."[112]

This quest to define moral predicates and invisible essences tied the bourgeois discourses of sexuality, racism, and certain kinds of nationalism in fundamental ways. Each hinged on the state's moral authority to defend the social body against degeneration and abnormality. As George Mosse has argued for nineteenth-century Germany, nationalism was animated by notions of bourgeois respectability and a "moral terror" that rigidly defined what was deviant sex and what was not.[113] Nationalist discourse staked out those sexual practices that were nation-building and

---

109. As Michael Banton notes for the case of nineteenth-century racial typologies: "the notion of type was a convenient one because it was not tied to any particular classificatory level in zoology, so that it was easy to refer to the physical types characteristic of particular nations, to 'types of cranial conformation,' or to say that a skull 'approximates to the Negro type' without having to establish just what that type was" (The Idea of Race 31).

110. Etienne Balibar, "The Paradoxes of Universality," Anatomy of Racism, ed. David Goldberg (Minneapolis: U of Minnesota P, 1990) 285.

111. Quoted in Etienne Balibar, "Fichte and the Internal Border: On Addresses to the German Nation," Masses, Classes, Ideas 61–87.

112. J. A. Nederburgh, Wet en Adat (Batavia: Kloff, 1898) 87–88.

113. George Mosse, Nationalism and Sexuality (Madison: U of Wisconsin P, 1985).

race-affirming, marking "unproductive eroticism, as Doris Sommer has so well shown, "not only [as] immoral, [but as] unpatriotic."[114]

In such a frame, the discourse of middle-class respectability was double-billed, playing several roles. Bourgeois women in colony and metropole were cast as the custodians of morality, of their vulnerable men, and of national character. Parenting, and motherhood specifically, was a class obligation and a duty of empire.[115] In short, the cultivations of bourgeois sensibilities were inextricable from the nationalist and racial underpinnings of them. Whether Foucault assumed these links or underestimated their importance is unclear. In volume 1, he simply referred to the "Hitlerite politics of sex" as an "insignificant practice" [HS:150]. But Nazism's politics of sex and reproduction were not insignificant by any stretch of the imagination. Feminist historians have shown how significant cults of manliness, motherhood, homoeroticism, and misogyny were to the racial politics of Nazi rule.[116] In Foucault's lectures, where one might expect such connections to be elaborated, they are not. It is normalization that drives racism. The proliferation of sexualities and racisms that Nazi nationalism underwrote is not part of that account.

Feminist critics have long criticized Foucault's concern with sexuality and not gender, his lack of attention to differential access to power eclipsed by a focus on diffused power relations throughout the social body at large.[117] But the problem may be broader still. By not engaging the significance of the nineteenth-century discourses of nation and empire and the gender-specific nature of them, the cultivation of the bourgeois self and its sexual deployments remain rooted in Europe and *inside* the bourgeois

114. Doris Sommer, "Irresistible Romance: the Foundational Fictions of Latin America," *Nation and Narration* ed. Homi Bhabha (London: Routledge, 1990) 87.

115. Anna Davin, "Motherhood and Imperialism," *History Workshop* 5 (1978): 9–57.

116. Mosse, *Nationalism and Sexuality*; Klaus Theleweit, *Male Fantasies* (Minneapolis: U of Minnesota P, 1989); Claudia Koontz, *Mothers in the Fatherland* (New York: St. Martin's P, 1987).

117. See, for example, Biddy Martin, "Feminism, Criticism and Foucault," *New German Critique* 27 (Fall 1987): 3–30; Judith Newton, "History as Usual: Feminism and the New Historicism," *Cultural Critique* (Spring 1988): 87–121. Other efforts to explore the productive tension between Foucault and feminism include Caroline Ramazanoglu, ed., *Up against Foucault* (London: Routledge, 1993) and for a less inspired effort Jana Sawicki, *Disciplining Foucault: Feminism, Power and the Body* (London: Routledge, 1991) and Lois McNay, *Foucault Feminism* (Boston: Northeastern UP, 1992). None of the above deal directly with Foucault's historical arguments or engage his formulation of those "four strategic unities" in which women are absent but figure so strongly.

nation, rather than constitutive of it. Foucault may have alluded to the metonymic quality of the bourgeois body for the nation, but left us to show that its cultivation and unique sexuality was nourished by a wider colonial world of Manichean distinctions: by Irish, "Mediterranean," Jewish, and non-European Others who provided the referential contrasts for it.

By marginalizing the link between nationalism and desire in both his genealogy of racism and his history of sexuality, Foucault eclipses a key discursive site where subjugated bodies were made and subjects formed. The technologies of sexuality that concerned Foucault were productive of power in specific ways that targeted disciplined sentiment as much as normalized sexuality in the governing of oneself. The knot that bound subversion to perversion could only be undone if people themselves believed in the sexual codes of the moralizing state, if personal affect and sentiments could be harnessed to national projects and priorities for racial regeneration.[118] Doing so was no easy task. It first required identifying where disaffections were produced, where children's 'instincts' were schooled, how early, and by whom. It required distinguishing those contaminations of the social environment from those reproduced in the intimate confines of bourgeois homes. It is this subject to which we turn in the next chapter.

118. Two dazzling works on this subject include Lauren Berlant's discussion of the "harnessing of affect to political life through the production of a national fantasy" in The Anatomy of a National Fantasy: Hawthorne, Utopia and Everyday Life (Chicago: Chicago UP, 1991) 5, and Doris Sommer's masterful analysis of how bourgeois goals of nationhood coordinated "sense and sensibility, productivity and passion" in Latin American novels in Foundational Fictions: The National Romances of Latin America (Berkeley: U of California P, 1991) 14. Also see my "A Sentimental Education" in Fantasizing the Feminine, 1996.

V

DOMESTIC SUBVERSIONS AND CHILDREN'S SEXUALITY

[It] was not the child of the people, the future worker who had to be taught the disciplines of the body, but rather the schoolboy, the child surrounded by domestic servants, tutors, and governesses, who was in danger of compromising not so much his physical strength as his intellectual capacity, his moral fiber, and the obligation to preserve a healthy line of descent for his family and his social class. (HS:121)

The emergence in the eighteenth century of a discourse on children's sexuality and the power relations generated by it plays a central part in Foucault's biohistory, joining several of his projects in ways that have only been partially explored. He calls upon it to instantiate his rejection of the repressive hypothesis, to repudiate both Marx and Freud, and to specify those mechanisms and techniques of power that operate in productive, intimate, and capillary form. Despite this emphasis, Foucault's treatment of the "pedagogization of children's sexuality," like volume 1 of The History of Sexuality, is schematic and telegraphic. But, like that volume, it invites us to do something more. Specifically, it is from the vantage point of race-making and nation-making that his interest in this discourse on children's sexual precocities dovetails with our own. If this was one of the principal discursive sites where bourgeois culture defined and defended its interests, in colonial perspective it was also one of the key sites in which racial transgressions were evident and national identities formed. It was a discourse in which the distribution and education of desire was lodged in that "tiny, sexually saturated, familial space" (HS:47). This space contained and revamped intrafamilial relations, as Foucault argued. But it also did something more. It was here that those with other class and cultural sensibilities—domestic servants and nursemaids in particular—played a crucial role.

Foucault's analysis of the discourse on children's sexuality highlights both the power of his vision and the vagaries of his argument. In rejecting both Marx and Freud so boldly, he nonetheless still underestimated the range of other power relations that this discourse on children called up for scrutiny and brought into play. Knowledge and control of servants within middle-class homes, and the seductions attributed to them, were part and parcel of the normalizing regime of that discourse in crucial ways. It was clearly not only the moral dispositions of children and parents that came under surveillance, but the *relations* between those [white] family members and those who served them. Both groups were held partly responsible for the perversions, subversions and unmanaged sentiments that contaminated bourgeois homes.

In fact, Foucault's assault on Freudian analysis might have taken an even stronger turn if he had looked at the strained positioning of servants within it. Not only did Freud eventually absolve parents of committing child abuse when he rejected his earlier theory of seduction, as Jeffrey Masson has argued.[1] In the end, Freud embraced a common trope of nineteenth-century bourgeois society, a folk theory of seduction and adult pathology that attributed the few "real" abuses of children, not to middle-class parents, but to the promptings and imaginings of the desiring child on the one hand and to the immorality of servants on the other.[2]

Foucault took a different tack. In *The History of Sexuality*, the "pedagogization of children's sex" is presented as one of the "four strategic unities" that emerge in the early eighteenth century where the mechanisms of knowledge and power centered on sex (HS:101–102). These discourses on children's sexuality were founded on two assertions:

> that practically all children indulge or are prone to indulge in sexual activity; and that, being unwarranted, at the same time "natural" and

1. Jeffrey Moussaieff Masson, *The Assault on Truth* (New York: Farrar, Straus and Giroux, 1984).

2. Masson notes that Freud's range of reading materials (and those he marked with marginalia) included a large number that targeted servants as the perpetrators of child abuse, and suggests that "it would be interesting to follow [Freud's] thinking about the role of servants in this respect [to sexual assault on children]. For here was a class of people who could be accused with complete safety" (218). Masson makes no reference to, and thus would seem to be unaware of, how common such accusations were among a much wider community than the medical profession in the nineteenth century (see esp. 125–127, 218).

"contrary to nature," this sexual activity posed physical and moral, individual and collective dangers . . . Parents, families, educators, doctors, and eventually psychologists would have to take charge, in a continuous way, of this precious and perilous, dangerous and endangered sexual potential. (HS:104)

The texts on which Foucault drew focused on the imputed sexual potential of children, but his analysis of them did not. He looked instead to the forms of knowledge generated by those fears and to the range of power relations engendered among *almost* everyone else. The eighteenth- and nineteenth-century war against masturbation was, for him, the quintessential example of a discourse designed not to curtail a practice, but to produce new "local centers" of power-knowledge, "lines of penetration" that allowed more intimate surveillances of children and their guardians in public institutions and in the home. (HS:42) Despite the scattered references to children's sexuality in volume 1, like the subject of race, these references mark a set of issues that were to be analyzed in greater depth. Volume 3 of the projected six volumes was to be entitled *Croisade des enfants* (The Crusade for Children).

Foucault hinted at the salience of this discourse on children's sexuality to the formulation of biopower in volume 1, but in a number of other contexts he turns to it as well. One is his summary of the Collège de France lectures of 1974–75 given in the year preceding those on race.[3] Devoted to "abnormals," not children or sexuality per se, the seminar nevertheless dealt in large part with the sexualized child and the discourse of masturbation. There Foucault describes the historical development of a taxonomy of abnormality, three categories of "abnormal persons" associated with distinct regimes of power: the "human monster" of the Middle Ages and Renaissance, the individual "to be cured" in the seventeenth and eighteenth centuries, and finally the "onanist"—the masturbator—an eighteenth-century persona whose emergence "correlated with the new relations between sexuality and familial organization, with the new position of the child in the parental group, with the new importance accorded to the body and health" (RC:76). The "sexual body of the child" appeared then with a new form of biopower, signifying at once a "rupture" with a long prehistory of bodily interdictions and their reinscription.

When asking why this discourse emerged in the eighteenth century,

3. See Michel Foucault, *Résumé des Cours 1970–1982* (Paris: Julliard, 1984), "Les anormaux" 73–81.

it is the repressive hypothesis that he rejects. *Contra* Reich, how could it be accounted for "by a process of repression tied to the new exigencies of industrialization," if this crusade at the time never took the form of a "generalized sexual discipline" (RC:77)? On the contrary, "it addressed itself, in a privileged manner, if not exclusively, to adolescents and children, and more precisely still, to those of rich and comfortable families. It places sexuality, or at least the sexual use of one's own body as the origin of an undefined series of physical problems whose effects could be felt in all forms and at all stages of life" (RC:78). Thus, he dismisses a Reichian Freudo-Marxist analysis on two grounds: because the discourse on children's sexuality was initially directed at bourgeois not working-class families and it was a discourse that expressed rather than repressed sex. If the child was partly responsible for abuses of its own sexual body, it was others who were called on to witness the child's transgressions and who were ultimately to blame. Middle-class parents were "denounced as the true culprits: [due to their] lack of surveillance, negligence, and especially lack of interest in their children, their bodies and their conduct" (RC:78). It was the fault of parents who entrusted their children to "wet nurses, domestics, tutors, all these intermediaries regularly denounced as the initiators of debauchery" (RC:78)

What power relations are intensified, and who is really to blame? Foucault looked not to relations between middle-class adults and their servants, nor to those between those "initiators of debauchery" and their charges, but to a new web of physical and moral ties between parents and children in which desire and power were knotted, "necessitating a control and an external medical knowledge to arbitrate and regulate these new relations between the obligatory vigilance of parents and the fragile, sensitive, excitable bodies of children" (RC:79). Foucault writes:

> The crusade against masturbation translated the arrangements of the restricted family ([made up of] parents, children) into a new technology of power-knowledge. To put into question children's sexuality and all the anomalies for which it was held responsible, was one of the methods of constituting this new technology. (RC:79)

Each of these types of "abnormals" were both inscribed in "autonomous systems of scientific reference," and joined in the nineteenth century by three basic phenomena: one, by the emergence of a general theory of degeneracy that socially and morally justified all sorts of techniques to "spot, classify, and intervene" in the lives of abnormals; two, by the creation of a dense institutional network that could take in abnormals and serve as an instrument for the "defense of society"; and finally, by a shift whereby the most recent problem of infantile sexuality would come to overlap with these two earlier ones to become the richest explanatory principle of a range of anomalies in the twentieth century (RC:80). These make up a familiar constellation. We might remember from chapter 2 that the discourse on race, like that on "abnormals," emerged as part of society's defense against its "enemies within." Children now enter on both sides of that equation, for theirs is both an endangered and dangerous sexuality. They must be protected against exposure to the dangerous sexuality of the racial and class Other, not because their sexuality is so different, but because it is 'savage,' unrestrained, and very much the same. This discursive connection between the 'savage as child' and 'child as savage' is not one that Foucault makes, but it will be crucial to us. Both representations were constructs of a civilizing, custodial mission and a theory of degeneracy whose bourgeois prescriptions would turn on the contrast and equation between the two.[4]

Foucault ends the résumé of the 1975 lectures obliquely relating the discourse on masturbators to those "technologies of security" on which he will focus the following year:

> Since 1970, the seminar series has dealt with the slow formation of a knowledge and power of normalization, deriving from traditional juridical procedures of punishment. The seminar of 1975–76 will end this cycle with a study of the mechanisms by which, since the end

---

4. This relationship between the "endangered" and the "dangerous" is not a point that escapes Foucault. While he makes no connection between the two here, he did elsewhere. In a debate on France-Culture in 1978 with Guy Hocquenghem and Jean Danet, Foucault discussed the new nineteenth-century technologies surrounding children's sexuality and the making of those layers of the population that must be "protected," in this way:

> One comes to have a society of dangers, with, on the one hand, those put in danger; and on the other those who bear danger: And sexuality will no longer be a conduct with certain precise interdictions; but . . . will become a kind of danger that prowls, a sort of omnipresent phantom . . . that will play itself between men and women, between children and adults. . . . Sexuality will become this menace in all social relations, for all ages, in all relations between individuals. It is there, on [the basis of] this shadow, this phantom, this fear that power will try to take hold through an apparently liberal and in any case general set of laws; And we will have a regime of control over sexuality." ("La Loi du Pudeur," *Recherches* 37 (April 1976): 77–78)

of the nineteenth century, claims were made to "defend society." (RC: 80–81)

As we know, the 1976 lectures did not begin with the late nineteenth century, but with a discourse on race some three centuries earlier. And while the historical content of the seminar did not speak to the issue of children, Foucault's discussion of power in the second lecture drew on the discourse on infantile sexuality to make his argument. Again, he poses the same basic question: "Given the domination of the bourgeois class, how can one understand the repression of infantile sexuality" (CPH:215)? Here, too, he answers that analyses such as Reich's are just too "glib" insofar as "anything can be deduced from the general phenomenon of the domination of the bourgeois class," even its very opposite, an encouragement of sexual precociousness not its repression (CPH:216).

Foucault asks us instead to look at the techniques and procedures that "came to represent the interests of the bourgeoisie" but not to stop there, for it was "not the bourgeoisie itself which thought that madness had to be excluded or infantile sexuality repressed" (CPH:216).

> What in fact happened instead was that the mechanism . . . of the surveillance of infantile sexuality began from a particular point in time, and for reasons which need to be studied, to reveal their political usefulness and to lend themselves to economic profit, and that as a *natural consequence all of a sudden*, they came to be colonized and maintained by global mechanisms and the entire State system . . . The bourgeoisie is interested in power, not in madness, in the system of control of infantile sexuality, not in that phenomenon itself (CPH:217) [my emphasis]

If a "system of control" is what is at stake for the bourgeoisie and not the phenomenon of infantile sexuality itself, why this emphasis on children? From what other scholar would we accept such vagaries that would explain a technology of power emerging "all of a sudden" and as a "natural consequence" of political utility? While Jacques Donzelot, in *Policing the Family*, has gone far to give this process more reason and more flesh, Foucault's account does not. He wavers between an assessment of the discourse (and set of practices around infantile sexuality) as a unique one that defined the bourgeois body, and as a generalized discourse that went far beyond the interests of any particular class.

Part of the problem stems from how Foucault locates the political field in which moralizing regimes thrived. He seems to exclude (or is it that he assumes?) the extent to which specifically nationalist discourses and agendas shaped the new priorities of bourgeois domesticity and its moral prescriptions. Alan Sheridan generously suggests that Foucault demonstrated how "the bourgeoisie was able to identify its fortunes more and more with the nation state," how "its concern with its own inherited and carefully preserved health was extended to the national races."[5] But if this were the case, why did Foucault resort to this "all of a sudden" appearance of a discourse on children's sexuality? The historiography on nationalism and pedagogy, on patriotism and the moral training of children suggests that there was nothing "all of a sudden" about the concern for children's sexuality at all. The moral mission of bourgeois liberalism invested enormous cultural capital, and specifically pedagogic energy, to make children into moral citizens and to attach those skills of self-discipline and the learning of civilities to the strength of the nation, to the "redemption of the republic" (in the case of the U.S.), and to the survival of a master race.[6]

If the task of the state is, as Gramsci defined it, to "educate consent," then it should be no surprise that childrearing practices also would have been directed at extracting consensus. As part of that process, childrearing practices turned from "physical coercion to psychological maneuvering," focusing on restraint of passion and individual self-control in which the mother was cast in a model role.[7] This observation does not contradict Foucault. On the contrary, it ties his discursive genealogy on childhood sexuality firmly back into the histories of nationalist and liberal projects in ways that account for its "suddenness" and place these campaigns for the preservation of children and race in a biohistory of wider imperial breadth.

While Foucault's summary of his 1974–75 course situates his analysis of the construction of children's sexuality within the context of his work on discipline and normalization from 1970, elsewhere he sought a somewhat different frame. In an unpublished talk delivered sometime in the mid

5. Alan Sheridan, Michel Foucault: The Will to Truth (London: Tavistock, 1980) 191.

6. See Bernard Wishy, The Child and the Republic: The Dawn of American Child Nurture (Philadelphia: U of Pennslyvania P, 1967) 181.

7. See Nancy Cott, "Notes Toward an Interpretation of Antebellum Childrearing," Psychohistory Review 7.4 (1973): 20.

1970s entitled "Infantile Sexuality," Foucault referred to his current work on sexual repression as a "sequel" to the history of madness, published more than a decade earlier. It is a curious text on several counts. Despite its title, only the five final pages of this twenty-three-page manuscript have anything to do with the discourse of masturbation and less to do with children. Most of the text is an earlier (or is it a later?) version of chapter 1 of *The History of Sexuality*. It rehearses the notion of power as productive rather than negative and rejects what he called the "hysterical model" of the repressive hypothesis (in the sense that repression produces a "hysterical" cultural outburst).

The section on masturbation, albeit brief, is of interest because in it Foucault sees the emergence of a new meaning attached to masturbation. It is no longer cast as one of many sexual sins focused on the relationship between individuals, but on the sin of "caressing oneself," of one's relationship not to other bodies but to one's own. Foucault describes a turn away from "forbidden relationships" enacted to the production of new truth claims about individuals who now can be known not by their actions, but by what they desire. With this shift in the eighteenth century, children's sexuality will emerge as both a "privileged point" of control, pleasure, and as a target of power. In an interview in 1976, Foucault put it this way:

> What was important was the reorganization of the relations between children and adults, parents and educators: it was an intensification of intra-familial relationships, it was childhood which was at stake for the parents, the educational institutions, for the public health authorities; it was childhood as the breeding ground for the generations to come. At the crossroads of body and soul, of health and morality, of education and training, children's sexuality became at the same time a target and an instrument of power. . . . It was precarious, dangerous to be watched over constantly. . . . The objective was not to forbid. It was to constitute . . . a network of power over children.[8]

It was also to do something more; to identify children not only as heirs to their parents, but also to the national patrimony and to the race. It was to constitute them as sexual objects of desire as well. Foucault's unpublished talk on infantile sexuality is one of the few places where he explicitly ties

8. "End of Monarchy," interview, n.d., c. 1977, *Foucault Live* (New York: Semiotext(e), 1989) 141.

the prohibition on masturbation to a corresponding "parental obligation" of "incestuous intent," leaving unspecified whether this was a possible or a necessary correlation.[9]

If the identification and management of desire was the "real" target of this technology, the reader is still left with only the vaguest sense of what range of desires put bourgeois children at risk. Was it the desires of peder-ast pedagogues and of perverse parents for children or more importantly the desires animated in the children themselves?[10] Less focused here on the production of desire than the production of power, Foucault seems to assume that the object of children's sexual desire was auto-erotic, centered on themselves. But the housekeeping manuals, childrearing guides, and pedagogic and medical texts from the nineteenth century offer a differ-ent rendering of this nexus of knowledge/power/sexuality than Foucault chooses to tell. They focus not only on masturbation, but on the more gen-eral lack of self-control, civility, and restrained desire that children, in their "savage"-like behavior, displayed. These were, significantly, the very same characteristics attributed to those who served and administered to their needs. It was feared that servants and middle-class children would have sex but the ties might go deeper still, for it was sentiments and unseemly dispositions they were feared to share and enjoy as well.

Studies of domestic service in early modern Europe would certainly point in that direction. European discourses on the dangers of wet nurses and nursemaids for the identity formation of noble and middle-class chil-dren have a long genealogy, suggesting that nursemaids were seen to enjoy a special power over their charges. A baby was thought to absorb the "per-sonality traits" of his nurse when he drank her "whitened blood."[11] One seventeenth-century French doctor took as a given that breastmilk "had

9. *The History of Sexuality* alludes to the "perpetual incitement to incest in the bourgeois family" but makes no direct link between the discourse on masturbation and incestuous sex. See 129–130.

10. On the "enjoyment in intervening" and the "sexual excitement and sexual satisfaction" gen-erated by the surveillance of children's sexuality see the 1983 interview with Stephen Riggs, "The Minimalist Self," *Michel Foucault: Politics, Philosophy, Culture.Interviews and Other Writings 1977–1984*, ed. Lawrence D. Kritzman (New York: Routledge, 1990) 9.

11. Cissie Fairchilds, *Domestic Enemies: Servants and their Masters in Old Regime France* (Baltimore: Johns Hopkins UP, 1984) 195. Also see Elizabeth Wirth Marvick's "Nature versus Nurture: Patterns and Trends in Seventeenth Century French Child-Rearing," *The Evolution of Childhood*, ed. Lloyd Demause (New York: Psychohistory Press, 1974) 259–301, who argues that "the nursing relation-ship was seen as more profoundly influential on the developing nature of the child than the pre-natal experience" (264).

the power to make children resemble their nurses in mind and body, just as the seed makes them resemble their mother and father."[12] Marc Shell argues that Montaigne was not alone in holding that "interfamilial and interspecies collactaneous kinship [could] take precedence over intrafamilial consanguinity."[13] In fact, French medical experts in the late eighteenth century debated whether children fed on the milk of extraspecies animals became "essentially animals."[14] Some advice manuals of the period characterized the milk of wet nurses as "alien and bastard."[15] According to Shell "kinship by consanguinity and kinship by collactation amount[ed] to the same thing."[16] Still, in the nineteenth century, child "experts" warned that "the blood of the lower-class wet nurse entered the body of the upper class baby, milk being thought to be blood frothed white."[17] Foucault's concern to show that the technologies of sex were initially designed to affirm the bourgeois self eclipses an important dynamic: how much these discourses were constructed around a spectrum of stereotypic Others, epitomized in the servant class against which the boundaries of the bourgeois self were drawn. Foucault introduces that possibility but does not pursue it when he writes:

> The separation of grown-ups and children, . . . the relative segregation of boys and girls, the strict instructions as to the care of nursing infants (maternal breast-feeding, hygiene), the attention focused on infantile sexuality, the supposed dangers of masturbation, the importance attached to puberty, the methods of surveillance suggested to parents, the exhortations, secrets and fears, the presence—both valued and feared—of servants: all this made the family . . . a complicated network,

12. Demause 195.

13. Marc Shell, Children of the Earth: Literature, Politics and Nationhood (New York: Oxford, 1993) 143.

14. Shell, Children of the Earth 143.

15. Marie Anel Le Rebours, Avis aux mères qui veulent nourir leurs enfants (Paris, 1767) quoted in Shell 159.

16. Shell 10. Shell writes: ". . . a nurse-mother, or wet nurse, transmits familial kinship—and hence species kind—through her milk just as a consanguineous parent transmits kinship through blood" (158).

17. Lloyd Demause, "The Evolution of Childhood," History of Childhood Quarterly: The Journal of Psychohistory 1 (1974): 536. Also see Jonathan Gathorne-Hardy, The Rise and Fall of the British Nanny (London: Hodder and Stoughton, 1972), who argues that "belief in the transference of characteristics by breast milk continued almost up to the present day" 41.

saturated with multiple, fragmentary, and mobile sexualities. (HS:46) [my emphasis]

Thus it was not only children who were confined and whose sexuality and conduct was condemned. Jacques Donzelot argues that the problem of house servants was "the guiding thread" of eighteenth-century debates about the ills of urban migration, the decadence of cities, the ill-health of bourgeois children.[18] The profusion of nineteenth-century guidebooks on the "art of bringing up young children" focused on the central theme of protecting children from the cultural and sexual seductions of those charged with their care. Krafft-Ebing's widely read and reprinted text on sexual pathology remarked not on what children did with their own bodies, but graphically described how "Maids . . . masturbated children who had been entrusted to them."[19] The structure of the sentence itself seems at odds with the dictionary definition of "masturbation" as a genital manipulation by which one excites *oneself*. But Krafft-Ebing's grammar was neither incorrect nor strange. In fact it represented a common use of the verb "to masturbate," not as a self-contained act, but as an imagined social relationship between nursemaids and the 'apprentice' child in their care. Nursemaids and other domestics were thought to perform "intimate functions" for children under their control. While the transgressions of servants were certainly feared, danger also emanated from the desires provoked in middle-class children and adults for them.[20]

That Freud's theories were in some way influenced by this discourse on servant-child sexuality seems plausible from several sources. Krafft-Ebing's text was certainly one Freud owned and read. But how this discourse might have shaped his understanding of child development is more difficult to tell. If Freud subscribed to the myth of the promiscuous servant for some of his analyses, Bruce Robbins argues that he completely effaced the reality of sexual desire of employers for their servants in others. Robbins holds that Freud's oedipal theory itself helped to assure both a silence around "the massive intrusion of desire for servants into the lives of the servant-keeping classes in this period," as well as a misrecogni-

18. Jacques Donzelot, *The Policing of Families* (New York: Random House, 1979) 15.

19. Richard von Krafft-Ebing, *Psychopathia Sexualis, mit besonderer Berucksichtigung der contraren Sexualempfindung: Eine klinisch-forensische Studie* (Stuttgart: F. Enke, 1892) 375.

20. Bruce Robbins, *The Servant's Hand* (Durham: Duke UP, 1986) 199–200.

tion of what that desire for servants inspired; namely, both "dependence" on, and "identification" with, them.[21] Stallybrass and White contend that Freud's systematic displacing of the nurse with the mother in his formulation of the oedipal complex, allowed him to "rewrite unconscious desires in closer conformity to the endogamous rules of the bourgeoisie"—one paradoxical tenet being that "to desire one's mother [was] . . . more acceptable than to desire a hired help."[22] Both accounts are indebted to a discerning essay by Jim Swan that analyzes the role of Freud's *kinderfrau* in his own life and theory in light of the crisis conditions of the European bourgeoisie after 1848 and with respect to the socio-economic position of this Czech working-class woman in Freud's German bourgeois home.[23] Both omit an element that Swan's analysis underscores: namely, that the affection, shame, and desire invoked in Freud by his *kinderfrau* were matters of racial as well as class transgression.[24]

Stallybrass and White, and Robbins draw on Foucault to do with Freud what Foucault did not. They register not only that Freud's intra-familial focus was part of the making of a bourgeois moral order, but unlike Foucault, they show how Freud's turn from a focus on *acts* to *desire* (a shift that very much concerned Foucault) produced systemic omissions from Freud's analysis.[25] They prompt us to question how much these imagined, real, and erased relations of power and pleasure with servants, and the discourse on the promiscuities attributed to them, shaped the eroticized landscape in which children were taught, and adults prescribed, the cultivations of their bourgeois selves. These were not the only sorts of contaminations from which small children had to be protected and which their proximity to servants held in store. Sex was perilous, but there was

21. Robbins, *The Servant's Hand* 200.

22. Peter Stallybrass and Allon White, *The Politics and Poetics of Transgression* (London: Methuen, 1986) 159.

23. Jim Swan, "Mater and Nannie: Freud's Two Mothers and the Discovery of the Oedipus Complex," *American Imago* 31, 1 (Spring 1974): 1–64.

24. Swan, "Mater and Nannie" 35–36. Swan draws a parallel between the position of Freud's *kinderfrau* and "black Mammies" in the American slaveholding South, arguing that "race—Freud's Jewishness"—is a factor that is more important than has been indicated so far" (36). For an account that confronts the extent to which anti-semitism and Freud's Jewishness shaped his psychoanalytic theory (and prompted his efforts to universalize the pathologies attributed to Jews) see Sander Gilman, *Freud, Race and Gender* (Princeton: Princeton UP, 1993).

25. See Swan, "Mater and Nannie" 13.

equal danger in loss of character, altered class and racial identities, and the alienation of children's affections.

On Whiteness and Native Nursemaids

She never remembered seeing familiarly anything but the dark faces of her Ayah and the other native servants, and as they always obeyed her and gave her own way in everything, because the Mem Sahib would be angry if she was disturbed by her crying, by the time she was six years old she was as tyrannical and selfish a little pig as ever lived.[26]

Discourses on children's sexuality found symptomatic resonance in the colonies. But in this force field, questions of racial contagion were more explicitly and centrally framed. These discourses were animated by fears that turned less on children touching their own bodies than on their relationship to those bodies that should not touch them. In the Indies, sexual danger was part of a wider politics of contamination in which the susceptibilities of children's bodies and minds represented a range of cultural intrusions that threatened the European colonial home.

As James Clifford has noted, "in western writing, servants have always performed the chore of representing 'the people'—lower classes and different races."[27] In colonial discourse, the "lower orders"—be they servants, "Indos," native mothers and/or their native lovers—were the sources of sexual arousal, moral deviance, misguided reason, and the objects of control.[28] But the representation was ambiguous as well: native servants might serve at once as a foil for European restraint and, as Win-

---

26. Frances Hodgson Burnett, *The Secret Garden* (1910; London: Purnell, 1975) 2.

27. James Clifford, *The Predicament of Culture* (Cambridge: Harvard UP, 1988) 4. Also see Robbins, *The Servant's Hand*, and Stallybrass and White, *Politics and Poetics*, chapter 4.

28. It is not surprising, therefore, that Frances Hodgson Burnett, who wrote with such authority on colonial servants in the opening pages of *The Secret Garden*, never lived in India nor visited it after she emigrated from England to the southern United States at the age of sixteen. What is striking is how much her moral tale of personal transformation—of an affectless, indulged child raised by servants in India who grows into a sensitive, independent, and sentient being in British air and on British soil—so faithfully reproduces the discourse on the dangers of servant-child relations represented in colonial pedagogic and housekeeping manuals. See Ann Thwaite, *Waiting for the Party: The Life of Frances Hodgson Burnett, 1849–1924* (New York: Scribner, 1974). Also see the reviews of *The Secret Garden* in G. Senick, ed., *Children's Literature Review*, 24 (London: Gale Research, Inc. 1991) 21–51. None refers to the colonial backdrop of the novel or to the racist imagery in it.

throp Jordan has argued for the generic "savage" in the British imagination, as a mirror for "attributes which they found first but could not speak of in themselves."[29] Represented as both devotional and devious, trustworthy and lascivious, native servants occupied and constituted a dangerous sexual terrain, a pivotal moral role. While Clifford may be right that servants were the "domesticated outsiders of the bourgeois imagination," it was their very domestication that placed the intimate workings of the bourgeois home in their knowing insurrectionary hands and in their pernicious control.[30]

Perhaps one of the most common observations about the racial discourse of colonialism is the patriarchical, protective familial metaphors in which it was cast.[31] Students of colonial discourses in Africa, Asia, and the Americas have often commented on a common thread: namely, that racialized Others invariably have been compared and equated with children, a representation that conveniently provided a moral justification for imperial policies of tutelage, discipline and specific paternalistic and maternalistic strategies of custodial control.[32] But this equation of children and primitive, of children and colonized savage was not operative in overtly racist, colonial discourse alone. If we look to the childcare manuals of the

29. Winthrop Jordan, *White over Black* (Chapel Hill: U of North Carolina P, 1968) 40.

30. Clifford's ironic allusion to a "domesticated" outsider, like that of Robbins, implies someone not domesticated at all, merely someone standing in for "groups marginalized or silenced in the bourgeois West," someone who can be looked at 'up close,' with "curiosity, pity and desire" (4).

31. Certainly such felicitous images of government were not only invoked in the colonies. As Lynn Hunt has argued, an appreciation of the "family romance" that "helped to organize the political experience of the [French] revolution" could subvert public and private authority as much as it could bolster such authority. Hunt's work addresses the "interweaving of private sentiments and public politics," and how this image of paternal obligation and the dismantling of parental prerogative were joined to play a pivotal political role. *The Family Romance of the French Revolution* (Berkeley: U of California P, 1992). Also see Melvin Yazawa's study of the founding of the American republic, where he argues that colonial writers "turned to the traditional familial paradigm of patriarchal authority" when they "sought a model for the conception of a polity that combined restraint with affection." *From Colonies to Commonwealth: Familial Ideology and the Beginnings of the American Republic* (Baltimore: Johns Hopkins UP, 1985) 19.

32. The examples are too numerous to cite. See, among many others, Ashis Nandy in *The Intimate Enemy* (New York: Oxford UP, 1983) 11–18, on the "homology between childhood and the state of being colonized"; Ronald Takaki in *Iron Cages* (Seattle: U of Washington P, 1979) 109–28, on the black 'child/savage' in Jacksonian politics; Syed Alatas in *The Myth of the Lazy Native* (London: Cass, 1977); V. G. Kiernan in *The Lords of Human Kind* (London: Wiedenfeld and Nicolson, 1969) 243.

eighteenth and nineteenth centuries, the same equation is present, but the other way around. Children are invariably othered in ways that compare them to lower-order beings, they are animal-like, lack civility, discipline, and sexual restraint; their instincts are base, they are too close to nature, they are, like racialized others, not fully human beings.[33]

What is striking is how much the middle-class impulse to prescribe children's social, and specifically sexual, behavior was based on a racialized language of class difference. The social grammar of prescriptions for making a child into a bourgeois adult rested on distinctions that affirmed the virtues of whiteness and the moral highground of bourgeois civilities at the same time. If we are looking to trace the embeddedness of race in the cultivation of the bourgeois self, it may be that this prescriptive discourse on childrearing is a place to turn. If to be a respectable bourgeois adult meant that one acquired a set of behaviors that prescribed restraint and civility, they also *proscribed* something else: namely, that these were attributes in which racial and class "lower-orders" did not share. Nancy Armstrong, as we have seen, reads housekeeping manuals as texts that prefigured the bourgeois way of life they represented. But they may have done something more. For becoming adult and bourgeois meant distinguishing oneself from that which was uncivilized, lower-class, and non-European.[34] Carolyn Steedman's observation that "a perception of childhood experience . . . [can provide] the lineaments of adult political analysis," suggests that these lay and professional discourses on childrearing may have much to tell us; certainly about the world that adults construed, but also how children were socialized to perceive the categories of the social world in which they would share.[35]

Norbert Elias' contention in *The Civilizing Process* that children's fears are reproduced "more or less automatically" is a facile rendering of a complicated process of socialization of which Locke, among others, have long been aware.[36] For in rehearsing repeatedly what a child must shed to be-

33. As Ashis Nandy in *The Intimate Enemy* notes, without further elaboration: "the theory of social progress was telescoped . . . into the individual's life cycle in Europe" (15).

34. On this notion of "distinction" in the making of the bourgeois man (sic) see Jean-Paul Sartre, *Critique de la raison dialectique* (Paris: Gallimard, 1960) 717 quoted in Swan, "Mater and Nannie," 24 and Bourdieu's extensive rendering in *Distinction: A Social Critique of the Judgement of Taste* (Cambridge: Harvard UP, 1984) esp. 247–248.

35. Carolyn Steedman, *Landscape for a Good Woman* (New Brunswick: Rutgers UP, 1986) 14.

36. Norbert Elias, *Power and Civility* (1939; New York: Pantheon, 1982) 328.

come an adult, these verbal and written injunctions also rehearsed a social hierarchy and racial taxonomy of libidinal desire and uncivilized habits that bourgeois children would have to shed to become fully human, adult, and European. This is not to suggest that race was always the dominant metaphor in these texts. But it should alert us to the issue raised in chapter 4, namely, that the language of class distinction was often racialized in ways that more conventional historical sources might not suggest. At the very least, the observation should disrupt our neat, discrete, and discipline-bound readings. It should put into question how these protective, moral missions that targeted middle-class children, racialized Others and abnormals overlapped in the anxious and self-affirming discourses of the nineteenth-century bourgeoisie.

Aries characterizes the eighteenth century as one that revealed a new "respect" for children; Foucault saw it as the century of adult power and pleasure in surveilling their sexualization.[37] The two may be compatible but not necessarily so. For "respect" was not what much of the discourse and guides to childcare were about. Liberal philosophers, colonial policymakers, and nationalist thinkers shared an overwhelming concern with the dispositions of very small children and the malleabilities of their minds. All attended to the importance of breeding self-disciplined children and to the dangers of servants in the home. For each, the family was where a child's sense of personhood, citizenship, and sexuality could be subverted, perverted, or well formed.

For the eighteenth century, Locke's writings set the tone. He was explicit on the importance of education and home rearing in particular, for shaping "human nature." Uday Mehta notes that Locke was preoccupied with the "orchestrated social environment of domestic space" in which small children were to be habituated to the practices that would "appear natural" to them as adults later on.[38] But Locke also held that this internalization

37. Philippe Aries, *Centuries of Childhood: A Social History of Family Life* (New York: Knopf, 1962) 109.
38. See Uday Mehta's *The Anxiety of Freedom* (Ithaca: Cornell UP, 1992) esp. 131–54. Note that Locke did not take for granted that a child's fears were reproduced "more or less automatically" as Elias did centuries later. Margaret Ezell notes that Locke's *Some Thoughts concerning Education* (1693) was a widely read essay that went through over a dozen editions before the mid-eighteenth century. Like Mehta she makes the important point that Locke strictly advised "isolating children from servants"—a directive not unrelated to his conviction that education was principally a task of "cultivation" and of instilling morality. She writes that he shared with Daniel Defoe

of bourgeois standards was easily undermined by the "folly and perverse-
ness of servants." Children found "a refuge and relief in the caresses of
those foolish flatterers, who thereby undo whatever the parents endeavor
to establish."[39] His treatise on education warned parents to keep their
children from "the Taint of your servants," from the "ill effects" of those
"unbred and debauched" persons who might make "court to them . . . and
make [your children] in love with their conversation."[40] Locke's counsel
speaks to more than sexual transgressions. Children's desires to be in the
company of servants exposed them to "the contagion of these ill prece-
dents, both in Civility and Vertue." What could be undermined was their
acquisition of the cultural competencies of class and race as well.[41]

This fear of the influence of servants on children was not an altogether
new theme in upper class discourse, but in the eighteenth century it was
sexualized in new and varied forms.[42] Jacques Donzelot argues that campaigns for the preservation of children in the eighteenth-century France
"came to mean . . . putting an end to the misdeeds of domestic servants,
creating new conditions of education that would be capable of counteracting the harmful effects suffered by the children entrusted to them. . . ."[43]
References to the sexual promiscuities of servants were already common
in the eighteenth century, but specific warnings against the sexual abuse
of children by servants in the nineteenth century became yet more persis-

---

the belief that "early education in the family has political importance" ("Locke's Images of
Childhood" *Eighteenth-Century Studies* 17 [Winter 1983/1984]: 139–55). Not unlike Locke, Bourdieu
argues that children are not taught by trial and error. Instead, they grasp the rationale, the
theory underlying any set of practices and are given a set of "structural exercises" that allow
them to habituate themselves to their social worlds. *Outline of a Theory of Practice* (Cambridge:
Cambridge UP, 1991) 87–88.

39. Locke quoted in Mehta, *Anxiety of Freedom* 146.

40. John Locke, *Some Thoughts concerning Education*. 1693 (Menston, England: Scolar Press, 1970)
70–72.

41. Locke 70.

42. Aries (*Centuries of Childhood*) writes that "the stress laid by the moralists on the need to separate
children from the varied world of 'the servants' shows how well aware they were of the dangers
presented by this promiscuity of children and servants" (117). Also see Jean-Louis Flandrin,
who notes how important it became to prevent children from being "corrupted" by contact
with servants. *Familles: Parenté, Maison, Sexualité dans l'ancienne société* (Paris: Hachette, 1976) 142.

43. Jacques Donzelot, *The Policing of Families* (New York: Random House, 1979) 16.

tent and direct.[44] Steven Marcus notes for *My Secret Life*, the famed sexual autobiography of the mid-nineteenth century, that in "scenes of childhood seduction and masturbation," the "nursemaid occupied the chief role."[45] In the U.S., infantile masturbation was a "sign of moral and physical degeneration," caused by "the low and depraved character" of nurses and "licentious domestic[s]."[46] In the Netherlands, a new science of domestic medicine warned burgerlijk mothers against leaving their children's rearing to such "lowly beings," exhorting them to manage their children's bodies in ways that would both protect them *and* ensure that middle-class women would stay at home.[47] George Mosse describes a German nationalist discourse in which masturbation was perceived both as the "root cause of all loss of control" and the quintessential "anti-social act." Both Mosse and Foucault—the former focusing directly on nationalism, the latter not—describe the racial and sexual Other in the very same terms: in Mosse's words, echoing those Foucault repeated throughout his 1976 lectures, as "a danger to the security of the state."[48]

Discourses on the nation, race, and child development converged in other striking ways. Strict surveillance of domestic servants was one way

44. See, for example, Cissie Fairchild's study of servants in the *Ancien Régime, Domestic Enemies: Servants and their Masters in Old Regime France* (Baltimore: Johns Hopkins Press, 1984) 207. According to Jeffrey Masson, these were observations of particular interest to Freud, who, when he read Krafft-Ebing's *Psychopathia Sexualis*, checked the passage which read: "parents if you have children, beware of the morals of your servants" (127).

45. Marcus 168. James Kincaid, in a study of the children's sexuality in Victorian culture, writes: "So many books warn against nurses and servants that one wonders (a) why any were kept, (b) how they could reasonably have been made responsible for child sexuality, and (c) how it is no one blew the whistle on such obvious scapegoating" (175). Kincaid's answer: it served as a "very handy class biology, a notion that the lower orders not only are performing under much lower moral standards but a different bodily organization as well. . . ." James Kincaid, *Child-Loving: The Erotic Child and Victorian Culture* (New York: Routledge, 1992). Although Kincaid is certainly right to note this "handy class biology," he leaves the issue of servants otherwise unaddressed. His quick dismissal of the servant issue is surprising given his otherwise nuanced analysis of the relations of pleasure and power through which the ambiguous sexuality of the Victorian child was activated and displayed.

46. As Bernard Wishy in *The Child and the Republic* notes, many of the warnings were "basically, if veiledly, sexual" (40).

47. Van Hamelsveld 1791, quoted in Lily Clerkx, "De kinderjuffrouw. Opvoedster en dienstbode tussen ouders en kinderen," *Sociologisch Tijdschrift* 10.4 (1984): 676. Also see by the same author, *Moeders, kinderen en kinderopvang: veranderingen in de kinderopvang in Nederland* (Nijmegen: SUN, 1981).

48. George Mosse, *Nationalism and Sexuality* (Madison: U of Wisconsin P, 1985) 11.

to protect children; removal of them from the home was another. Class-specific theories of child development were exemplified in the first kindergartens and nurseries that emerged in Germany and England in the late 1820s and in the 1850s in the Netherlands. As distinct from the first nurseries for working-class children, called *bewaarscholen*, the kindergartens developed by Froebel in the 1830s appealed to the patriotic sensibilities of the middle-class and had a strong nationalist bent.[49] Spurred by the conviction that bourgeois households were providing "poor child management," the Froebel movement recommended that toddlers and even infants were better off in kindergartens than in an unschooled nursemaid's or servant's care.[50] Kindergartens were envisioned as "microcosms of the liberal state," stressing not only independence, but self-discipline, citizenship, and "voluntary obedience to general laws"—qualities that lower-class servants could not be expected to value, nurture, or protect.[51]

In the Indies, concern for children's moral environments, bourgeois identity, and sense of racial affiliation were deeply enmeshed. Virtually all the debates on the dangers of masturbation and sexual precocity for European children were concerned with whether these children could cultivate the sensibilities that will allow them to grow up European. Within these texts, masturbation was not something that European children were inclined to do on their own. They were encouraged and guided in such exercises in self-pleasure by servants, not taught to do it by themselves. Thus one colonial doctor's much-quoted 1898 handbook for European mothers in the Indies warned of the "extremely pernicious" moral influence of native nursemaids (*babu*) and advised that "children under no circumstances should be brought to bed by them and should never be permitted to sleep with them in the same room." *Babus* lulled their charges to sleep, he writes, "by all sorts of unnatural means . . . unbelievable practices

49. Ann Taylor Allen, "Gardens of Children, Gardens of God: Kindergarten and Daycare Centers in Nineteenth-Century Germany," *Journal of Social History* 19 (1986): 437. According to Taylor Allen, Froebel was strongly influenced by Fichte's emphasis on education in *Speeches to the German Nation*. In 1844, Froebel urged "German wives and maidens" to support kindergartens "for the welfare of the German but ultimately of all people, for the benefit of their own but ultimately of all children, as a blessing to this nation and ultimately to all nations" (quoted in Taylor Allen 437).
50. Michael S. Shapiro, *Child's Garden: The Kindergarten Movement from Froebel to Dewey* (University Park: Pennsylvania State UP, 1983).
51. Allen, "Gardens of Children" 439.

that alas occur all too often, damaging these children for their entire adult lives and that cannot be written here."[52] A housekeeping manual from the same period warned Dutch parents in the Indies that their children's innocence of sexual matters was compromised by "natives who impart it to them in a form and in a manner that is extremely undesirable for their upbringing. Knowledge is also power on sexual issues and not least for our future mothers."[53] Such fears died hard. A 1923 guide for Dutch mothers departing for the Indies emphatically urged: "If you are not absolutely sure of your children and your servants, then do not leave them together unattended!"[54] A few years later, De Banier, a prominent Indies' Christian paper, lauded the important role that European women now played in fostering domesticity (huislijkheid) and in counteracting the "pernicious influence of the babu."[55] As late as 1941, a popular account of European life in the Indies counseled "that association with native servants could carry grave spiritual and physical dangers for our children."[56] Unlike in Foucault's account, here was a discourse in which masturbation and sexual precocity were not natural proclivities of all children but only those subjected to tropical circumstances and/or to those of native or impure blood.[57] The focus is on the intensity of the environment; on the tropical heat and secreted recesses of the home, on the seductions that environment encouraged or allowed that could damage a child in its adult life.

Servants as a class were to blame, but others provided inappropriate sexual knowledge as well. Children of inlandsche kinderen, "colored" (kleurlingen) and those of native origin were considered to "hear and know about sexual matters" at a much earlier age. It was they who initiated their

52. J. J. Pigeaud, Iets over kinderopvoeding: raadgevingen voor moeders in Indie (Samarang: G.C.T. van Dorp & Co., 1898).

53. L. de Pagter, Het Sexuelle in de Opvoeding: een ernstig woord aan moeders en vaders (Jogjakarta: Buning, 1901).

54. Dr. C. J.Rutten-Pekelharing, Waaraan moet ik denken? Wat moet ik doen? Wenken aan het Hollandsche Meisje dat als Huisvrouw naar Indie gaat (Gorinchem: J. Noorduijn, 1923) 70.

55. De Banier, 9 November 1926: 1.

56. D. C. M. Baudin, Het Indische Leven (1927; 's-Gravenhage: H.P. Leopolds, 1941) 62.

57. Dutch scientific studies carried out after World War II still entertained this common European folk belief that sexual precocity was more marked in the tropics. See C. Veneklaas, Het Rassenconflict in de opvoeding in Indonesie, Mededeelingen van het Nutsseminarium voor Paedagogiek aan de Universiteit van Amsterdam, 44. (Batavia: J.B. Wolters, 1949) where a number of Dutch, German and American studies on the physiology and psychological "suggestibility" and "erotic reaction" of different "underdeveloped races" and "classes" are compared.

"pure European" playmates into such precocious pleasures, thus making the Indies an unsuitable milieu for them.[58] Contact with native adults and "less well-to-do Europeans" was of equal danger since, among them, all together "too much attention [was] given to sex." Thus in 1906 the Indies doctor, J. H. F. Kohlbrugge wrote from Utrecht:

> Most Europeans in the Indies do not see it as objectionable to have sexual relations outside of marriage. There are parents who drive their sons into the arms of prostitutes, women who drive their husbands, doctors who drive their patients, all excused by the so-called demands of the climate . . . I have mentioned all the factors that make an up-bringing in a European manner doomed to failure. They show us why it is impossible to cultivate a European in Java, regardless of whether the child is born from pure European parents or by crossing with another race.[59]

The sexual and moral danger posed by native servants was partially attributed to the cultivated sensibilities they neglected to provide, but more so to the excesses of bodily care offered in their stead. Native nurse-maids were commonly accused of destroying the character of the child by indulgence, not neglect, as Frances Hodgson Burnett portrays Mary in The Secret Garden. As van Geuns, editor of one of the popular Indische newspapers warned in a serialized piece on the "character formation of Indos," "the babu is synonymous with total servitude,"[60] and European children took full advantage of it. It was she who turned her charges into dependent no-goods with a "love of ease." In professional and popular discourse, "experts" portrayed European children in the colonies as irreparably "spoiled" in a double sense: too lavishly waited upon, they turned into "young tyrants" who treated their servants as "slaves" and thus such children lacked the "self-respect and independence" that later could make them into rational rulers and truly European.[61] This was a Hegelian servi-

58. M. W. F. Treub, "De Structuur der Indische Maatschappij," Nederland in de Oost: Reisindrukken (Haarlem: Tjeenk Willink, 1923) 94. For a statement a half century earlier on the overexposure of children in "colored" (as opposed to native) households to sexual matters see Dr. W. van Eyk, Het openbaar lager ondwerijs voor Europeanen in Nederlandsch-Indie (Deventer: Hulscher, 1870) 30.

59. J. Kohlbrugge, "Het Indische Kind en Zijne Karaktervorming," Blikken in het Zieleleven van den Javaan en zijner overheerschers (Leiden: Bril, 1907) 141–142.

60. M. van Geuns, "De karaktervorming der Indo's," Weekblad voor Indie, 11 December 1904, 2.

61. Treub, "De Structuur der Indische Maatschappij" 93. Compare the musings of "Mistress Mary" in the Secret Garden, described as a dulled, uncaring spoiled child upon her arrival from

tude of an empowering kind that could weaken and transform even a
Dutch-born child into another sort of sentient being.[62] Thus Kohlbrugge,
like many others, admonished those parents who allowed servants to
carry their children's satchels to school or to attend to their every whim:[63]

> The [European] child learns earlier to order than to listen; that a Euro-
> pean child hits a native servant, if the latter does not do what he [sic]
> wants is a very common phenomenon. Yet more striking is that the
> babus find this agreeable [sic]. But the corruption has already begun
> long before the child can hit, it begins with the infant who is taken out
> of his bed and carried about as soon as he cries; it continues when the
> child begins to eat; if he doesn't finish up his food, the babu runs after
> him with a plate and tries to give him a mouthful while he plays.[64]

Any reader with even a moderate familiarity with Javanese child rearing
practice would recognize some of these "indulgences" as the common
and culturally distinctive ways in which small children are reared.[65] What
servants embody here is excess of a particular kind: a piercing through of
Javanese culture itself. These "indulgences" clearly run against the grain
of Dutch bourgeois notions of self-discipline. But they also express a dis-
comfort with a different developmental calendar for children, the age at
which they are expected to walk, eat on their own, and abide by adult
rules of comportment. Kohlbrugge concluded, as did many of his professional compatriots, that it was "impossible to provide a child with a Euro-

---

India, who is shocked by the forthright speech of her young, new, Yorkshire maid, Martha:
> Mary listened to her with a grave, puzzled expression. The native servants she had been used
> to in India were not in the least like this. They were obsequious and servile and did not
> presume to talk to their masters as if they were equals. . . . Indian servants were commanded
> to do things, not asked. It was not the custom to say "please" or "thank you" and Mary had
> always slapped her Ayah in the face when she was angry. She wondered a little what this girl
> would do if one slapped her in the face . . . if she might not even slap back. (25–26)

62. Kohlbrugge, "Het Indische" 116.

63. A. de Geuns, "Moeten onze kinderen naar holland?" 't Onderwijs 36 (15 September 1906): 420;
Treub, "De Structuur" 93.

64. Kohlbrugge, "Het Indische" 116.

65. See Hildred Geertz's The Javanese Family (New York: Free Press of Glencoe, 1961), where she
describes childrearing practices in rural Java in the 1960s in ways that do not differ markedly
from the latter part of the description above.

pean upbringing" in the Indies, that the problem was less climate than the domestic personnel.[66]

While most of these assaults on children's upbringing directly targeted native servants, in a more veiled way they also condemned the mothering and moral qualities of native women. Given how common concubinary relations were between European men and those native women in their domestic (and sexual) service, the person of the mother and the accused native servant was often one and the same. Here was a veritable Freudian nightmare. Not only were *mater* and *kinderfrau* transposed and confused as Freud did in his dream analysis.[67] In the Indies discourse on the rearing of European children, the cultural incompetencies of native nursemaid and native mother were made virtually substitutable, the disastrous moral consequences for the child were the same. At issue was not a subconscious confusion of identity and desire, but a cultural and racial anxiety bred out of the ambiguous, unacknowledged and threatening role that native women played in creating the cultural habitus of what were claimed to be distinctively Dutch homes. Sexual desire for native bodies was not all that these fears were about. Proximity to the world of native servants led to individual and racial degeneracy, personal and political disaffection and identification. Stallybrass and White's comment on the dangers of intimate connections between maid and middle-class male child for the nineteenth-century British family life suggest a cultural logic that was very much the same:

> To become his parents' child, he must forgo those pleasures which he associated with serving maids. . . . The pure [bourgeois] child would grow up into the healthy parent only if he exhaled those 'evil spirits' which had already 'contaminated' him in the form of household servants.[68]

Accusations of moral degradation were not confined to native women, they were as forcefully directed at poor white and Indo mothers. If cultural

66. Kohlbrugge, "Het Indische" 117.

67. Among those who examine Freud's confused treatment of his mother and nursemaid in his early "erotic stimulations" see Swan, "Mater and Nannie"; Stallybrass and White, *Politics and Poetics*; and Robbins, *The Servant's Hand*. An early but less relevant account can be found in Kenneth Grigg's "'All roads lead to Rome': the Role of the Nursemaid in Freud's Dreams," *Journal of American Pyschoanalytic Association* 21 (1973): 108–126.

68. Stallybrass and White, *Politics and Poetics* 167.

contagions could seep through the well-heeled European colonial household, they saturated the homes of poorer European men whose partners
were most often native or Indo-European women. Indolence, sexual excess, haughtiness, abuse of servants and a disdain for labor were considered (by such doctors as Kohlbrugge) strong evidence of the "character
faults" and neglected upbringing of Indo youths, the principal causes of
pauperism and political discontent among them.[69] Kohlbrugge fantasized
that if only one could "give the Indo another mother . . . he [would] be
otherwise!" But even he "alas" knew "it could not be done."[70] More real-
istic solutions were at hand. Other authorities, such as one Dr. W. Horst,
promoted the establishment of Indies nurseries for the European poor
with the express design of removing Indo children from the "damaging
influence of native and Malay-speaking mothers," thereby including in
the category of maternally inept native women, those who might be of
"mixed parentage," creole, and nativized Europeans.[71] A well-cited pedagogic handbook on the virtues of establishing Froebel nurseries for poor
Europeans in the Indies put it clearly:

> Would not such a little school be a heaven on earth for the child of
> the Indische popular classes who often vegetates amidst chickens and
> dogs in a village hut tended—not raised—by a mother, who does not
> know what rearing is? Would not even the strongest opponents of
> [nurseries], they who find it unnaturally cruel to take the child away
> from its natural mother have no objection? We know that no prepa-
> ratory school can *entirely* take the place of . . . the *'moederschool'* [that
> schooling that only mothers can provide] but how many mothers are
> capable of managing [one]?[72]

Criminality among children of mixed-descent was also considered to
have sexual roots. It was native mothers who sapped the energy of boys
and men, procuring "native concubines" for their sons "at a very early
age." Schools for Indo girls were introduced on the similar premise that by

69. Kohlbrugge, "Het Indische" 119.
70. Kohlbrugge, "Het Indische" 127.
71. Dr. d.W. Horst, "Opvoeding en onderwijs van kinderen van Europeanen en Indo-
Europeanen in Indie," *Indische Gids* II (1900): 989. But Horst also blamed those women who gave
their young the choice to speak "the Malay of their babus" or their own native Dutch tongue,
since the children would inevitably choose Malay (990).
72. Th. J. A. Hilgers en H. Douma, *De Indische Lagere School* (Weltevreden: Visser, 1908) 10–11.

the age of fourteen their own homes were not "safe" because "seduction, concubinage, and prostitution" confronted children at every turn.[73] Diatribes against the native mothers of métis children in French Indochina in this period are resonant. The mothers' example of "debauchery, sloth, and immorality" would turn the girls to prostitution, the boys to "vagabondage, extortion and theft."[74] Schooling was deemed a critical moral intervention—a protection and antidote to the sexual excesses to which youths were exposed outside the family but more importantly within it.

These discourses thus take as their target not the sexuality of children so much as the dangers posed by alien cultural longings and sexual enticements, disrupting the sense of European bourgeois culture in which European children rightfully belonged. These debates make clear that the cultivation of the bourgeois self required a host of calibrated administerings that in excess or dearth could divert its growth. Children required an environment cordoned off from nursemaids, from their native mothers, from those conduits of sentiment that would incline them not only to "babble" but "to think and feel" not in Dutch, but in Malay or Javanese.[75] If the notion of "evil spirits" were figurative in the bourgeois imagination in Europe as the above quote from Stallybrass and White suggests, in the Indies it took much more concrete form. European mothers were cautioned against the "duveltje" (little devil) of Malay and of the sorts of cultural sensibilities that such linguistic competence might convey. Servants who told children Javanese ghost stories were to be guarded against as well: fearfulness, superstitiousness, and the "nervous irritability" of European children were all attributed to such stories (and their raconteurs).[76]

73. I. J. Hissink Snellebrand, "Wat is te doen in het belang van de Indische paupermeisjes en tot versterking van het Nederlandsche element in Nederlandsch-Indie," Indische Genootschap. General Meeting of 22 November 1910, 41.

74. Archives d'Outre-Mer. Amiraux 7701, 1899, "Statute of the "Société de protection et d'èducation des jeunes métis français de la Cochinchine et du Cambodge."

75. Kohlbrugge, "Het Indische."

76. Thus, a 1920 article in a popular Indies Dutch language paper warned European parents against leaving their children to play in the vicinity of native servants, and noted that "the danger that nursemaids frighten the child with [ghosts] is not fictive. For the most part children's nervousness and fear derive from it" ("Iets over kinderopvoeding in Indie," Indie 3.52 (March 1920): 847. Also see Dorothée Buur's Indische Jeugdliteratuur (Leiden: KITLV, 1992), an annotated bibliography of children's literatures of the Netherlands Indies. Buur lists a number of stories in which the babu tells such frightening tales that the child can either not sleep or becomes fearful and superstitious both by day and night (62, 164).

This susceptibility of children to native affinities and sexual immoralities underwrote a sustained political discourse from the mid-nineteenth to mid-twentieth century over distinctions between education (*onderwijs*) and upbringing (*opvoeding*)—prompting a tense debate over whether the colonial state should be responsible for both. Such debates over education versus upbringing were of course not specific to the colonies, but there one finds particularly strong racial inflections in the ways they were framed. For while these debates raised Lamarckian questions about the effects of social and climatic surroundings on individual character, political disposition was as much at issue. Thus questions about the "character" of those creole whites whose psychological makeup was seen as distinct from the European-born Dutch addressed their political propensities as well as their affective character. Here was a population who were seen as potentially oppositional to the continued supremacy of metropolitan interests and the colonial state. As early as 1848, the Dutch Minister of Colonies fought against educating European children in the Indies rather than Holland on the grounds that "this upbringing will have the result that these children who are frequently suckled with the breastmilk of Javanese wet nurses along with their native children, at a more advanced age, will lack any sense of unity with Europeans."[77] While the use of native wet nurses for European children was a common practice on South Africa's Cape through the early nineteenth century and among British memsahibs in nineteenth-century India, it was not in the Indies.[78] But suckling of mixed-blood children by their native mothers certainly was. In any case,

77. Algemeen Rijksarchief, Koloniaal Verbaal 1848/x, no.389, 22 September 1848.

78. On Indian wet nurses in British India, see Nupur Chaudhuri, "Memsahibs and Motherhood in Nineteenth-Century Colonial India," *Victorian Studies* 31.4 (1988): 517–36. On the topic of wet nurses on South Africa's Cape, Samuel Hudson wrote:

> . . . the young children are generally placed with the female slaves, few [settler women] taking upon themselves the office of a Mother. This in my opinion lays the first foundation for all the Vicious habits they contract of them: caresses and instances I could bring forward when the licentious curses of these domestic slaves are considered more by these discarded children than [those of] their real mothers are . . . the first thing they learn is to deceive the parent and keep their intercourse with their enamerados [young lovers] a secret so that by the time they are able to discriminate they are initiated into all the mysteries of duplicity and not infrequently of dishonor.

See Robert Shell, "Tender Ties: Women and the Slave Household, 1652–1834," *The Societies of Southern Africa in the 19th and 20th Centuries*, vol. 17 (London: University of London, 1992) 13–14.

what was at issue was not suckling, but a folk theory of contamination that posited tenacious psychological attachments of children to native mothers and maids that even nurseries for infants could not arrest.[79] Some nursery advocates, such as Dr. Horst, had faith that a "Dutch spirit" could be instilled in carefully controlled contexts "under the directorship of cultivated, wise, and suitable women for the rearing of young children.[80] But for many educational commentators the "kneadable" age of four to seven years old was already too late. European middle-class values had to begin, as one Dutch schoolmaster opined "at the beginning in the mother's arms"—or more to the point out of them.[81] By the mid-nineteenth century, the notion in Europe that "the nation comes from the nursery," that "the history of nations is determined not on the battlefield but in the nursery" was heard again and again.[82] It was an observation that European colonial authorities had been making for some time. For them, the stakes were high. Something perhaps more dangerous and intimate than European rule was at risk in the colonies; not whether their sons and daughters would lack some abstract affection for a particular European motherland, but whether in their crisis of racial and national identity, in their alienation from French, Dutch and British civilities, they would become déraciné and patricidal.

In contrast to the stereotype of the fixity of the racial other, bourgeois white identities, both child and adult, were more vulnerable, unstable and susceptible to change. Protection from this fear demanded a rerouting of desires, a displacement of eroticism, an externalization of arousal to a native or mixed-blood surrogate self. Servants could steal more than the sexual innocence of European children, but the sentiments that under-

79. Chaudhuri notes that although the practice was encouraged by British physicians to protect the European mother's health, such critics as Flora Anne Steel remarked that "some Anglo-Indians also feared that milk of 'native women' might contaminate an English child's character" (529). Also see Marc Shell who characterizes this intimate relationship as one of "affective kinship" following, among others, Montaigne who called the feelings of the nurse-mother for the nursing child a "bastard affection" marked by a "greater solicitation for the preservation of the borrowed child than for their own" (quoted in Shell 158).

80. D. W. Horst, "Opvoeding en onderwijs van kinderen van Europeanen en Indo-Europeanen in Indie," *Indische Gids* 2 (1900): 990.

81. Otto van Knaap, "De Verindisching van ons Nederlandsche," *De Indische Gids* (1902): 1871–72.

82. Quoted in Kincaid, *Child-Loving* 82 and Davin, "Motherhood and Imperialism" 29.

wrote their identification as European. E. P. Thompson once described the shared goal of nineteenth-century utopias as the "education of desire."[83] This, not surprisingly, is what the bourgeois vision of a colonial utopia was contingent on as well. Understanding the hazards of other cultural longings entailed in prescriptions for adults and children leads us to the deep structuring of colonial power, back to Freud and Foucault and to the racial grammar on which imperial distributions of desire rests.

83. E. P. Thompson. *William Morris: Romantic to Revolutionary* (N.Y.: Pantheon, 1977 [1955]): 791. Also see Ruth Levitas, *The Concept of Utopia* (New York: Philip Allan, 1990).

VI

THE EDUCATION OF DESIRE AND

THE REPRESSIVE HYPOTHESIS

One should not think that desire is repressed, for the simple reason that the law is what constitutes desire and the lack on which it is predicated. Where there is desire, the power relation is already present; an illusion, then to denounce this relation for a repression exerted after the event; but vanity as well, to go questing after a desire that is beyond the reach of power. (HS:81)

Judith Butler has characterized volume 1 of The History of Sexuality as a history of western desire, but I am not sure this is the case.[1] In fact desire is one of the most elusive concepts in the book, the shibboleth that Foucault discards and disclaims. For Foucault, there is no "original" desire that juridical law must respond to and repress, as for Freud. On the contrary, desire follows from, and is generated out of, the law, out of the power-laden discourses of sexuality where it is animated and addressed.[2] Contra Freud's contention that "civilization is built up upon a renunciation of

---

1. See Judith Butler's *Subjects of Desire: Hegelian Reflections in Twentieth-Century France* (New York: Columbia UP, 1987) for an informed and accessible treatment of the philosophical debate on desire and Foucault's position within it. See especially 186–229 for her helpful discussion of the commonalities and differences in approaches to desire by Lacan, Deleuze, Derrida and Foucault, a subject I do not broach here.

2. Judith Butler puts Foucault's position this way:

> The law that we expect to repress some set of desires which could be said to exist prior to law succeeds rather in naming, delimiting and thereby, giving social meaning and possibility to precisely those desires it intended to eradicate. (*Subjects* 218)

Other attempts to define what is distinctive about Foucault's notion of desire offer only a sparse roadmap to it. See, for example, Scott Lash, "Genealogy and the Body: Foucault/Deleuze/Nietzsche," *Theory, Culture, Society* 2.2 (1984): 1–17 whose discussion of desire centers more on Deleuze and Guattari, than Foucault.

instinct," Foucault took as his task specification of the historical moment in the mid-nineteenth century when "instinct" emerged into discourse, analysis of the cultural production of the notion of "sexual desire" as an index of individual and collective identity.[3] Since the "truth" of our sexual desire (the premise that we can know ourselves if we know that truth of that primal sexual instinct hidden within us) is not a starting point for Foucault, knowledge of our "true desires" cannot be a condition of critique. It must be a historically constituted *object* of it.[4] Foucault does not dismiss Freudian models all together, but, as John Rajchman notes, assumes a "kind of practical and historical doubt about their use . . . with the suggestion that there may be more to the historical determination of sexual desire than the prevention of our capacity to publicly formulate it."[5]

The paradox of volume 1, however, is that while sexuality inscribes desire in discourse, Foucault's discussion of the discourses and technologies of sex says little about what sorts of desires are produced in the nineteenth century and what people do with them.[6] We know that the confessional apparatus of "medical exams, psychiatric investigations, pedagogical reports, and family controls" were mechanisms of both pleasure and power, but it is left for us to examine in particular political contexts, how that pleasure is distributed, how desire is structurally moti-

---

3. Sigmund Freud, *Civilization and Its Discontents* (New York: Norton, 1961) 45. For Foucault, "instinct" emerged as a medical object in the 1840s (see *Power/Knowledge* 221).

4. John Rajchman, *Michel Foucault: The Freedom of Philosophy* (New York: Columbia, 1985) 91.

5. Rajchman, *Michel Foucault* 91.

6. In the introduction to *The Uses of Pleasure* (1985), volume II of *The History of Sexuality*, Foucault explains the shift in his analytic trajectory and why he will "recenter [his] entire study on the genealogy of the desiring man." While this recentering on "the hermeneutics of the self" and a "general history of the 'techniques of the self'" is described as a new venture, there is already strong evidence of this concern in volume one. There the *dispositif* of sexuality forms the basis on which the cultivation of the [bourgeois] self is predicated, evinced in a bourgeois concern for governing and conveying how to live. A focus on "the cultivation of the self" is already there: the shift is in the larger frame in which Foucault historicizes that phenomenon. In volume I, Foucault identified "the cultivation of [the bourgeois] body" as crucial to the bourgeoisie's dominance (HS:125). In volume II, the nineteenth-century management of "how to live," described in the last of his 1976 Collège de France lectures, provides the analytic focus for a broader enquiry, not confined to nineteenth-century bourgeois culture. It is reformulated as the key to a deeper historical genealogy and addresses another agenda. What is *not* set out in volume one is a "history of desiring man" (UP:6).

vated, what specific "spirals" of pleasure and power are displayed (HS:45).[7]
Foucault presents his project as one that will "define the regime of power-
knowledge-pleasure that sustains the discourse on human sexuality in our
part of the world" (HS:11). But once we turn to question the distributions
of desires, to "discover who does the speaking" in the geopolitical mapping of desiring subjects and desired objects, "our part of the world"
becomes more than an innocuous convention, but a porous and problematic boundary to sustain. For that boundary itself, as we know, took as
much discursive and political energy to produce as that which bound sex
to power, and the "truth" of identity to sex.[8]

If the founding premise of Foucault's analysis is to trace how sexual
desire is incited by regulatory discourses, one might expect colonial studies, so influenced by him, to have embraced more of his critique than it has
actually done. We have looked more to the regulation and release of desire
than to its manufacture. We have hardly even registered the fact that the
writing of colonial history has often been predicated on just the assumption that Foucault attacked; the premise that colonial power relations can
be accounted for and explained as a sublimated expression of repressed
desires in the West, of desires that resurface in moralizing missions, myths

7. Foucault's notion of power shared with, and was clearly influenced by, Deleuze and Guattari's understanding of desire as embodying productive and generative properties (as opposed
to Freud and Lacan's psychoanalytic emphasis on "lack") and it was Foucault who wrote the
laudatory preface to Anti-Oedipus. But Deleuze and Guattari's approach influenced Foucault's conception of power more than his treatment of desire. For La volonté du savoir is not about what
desire produces but what produces desire, i.e, those regulatory discourses of sexuality that have
made us believe that true knowledge of ourselves is accessible if we know our "inner sexual
drives." Despite this debt, there were differences. According to Butler, Deleuze and Guattari,
unlike Foucault, retained a "precultural notion of 'true desire,'" thereby undermining their
historicization of it (1990: 215, 219). Didier Eribon too, who otherwise describes Lacan and
Foucault's pre-1976 relationship as one more of "affinity" than influence, holds that Foucault's
formulation of the repressive hypothesis "targeted" Anti-Oedipus, Lacanian psychoanalysis and
represented a clear break with Lacan. Didier Eribon, Michel Foucault et ses contemporains (Paris:
Gallimard, 1994) 249, 257.
8. Others have also noted the lack of an analysis of desire in volume I. Baudrillard, for very
different reasons, has argued that ". . . in Foucault power takes the place of desire. It is there
in . . . a network, rhizome, a contiguity diffracted ad infinitum. That is why there is no desire in
Foucault: its place is already taken." Jean Baudrillard, Forget Foucault (New York: Semiotext, 1977)
17–18.

of the "wild woman," in a romance with the rural "primitive," or in other more violent, virile, substitute form.

In colonial historiography, questions of desire often occupy a curious place. While the regulation of sexuality has come center stage, Foucault's reworking of the repressive hypothesis and thus the cultural production of desire has not. Although sexual desire, as expressed, repressed, made illicit, misdirected, inherited, and otherwise controlled has underwritten European folk theories of race from the seventeenth to twentieth centuries, desire is often suspended as a pre-cultural instinct to which social controls are applied, a deus ex machina, given and unexplained. Much mainstream colonial history has preceded not from a Foucauldian premise that desire is a social construct, and sex a nineteenth-century invention, but from an implicitly Freudian one.[9] While Freudian language has certainly permeated other branches of history and other disciplines, the specific and varied invocations of Freudian models in colonial studies— and the effects of their often silent presence—have neither been fully acknowledged nor explored.[10]

The relationship between Freudian models and Foucauldian critiques in the writing of colonial history has been a more complicated relationship than one might expect. Some analytic debts have been more quickly acknowledged than others. But saying "yes" to Foucault has not always meant saying "no" to Freud, not even for Foucault himself. Despite Foucault's rejection of the repressive hypothesis, there are surprising ways

9. This is not to suggest that the notion of "sexual instinct" first appeared with Freud. On the contrary, representations of African sexuality at least from the 1500's attributed primal lust, licentious instincts, unbridled sexual appetite and a propensity for "Venery" to the racialized Other long before Freud theorized the place of the libido in the workings of the human unconscious. See, for example, Karen Newman, "'And Wash the Ethiop White': Feminist and the Monstrous in Othello," *Shakespeare Reproduced*, eds. Jean E. Howard and Marion F. O'Connor (New York: Methuen, 1987). Sander Gilman argues that what Freud did was to to treat those sexual and mental pathologies, long associated with the Jew and the Black, not as racial attributes but as consequences of civilization itself. See Sander Gilman, *Freud, Race, and Gender* (Princeton: Princeton UP, 1993). What would be interesting to explore further is how these earlier discourses on racialized lust were, malgré Freud, recuperated in a nineteenth-century racial discourse that drew on Freud to lend added credence to arguments that the racialized Other was driven by sexual instincts that required a civilizing imperial mission to control and contain.

10. For a query into the theoretical bases for applying Freud to historical analysis see Dominick LaCapra's essay "History and Psychoanalysis," *Soundings in Critical Theory* (Ithaca: Cornell, 1989) 30–66.

in which their projects can and do converge. For Freud, sexual desire is a cause; for Foucault, an effect. Freud accounts for the psychological aetiology of perversions, Foucault looks to the cultural production and historical specificity of the notions of sexual pathology and perversion themselves. The differences are striking but so are some of the points on which they are complementary, if not the same. Both were concerned with boundary formation, with the "internal enemy" within. For Freud, cultural conventions arise out of the psychological contortions of the individual at war with her or his own subliminal desires. As Julia Kristeva writes, "Freud does not speak of foreigners: he teaches us how to detect foreignness in ourselves."[11] For Foucault, the cultural conventions of racism emerge out of social bodies at war with themselves. Thus when Michael Rogin, in an essay on liberal society and the Indian question in U.S. history, argues that attitudes toward native Americans were personalized and conceived as a "defense of the [American] self"—what Foucault would call a defense of society against itself—it is Freud he draws on, but Foucault who might have subscribed to Rogin's language of "defense" as well.[12] Or inversely, we might look to Edward Said's supremely Foucauldian analysis of Orientalist discourse and Western domination where Freud's notion of projection, of the Orient as the West's "surrogate self" is a crucial but buried part of his argument.

This chapter addresses two problems: the ways in which the language of Freud has entrenched itself in the general field of colonial studies, and the tangled coexistence of Freud and Foucault more specifically in analyses of colonial racism. If Foucault has led us to the power of discourse, it is Freud that has, albeit indirectly, turned us toward the power of fantasy, to imagined terror, to perceived assaults on the European self that made up the anxious and ambivalent world in which European colonials lived.[13] It is Freud after all, via Fanon, who as Homi Bhabha writes, located how "the deep fear of the Black figured in the psychic trembling of Western

---

11. Julia Kristeva, *Strangers to Ourselves* (New York: Columbia UP, 1991) 191.

12. Michael Rogin, "Liberal Society and the Indian Question," *Politics and Society* (May 1971): 269–312 esp. 284.

13. Clearly not all students of colonialism (myself included) who have attended to European colonials' anxieties in the face of their illegitimate rule are well versed in or intended to draw on Freud's arguments. My point is to acknowledge how much a Freudian, and more general psychologically oriented assessment of motivation, have underwritten what are ostensibly very different sorts of economic, political and sociological analyses.

sexuality."[14] Fanon was not alone. Octavio Mannoni, Albert Memmi, and Ashis Nandy have each drawn on a Freudian psychoanalytics to provide a *contre-histoire* of colonialism, a way to access the subjugated knowledges and psychology of domination of colonized Man (sic). I am not proposing that the task in colonial studies is to abandon Freudian concepts, but only the unreflexive use of them. We need to be aware of the varied analytic work we expect them to do, to distinguish, for example, when the concepts of repression, displacement, identification and projection that saturate so much of colonial historiography serve to clarify historical processes of empire—or, more frequently, are invoked to substitute for an analysis of historical depth.[15]

Subjecting the use of Freudian models to scrutiny requires doing so of Foucault's as well. Does embracing Foucault's statement that "sexuality is a dense transfer of power," charged with "instrumentality" run the risk of reproducing the very terms of colonial discourse itself, where everything and anything can be reduced to sex? Is Baudrillard's snipe that Foucault merely replaced one fiction of *homo economicus* with another, that of *homo sexualis*, valid?[16] And what is precluded by an economy of sex in which the genealogy of desiring subjects is only desiring men? While it may be in much colonial discourse that issues of sexuality were often metonymic of a wider set of relations, and sex was invariably about power, power was not always about sex. In these colonial contexts, discourses of sexuality often glossed, colonized, appropriated, and erased a more complicated range of longings and sentiments that, boiled down to sex, were made palatable as they were served up for immediate consumption.

There is overwhelming evidence that much colonial discourse, as Foucault's argument would suggest, has been framed by a search for the "truth" of the European bourgeois self through sex. This is not surprising. What is disturbing is that colonial historiography has inadvertently em-

14. See Homi Bhabha's injunction to re-engage Fanon and his Freudian sensibilities in "Remembering Fanon: Self, Psyche and the Colonial Condition," *Colonial Discourse and Post-Colonial Theory* eds. Patrick Williams and Laura Chrisman (New York: Columbia UP, 1994) 112–23 (originally published in 1986 as a Foreword to the republication of *Black Skin, White Masks*).

15. Among the best of the numerous recent re-engagements with Freud via Fanon, see Diana Fuss' critique of Fanon's treatment of interracial rape, femininity and homosexuality in "Interior Colonies: Frantz Fanon and the Politics of Identification," *Critical Crossings*, eds. Judith Butler and Biddy Martin, spec. issue of *Diacritics* 24.2–3 (Spring/Fall, 1994): 20–42.

16. Jean Baudrillard, *Forget Foucault* (New York: Semiotext, 1977) 30.

braced this notion of "truth" as well. Students of colonialism have often taken their readings of European sexual conduct in the colonies from colonial scripts themselves. Freudian notions of a repressed, sublimated and projected sexual impulse are invoked to explain political projects in instinctual psychosocial terms. In one version, desire is a basic biological drive, restricted and repressed by a "civilization" that forces our sublimation of it. Thus George Fredrickson in his history of white supremacy in the U.S. and South Africa suggests that Elizabethan repression of English sexuality may have incited the "secret or subliminal attractions" that were "projected onto Africans." [17] Gann and Duignan in their work on colonial Africa write that British imperial expansion was possibly "a sublimation or alternative to sex." [18]

If the repressive hypothesis is unacknowledged for these authors, it is not for others. Octavio Mannoni's postwar study of French-Malagasy colonial relations was centrally figured around the psychological coordinates and political consequences of European repression. [19] Fanon too explicitly called on psychoanalytic theory to explain racism as the projection of the white man's desires onto the Negro, where "the white man behaves 'as if' the Negro really had them." [20] Gilberto Freyre is perhaps most notorious for having attributed varied manifestations of colonial racial prejudice to the differences between the active libidos of the Portuguese, to the fact

17. George Fredrickson, *White Supremacy: A Comparative Study in American and South African History* (Oxford: Oxford UP, 1981) 100.

18. L. H. Gann and Peter Duignan, *The Rulers of British Africa, 1870–1914* (Stanford: Stanford UP, 1978) 240. As they explain:

Life overseas, away from family and friends, may have presented more opportunities or pressures to be promiscuous, officials had great power over the people they ruled, and black flesh may have seemed attractive merely because it was forbidden or was thought to be more 'natural.'

19. Octavio Mannoni, *Prospero et Caliban: Pyschologie de la Colonisation* (Paris: Seuil, 1950). Fanon's scathing assault in *Black Skin, White Masks* (83–108) on Mannoni's misguided analysis of the "so-called dependency complex of colonized people" coupled with Mannoni's gross generalizations about the roots of Malagasy national character both conspired to relegate him to the uncited and unworthy of critical review. Nevertheless, it is Mannoni who worked closely with Lacan whose revisions of Freud have in turn figured so prominently in some postcolonial theory. Shirley Turkel notes that Octavio and Maud Mannoni were considered among "the great barons," the "old guard of the Lacanian clinical tradition" and among "Lacan's loyal followers since the schism of 1953." See Shirley Turkel, *Psychoanalytic Politics: Jacques Lacan and Freud's French Revolution* (New York: Guilford Press, 1992) 259.

20. Frantz Fanon, *Black Skin, White Masks* (New York: Grove Press, 1967).

that they were so "highly sexed," in contrast to the more sexually conservative Anglo-Saxons.[21] According to Winthrop Jordan, Englishmen in the Renaissance projected onto the African "libidinal man" what "they could not speak of in themselves." Richard Drinnon in *Facing West*, a study of the metaphysics of Indian-hating and empire-building in U.S. history takes a systemic "repression" as the underlying theme of racial violence.[22] So too did George Rawick, who compared the Englishman's meeting with the West African to that of a "reformed sinner" who creates "a pornography of his former life."[23] By Rawick's account, this "great act of repression" left the Englishman identifying with "those who live as he once did or as he still consciously desires to live."[24]

For both Rawick and Jordan, racism emerged out of the unconscious realization by the English not that Africans were so different, but that they were frighteningly the same.[25] As Jordan put it, there was an

> irreconcilable conflict between desire and aversion for interracial sexual union . . . [It] rested on the bedrock fact that white men perceived Negroes as being *both alike and different* from themselves . . . Without perceptions of similarity, no desire and no widespread gratification was possible.[26]

For Jordan, some form of sexual desire is a given, while for Rawick, there is a hint that other motivating desires, besides those sexual, may have been at issue as well. David Roediger takes up just that theme in *The Wages of Whiteness* to specify the sort of nostalgic longings that racist "projections" entailed. He contends that the consensus achieved by a heterogeneous white working class in the nineteenth-century U.S. rested on an idea of blackness that embodied "the preindustrial past that they scorned and

21. Giberto Freyre, *The Masters and the Slaves* (New York: Knopf, 1946) 94.

22. Richard Drinnon, *Facing West: The Metaphysics of Indian-Hating and Empire-Building* (Minneapolis: U of Minnesota P, 1980). Although published in 1980, most of Drinnon's study was written in the mid 1970s just before *The History of Sexuality* appeared. Drinnon acknowledges his debt to Foucault's notion of a "carceral" society, but remains firmly committed to Freud's repressive hypothesis (xv–xvi).

23. George Rawick, *The American Slave: A Composite Autobiography* (Westport, CN: Greenwood Publishing Co., 1972) 132.

24. Rawick, *American Slave* 132.

25. Rawick, *American Slave* 133.

26. Winthrop Jordan, *White over Black* (New York: Norton, 1968) 137–38.

missed."[27] In Roediger's nuanced analysis, it is not *sexual* license that is longed for, nor *sexual* desire that is repressed, but desire in other forms, "longing for a rural past and the need to adapt to the urban present" of industrial discipline.[28]

In each of these versions of the repressive hypothesis, some combination of the Freudian notions of sublimated and projected desire is offered to account for racism and Europe's imperial expansion. Racism is treated as a historical construct, but repression of instinct remains the engine. The libidinal qualities imputed to the Other are understood as a product of racist fears, but sexual desire itself remains biologically driven, assumed, and unexplained. The underlying assumption is, as Martha Vicinus once so aptly called it, a "hydraulic model of sexuality" where "sex is always something to be released or controlled; if controlled it is sublimated or deflected or distorted."[29]

The notion that Western civilization has become increasingly restrictive and that the colonies have provided escape hatches from it runs deep in early Orientalist traditions and remains resonant in their contemporary popular form.[30] Hayden White, among others, points to a modern cultural anthropology that "has conceptualized the idea of wildness as the repressed content of *both* civilized *and* primitive humanity," of the "Wild Man . . . lurking within every man."[31] Sharon Tiffany and Kathleen Adams

27. David Roediger, *Wages of Whiteness* (London: Verso, 1991) 97. Thus Roediger writes: "Some concept of projection is necessary to understand the growth of a sense of whiteness among antebellum workers, who profited from racism in part because it enabled them to displace anxieties within the white population onto Blacks. But the process of projection was not abstract. It took place largely within the context of working class formation and addressed the specific anxieties of those caught up in that process" (101).

28. Roediger 109, 117.

29. "Sexuality and Power: A Review of Current Work in the History of Sexuality," *Feminist Studies* 8.1 (Spring 1982): 136.

30. See Sharon Tiffany and Kathleen Adams, *The Myth of the Wild Woman* (Cambridge: Schenkman, 1985), where these discourses on the eroticized native women are fully discussed. Louis Malleret's *L'Exotisme Indochinois et la Littérature Francaise* (Paris: Larose, 1934) offers a wonderful analysis of the erotics of the exotic and a comprehensive bibliography. For a recent take on the representation of the sexualized and passive Asian female "in the patriarchal Western psyche" and the long genealogy of it see L. Hyun-Yi Kang, "The Desiring of Asian Female Bodies: Interracial Romance and Cinematic Subjection," *Visual Anthropology Review* 9.1 (Spring 1993): 5–21.

31. Hayden White, "The Forms of Wildness: Archaeology of an Idea," *The Wild Man Within: An image in Western Thought from the Renaissance to Romanticism* (Pittsburgh: U of Pittsburgh P, 1972) 7.

have similarly argued that the anthropological idea of the sexualized "Wild Woman" has provided the "mirror in which we perceive ourselves."[32] Peter Gay's recent study of the bourgeois cultivation of hatred portrays male agents of empire as those who "satisfied their aggressive needs with abandon."[33] Ian Buruma, in an otherwise excellent review of a new edition of the famous Dutch colonial novel by Louis Couperus, *Hidden Force*, writes that "the European fear of letting go, of being 'corrupted' of going native, was to a large extent, I suspect, the northern puritan's fear of his (or her) own sexuality."[34] Philip Mason similarly notes that Rhodesian whites in the early twentieth century attributed to the "native," to "some dark and shadowy figure which they fear and hate, the desires they disapprove of most strongly in themselves . . . and when desire emerged, fear was not far away."[35]

Eroticized native bodies densely occupy the landscape of Western literary production and in the wake of Said's now enshrined critique of Orientalism, a profusion of literary and historical studies have catalogued the wide range of sexual and gendered metaphors in which the feminized colonies, and the women in it, were to be penetrated, raped, silenced and (dis)possessed.[36] But the sexual assault on women has provided more than the foundational imagery of imperial domination. Colonialism itself has been construed as the sublimated sexual outlet of virile and homoerotic energies in the West.[37] To argue, however, that different notions

32. Tiffany and Adams, *The Wild Woman* 6.

33. In Gay's Freudian analysis, racism and manliness provide the "alibis" for bourgeois aggression; deeply dependent on the notion of projection, Gay glaringly omits reference to Foucault.

34. Ian Buruma, "Revenge in the Indies," *New York Review of Books* August 11, 1994: 30–32.

35. Philip Mason, *Birth of a Dilemma: The Conquest and Settlement of Rhodesia* (London: Oxford UP, 1958) 244. Or, as put similarly in a more recent postcolonial critique of late colonial discourse by Ali Behdad: "the negative vision of the Oriental is important to the colonizer's identity because it provides him with an 'imaginary' Other onto whom his anxieties and fears are projected" (*Belated Travelers: Orientalism in the Age of Colonial Dissolution* [Durham: Duke UP, 1994] 79).

36. For studies that "reorient" Said's analysis in a gendered light see Sara Mill, *Discourses of Difference: an Analysis of Women's Travel Writing and Colonialism* (London: Routledge, 1991); Billie Mellman, *Women's Orients: English Women and the Middle East, 1718–1918: Sexuality, Religion and Work* (Ann Arbor: The U of Michigan P, 1992); Ali Behdad, *Belated Travelers* 1994, and Lisa Lowe, *Critical Terrains*, 1991.

On the "extraordinary fascination with and fear of racial and sexual difference which characterized Elizabethan and Jacobean culture" see Newman, " 'And wash the Ethiop White.' "

37. These images of an unrestricted libido let loose on colonial and post-colonial terrain remain tenacious leitmotifs in contemporary analyses of homoeroticism. See Kaja Silverman's analysis

of bourgeois manhood were merely confirmed by colonial ventures is to dilute a more complicated story. If the colonies were construed as sites where European virility could be boldly demonstrated it was because they were also thought to crystallize those conditions of isolation, inactivity, decadence, and intense male comradery where heterosexual definitions of manliness could as easily be unmade.

Freudian assumptions about the relationship between repression and desire hold fast. While Edward Said rightly notes how much the Orient has been conceived as "place where one could look for sexual experiences unobtainable in Europe," Ronald Hyam has taken that colonial discourse not as an object of critique but as a reasonable tool of analysis.[38] Hyam's *Empire and Sexuality* exemplifies a recent twist on the theme of an unrestrictive colony and a restricted west. He holds that empire provided "sexual opportunities" for European men when those in Britain were severely reduced. While explicitly deferring to Foucault's "model of sexual politics" to describe sexual attitudes in nineteenth-century Britain, the repressive hypothesis is what frames his argument and with it questions of power and racism remain out of his account.[39] For Hyam, among others, the colonies are a site for the "revenge of the repressed," an open terrain for European male ejaculations curtailed in the West.[40] Hyam's narrow focus on genitalia rather than gender, on the sexual fantasies of elite white males, on "sexual relaxation" rather than rape, is only part of his problem.[41] The

---

of T. E. Lawrence's homoerotic voyages ("White Skin, Brown Masks: The Double Mimesis, or With Lawrence in Arabia," *Differences* 1.3 (1989): 3–54), or Michelle Green's exploration of the sensual delights and opportunities for pleasure in post-war Tangiers for Paul Bowles and his compatriots, *The Dream at the End of the World: Paul Bowles and the Literary Renegades in Tangiers* (New York: Harper, 1992).

38. Edward Said, *Orientalism* (New York: Pantheon, 1978) 190.

39. Ronald Hyam, *Empire and Sexuality: The British Experience* (Manchester: Manchester UP, 1990) 58.

40. For a very different use of this notion of the "revenge of the repressed" see Malek Alloula's *Colonial Harem* where he analyses, and to some extent reproduces, the pornographic pleasures and power infused in erotic postcards of Algerian women as "illustrated forms of colonialist discourse" ([Minneapolis: U of Minnesota P, 1986] 120).

41. For a sharp critique of Hyam's attention to genitalia not gender, and to great white men not the racial politics of sexuality see Luise White's review of *Empire and Sexuality:The British Experience* in *The International Journal of African Historical Studies* 25.3 (1992): 664–65. On Hyam's euphemisms for sexual exploitation see Mark T. Berger's review (in *The Journal of Imperial and Commonwealth History* 17.2 (1988): 83–89) of an earlier paper entitled "Empire and Sexual Opportunity" on which the later book was based.

sexual politics of empire has never reduced to the opportunistic possibilities prompted by repressions in Europe alone.[42]

What gets clouded in such accounts is precisely where Foucault's analysis would lead us to turn. Colonial discourses of sexuality were productive of class and racial power, not mere reflections of them. The management of European sexuality in the colonies was a class and gender-specific project that animated a range of longings as much as it was a consequence of them. Nor were these confined just to the colonies. As Ian Buruma tells it, when he was growing up in the Hague in the 1940s and 1950s, the production of desire that continued to surround Eurasian "half-caste" girls ensured that they were still considered "hot."[43] But attention to the discourses on sexual desire only captures a small part of the psychological complexities that turned imitation into mockery, ambivalence into aggression, and reduced cultural nostalgia into a desire for—or prohibitions against—sex.[44]

Discourses about sexual contagions, moral contamination and reproductive sterility were not applicable to any and all whites, nor were they freefloating, generalized pronouncements that treated all bodies as equally susceptible and the same. These discourses circulated in a racially charged magnetic field in which debates about sexual contamination, sexual abstinence or spermatic depletion produced moral clusters of judgment and

42. For a review of a recently published set of books that work off this repressive model, see Bruce Robbin's "Colonial Discourse: A Paradigm and its Discontents," *Victorian Studies* 35.2 (Winter 1992): 209–14 where he similarly asks:

is the Empire to be conceived, as a number of the authors in these volumes seem to conveive it, as the "unconscious" of nineteenth-century culture, a repressed but definitive truth that is always already obliged to return? Or does an allegorical Freudianism of this sort soften the hard fact that the Empire *could* be successfully ignored, even by what has been judged highest in nineteenth-century culture? . . . Or to take another example of displaced Freudianism, is everything said by the colonizer about the colonized to be understood as a projection of the colonizer's anxieties? If imperialism required not just a rationale (the inferiority of the natives), but working knowledge of a certain objectivity that would aid in conquering and ruling, then projection probably is not the whole story. (212–13)

43. Buruma, "Revenge in the Indies" 32.

44. Homi Bhabha credits Fanon with having identified these colonial dislocations but I think Bhabha himself does it with much more subtlety and care. It is also, of course, Bhabha who exemplifies a welding of Foucauldian and Freudian analyses, via Lacan in many of the articles collected in his *The Location of Culture* (London: Routledge, 1994). Also see Michael Rogin's fine analysis of how blackface musicals drew on racial images to secure and resolve a nostalgic narrative of national identity in " 'Democracy and Burnt Cork': The End of Blackface and the Beginning of Civil Rights," *Representations* 46 (Spring 1994): 1–34.

distinction that defined the boundaries of middle-class virtue, lower-class immorality and the deprivations of those of colonial birth or of mixed-race.

Whiteness, Class and the Sexual Truth Claims for Being European

It is the pull of this racially charged field that I turn to here. The range of competing and converging myths of the sexualized Other that riddle European belles-lettres, colonial official texts and the sub-disciplines of nineteenth-century science have been the subject of a contemporary critical tradition for some time. Rather than rehearse them, I have another task: namely to take up Foucault's contention that desire was animated by discourses of sexuality and productive of new forms of power. It is a particular wedge of that discourse on European desire that interests me here, one that divided those Europeans who embraced European bourgeois respectabilities from those who did not. I want to look at how asymmetries in the production of the discourse of desire differed by gender and class, at how effectively these distinctions affirmed a shared notion of European bourgeois culture and its prescriptions for white normality.

And finally, in turning back to Foucault's claim that desire is not opposed to the law but produced by it, I ask what sorts of desires were incited by certain colonial discourses on moral reform and sexual regulation. What of those, for example, that spoke incessantly of the subversive dangers of mixed-bloods and their moral perversions? Those that reiterated the base sexual drives of common European soldiers and their homoerotic tendencies? Those Protestant dailies and weeklies in the Netherlands that proliferated in the 1880s, incessantly warning "every Dutch youngster" against the "indescribable horror and bestiality" that reigned in the Indies army barracks and the sexual dangers that awaited them?[45] Those that spoke to the sexual precocities of Indies youths and the passions that the tropics unleashed? These discourses not only recorded inappropriate desire, but created spaces for it as they struggled to define what was racially distinctive about bourgeois sexuality itself. They reaffirmed that the "truth" of European identity was lodged in self-restraint, self-discipline, in a managed sexuality that was susceptible and not always under con-

45. Hanneke Ming, "Barracks-Concubinage in the Indies, 1887–1920," *Indonesia* 35 (1983): 65–93, 79.

trol.[46] But they also confirmed that if "the colonized" were driven by an insatiable instinct, certain Europeans were as well.

The point is an important one because colonial enterprises produced discourses that were not only about a racialized sexuality and a sexualized notion of race. These colonial discourses of desire were also productive of, and produced in, a social field that always specified class and gender locations. It is the cultural density of these representations that interest me here. The fact that these discourses do not reduce to racial typologies alone suggests that the colonial order coupled sexuality, class and racial essence in defining what it meant to be a productive—and therefore successfully reproductive—member of the nation and its respectable citizenry.

What is striking about the sexual stories that European colonials and their metropolitan observers told about their own desires and thus about what distinguished themselves is how boldly they turned on defining and affirming the bourgeois order in specific ways. European children, as we have seen, were said to be susceptible to sexual desires in the tropics at a much earlier age than in Europe. This demanded a vigilance about their rearing, their cordoning off from "precocious Indies youths," repeated enumeration of the sexual dangers posed by servants and protection from a climate that encouraged "habitual licentiousness" at an early age.[47] Investments in a European-spirited education confirmed how much the European identities of these children had to be protected from the sexualized Other and how much those native adults and children with whom they came in contact had to be monitored and controlled. These discourses on children's sexuality were rooted in a racial grammar, confirming that education was a moral imperative for bourgeois identity and a national investment, designed to domesticate the sexual desire of children and to direct how they would later decide who to consider eligible recipients of it.

A basic tension in the sexual politics of colonial states was the prom-

46. Thus, in the brilliant turn-of-the-century novel, The Hidden Force, by Louis Couperus, sexual craving and passion activated by the Indies causes the demise of the main character and representative figure of colonial paternalism, Resident Van Oudjick, because "he is susceptible to it." See E. M. Beekman's superb analysis of this major piece of Dutch colonial literature in "The Passatist: Louis Couperus' Interpretation of Dutch Colonialism," Indonesia 37 (1984): 59–76. Also see Ian Buruma's review of the English edition, "Revenge in the Indies," cited above.

47. Grenfell Price, White Settlers in the Tropics (New York: American Geographical Society, 1939) 31.

ise of new possibilities for desiring male subjects and objects for them, but implemented policies that simultaneously closed those possibilities down. The regulatory policies that first condoned and then condemned concubinary relations between Asian women and European men activated as much discussion about the merits, pleasures and gratifications of these utilitarian relations as about the morally degraded nature of them.[48] In the name of British, French, and Dutch moralizing missions, colonial authority supposedly rested on the rigor with which its agents distinguished between desire and reason, native instinct and white self-discipline, native lust and white civility, native sensuality and white morality, subversive unproductive sexuality and productive patriotic sex.

But these Manichean lines were not always drawn with racial clarity. The class divisions that divided colonial discourses of desire distinguished subaltern white men from their middle-class counterparts in fundamental ways. European men of lower-class were repeatedly accused of giving into their biological drives at the cost of empire—and by more than contemporary colonial apologists. Thus Grenfell Price, in a publication of the American Geographical society as late as 1939, attributed the downfall of sixteenth-century Portuguese colonies to the "unbridled passions of the lower types of invaders."[49] Kenneth Ballhatchet notes that in eighteenth-century British India, "special provisions"—not applicable to the "educated English gentleman"—were made "for the sexual satisfaction of British soldiers because they came from the lower classes and so were thought to lack the intellectual and moral resources required for continence."[50] Eugene Genovese similarly notes that lower-class white men invariably were made responsible for the sexual abuses of slavery.[51]

In the Indies, the equation of common-class origins and unchecked licentiousness was much the same. Here, prostitution was excused on the grounds that a common European soldier had to satisfy his "natu-

48. See, for example, some of the following: Ducimus, "Het prostitutie-vraagstuk in het Indische leger," *Indisch Militair Tijdschrift* 1–6 (1902): 188–212 and 318–28; W. D. Koot, "Het Concubinaat" (no publisher, 1905); A. De Braconier, "het Kazerne-Concubinaat in Ned-Indie," *Vragen van den Dag* 28 (1913): 974–95; S. Weijl and W. H. Boogaardt, *Pro en Contra:Het Concubinaat in de Indische Kazernes* (Baarn: Hollandia, 1917).

49. Price, *White Settlers* 16.

50. Kenneth Ballhatchet, *Race, Sex and Class under the Raj* (New York: St. Martin's Press, 1980) 2.

51. Eugene Genovese, *Roll Jordan Roll* (New York: Pantheon) 421.

ral sexual appetites," "that a woman remains indispensable to him."[52] If thwarted from exercising his "natural" sexual urges, he would resort to "unnatural vices," specifically to masturbation or sexual relations with other men.[53] Concubinage with native women in the Indies army barracks was justified as preferable to homosexual contacts and social intimacies outside the state's control. But not everyone agreed. Debates over whether it was "healthy" for common soldiers to refrain from indulging their "sexual drive" also spoke to other concerns. One outspoken critic of the barrack-concubinage system, Dr. J. Kohlbrugge, admonished an Indies ethic in which the indiscriminant satisfaction of one's sexual tendencies was considered a "right," a "necessity," even "as in France, a *droit du travail*." He opined that the serious consequences of such a course were clear; a "paralysis of energy," a "disappearance of self-control," a "dampening of the desire to work"—all characteristics that described the native, absent in, and defining of, what was European.[54]

It is difficult to assess to what extent, what Foucault called the "discursive verbosity" that surrounded the sexual relations between European agents of empire and local women in fact animated new sorts of desires for such relations (HS:33). Whose pleasures and what sorts of desires were produced out of this careful surveillance is hard to tell.[55] What we do know is that because common soldiers were barred from marriage and poor European women were barred from the barracks, sexual accommodations of varied sorts prevailed.[56] Military officials condoned concubinage as a "necessary evil" on the grounds that it significantly lowered the subsis-

---

52. See Liesbeth Hesselink, "Prostitution: the Necessary Evil," *Indonesian Women in Focus*, eds. Elsbeth Locher-Scholten and Anke Niehof (Dordrecht, Holland: Foris, 1987), 206–07; and Verbaal 29 December 1903, no. 47, Minister of Colonies, quoted in Ming, "Barracks Concubinage."

53. S. Weijl and W. Boogaardt, *Het Concubinaat in de Indische Kazernes* (Baarn: Hollandia, 1917) 8.

54. J. F. H. Kohlbrugge, "Prostitutie in Nederlandsch-Indie," *Indisch Genootschap*, Algemene vergadering van 19 Februari 1901, 33.

55. On the fact that interracial sexual relations were more than a problem among low-level civil servants and the military rank and file see John Ingelson, "Prostitution in colonial Java," *Nineteenth and Twentieth Century Indonesia: Essays in honour of Professor J. D. Legge* (Clayton, Victoria: Monash UP, 1986) 123–40. Ingelson notes that in Surabaya in the 1860s there were also brothels "owned by Europeans, employing European women and catering for European men" (126).

56. See especially A. de Braconier who provides a summary history of the sexual arrangements of European soldiers since the seventeenth century in "Het Kazerne-Concubinaat in Ned-Indie," *Vragen van den Dag* XXVIII: 974–95.

tence requirements of soldiers without incurring higher wages or the increased medical costs that came with prostitution and a syphilitic rank and file.[57] The availability to European recruits of native women in sexual and domestic service—these "living grammar books" (levende grammaire) as they were sometimes called—was part of the male "wages of whiteness." This was a set of policies that legitimated the intimate regulation of the lives of common European soldiers and those Asian women who came in contact with them. But what is absent from, and usually unspeakable in, this discourse on "evil" is as striking as what it contained; the dangers of a homosexual European rank and file were implicitly weighed against the medical hazards of rampant heterosexual prostitution: both were condemned as morally pernicious and a threat to racial survival.[58]

While the moral dangers of homosexuality in these debates on concubinage often went unstated, strident moral disparagements were explicitly cast on those of inferior class and race. In this discursive terrain, the eugenic peril of mixing the "lower elements" of Europeans and Asians was supposedly illustrated by the dismal fate of the children of these mixed unions.[59] Referred to disparagingly as soldatenkinderen, the term itself im-

57. Those who supported concubinage argued that lifting the prohibition on marriage would raise military expenses three to five times above those under the concubinary system. See S. Weijl and W. H. Boogaardt, Pro en Contra: Het Concubinaat in de Indische Kazernes (Baarn: Hollandia, 1917) 11. In 1913, it was estimated that out of 34,000 European and native soldiers, forty percent of those classified as European had contracted some form of venereal disease, as opposed to only ten percent of the soldiers classified as native. According to Philip Curtin (Death by Migration. New York: Cambridge UP, 1989) "venereal disease was . . . the most important single cause of hospitalization in most nineteenth-century armies—at home or overseas" (156).

58. While the dangers of "unnatural desires" between men were more often assumed than discussed this was not always the case. In a debate over the merits of retaining barrack-concubinage one military official in 1893 noted that in the absence of women at the Gombong military compound, "far more than half of the young men quartered there were guilty of practicing unnatural vices [with other men]" (postscript to report dated 1893, in Verbaal 21-1-1903 quoted in Ming. 1983:69). Twenty years later the abolition of concubinage was again debated on similar grounds but with different resolution. The archbishop of Batavia held that "unnatural desires" could be "strictly controlled" but "not rooted out" (see Ming, "Barracks-Concubinage" 81).

59. For a brief discussion of the eugenics discourse in the Netherlands Indies see my "Carnal Knowledge and Imperial Power" (1991): 72–73. Cf. Jan Noordman (Om de kwaliteit van het nageslacht: Eugentica in Nederland, 1900–1950. [Nijmegen: SUN, 1989]) who argues that although many Dutch eugenists may have thought in terms of racial superiority, such statements were rare (129). While he is right that the valorization of "racial purity" was never made as explicitly in

plied illegitimate and sordid origins. Here was fertile ground for moral intervention and charitable goodwill, for extended debates about native prostitution and white pauperism, as well as obvious evidence for why managed sex and a moral upbringing should be of the state's concern and in its control. What was animated, however, were not only sexual fantasies and titillations about the barrack underworld, but a set of practical and perceptual "effects" that kept questions of racial mixing and racial clarity in clear view, where the desire to know the "truth" of race and sex, to know what caused European men "to go native" and European women to choose a native man, placed questions of moral deprivation and the psychological coordinates of racial belonging as favored and recurrent themes among the architects of military and civilian colonial rule.

The discourse that condoned concubinage and acquiesced to the biological drives of common European men did more than justify military policy. It distinguished those middle-class European men with a right to rule from both those decadent nobility and those class and racial commoners who did not. It identified men who degenerated out of the European camp, those betrayed by their desires from those Europeans guided by self-discipline and sexual restraint. It divided "men of character" and reason from men of passion. As importantly, as more restrictions were placed on concubinary arrangements for all civil servants and military staff at the turn of the twentieth century, it rehearsed and took solace in a specific narrative that concubinage only remained in those outposts where "cultivated marriageble European young women were scarce."[60]

Within this racialized economy of sex, European women and men won respectability by steering their desires to legitimate paternity and intensive maternal care, to family and conjugal love; it was only poor whites, Indies-born Europeans, mixed-bloods and natives who, as we might remember from the preceding chapter, focused just too much on sex. To be truly European was to cultivate a bourgeois self in which familial and national obligations were the priority and sex was held in check—not by silencing

---

the Netherlands as it was among racial hygienists in Germany, literature from the Indies on the mixed, Indo population calls into question Noordman's contention that a notion of racial superiority was of little import in Dutch eugenists' arguments.

60. AR, report on officers and civil servants living with a concubine from the Government-Secretary to the Governor-General of the Netherlands Indies, 8 March 1904. Also see R. A. Kern, "De kontroleurs en 't concubinaat," *Tijdschrift voor het Binnenlandsch Bestuur* 28.1 (1905): 250–52.

the discussion of sex, but by parcelling out demonstrations of excess to different social groups and thereby gradually exorcising its proximal effects. Desires for opulence and sex, wealth and excess were repeatedly attributed to creole Dutch and lower-class Europeans, to those with culturally hybrid affiliations and/or of mixed-blood origin. Once again, persons ruled by their sexual desires were natives and "fictive" Europeans, instantiating their inappropriate dispositions to rule.

Pleasure, Power and the Work of Scientific Pornography

The discourses of desire that surrounded European colonial women reflect some predictable qualities of nineteenth-century gender ideology, but not in all ways. We know the received, official script, that white women were encased in a model of passionless domesticity, mythologized as the desired objects of colonized men, categorically dissociated from the sexual desires of European men and disallowed from being desiring subjects themselves. As custodians of morality, they were poised as the guardians of European civility, moral managers who were to protect child and husband in the home. But clearly some women saw other options and made sexual and conjugal choices that speak to other possible scenarios, and other stories. European women who veered off respectable course were not only stripped of the European community's protection of their womanhood, but disavowed as good mothers and as true Europeans. Thus the Indies mixed-marriage law of 1898 relegated those European women to native status who chose cohabitation over marriage and chose native men over the European-born on the argument that if these women were really European they would never have made such inappropriate choices.[61]

In Dutch colonial novels, women of European status but of Indies birth, or of mixed-blood and common class origin appear as sensual, erotically charged beings, driven by passion in ways that "pure-blood" middle-class European women void and supposedly bereft of desire were not.[62] Each of these representations of bourgeois propriety and the social norms they

61. See my "Sexual Affronts and Racial Frontiers . . ." for discussion of the racial issues that surrounded the mixed marriage judicial debates.
62. Again see Couperus' *Hidden Force* where sexual passion circulates in a creole, Eurasian, Javanese world of illicit liaisons around the transgressions of Leonie, the creole wife of a colonial resident, not Eva, that woman who is educated, cultured and truly European.

prescribed hinged on the presence of other actors, on a marking of their sexuality as the essence of what kinds of human beings they were, as indexical of the social category to which they truly belonged. These discourses of sexuality could tell not only the truth about individual persons, but about racial and national entities. They linked subversion to perversion, racial purity to conjugal white endogamy, and thus colonial politics to the management of sex.

The production of new sites and strategies of colonial control engendered by the discourse on sexuality is easier to identify than the production of the "incessant spirals" of pleasure and power that Foucault would suggest it allowed. For the "talking cure" about sex in the colonies was voyeuristic and visual and not primarily in the confessional mode. It addressed less directly the "truth" of one's own desires, than a phantasmic litany of sexual specifications and excesses that distinguished these Others from European bourgeois selves.

A "gynecological study," Women in Java, published simultaneously in Semarang and Amsterdam by a Dr. C. H. Stratz in 1897 is exemplary of that mode.[63] Here the sexual pleasures of scientific knowledge join with the pornographic aesthetics of race. The "pleasures" infused in Stratz's study derive only in part from its full-front illustrations of naked nubile women's bodies with their arms raised and hands clasped behind their heads.[64] For this quintessential example of "scientia sexualis" is a guide to racial taxonomies and racially attributed psychological and physiological characteristics as well.

What does this pornographic racial taxonomy entail? Preceding the photos, the study is introduced with an analysis of different races, of those "colored" who morally "lag behind those of "the pure race" and of the Javanese who are "very indolent, fearful, without initiative and who have

63. Re-presentations of that mode have appeared in the form of postcolonial critique for some time, and some might argue that there is no longer reason to give space to such degradations here. University of Minnesota Press' high gloss coffee-table format for Malek Alloula's Colonial Harem—which literally takes the viewer through the progressive baring of Algerian women's bodies—is a case in point of this 'double-exposure.' Sander Gilman's study of the iconography of prostitutes and Hottentot women might be cited on similar grounds. While my analysis of the "scientific" study below omits both the photos accompanying that piece and its most explicit descriptive obscenities, I do not hold that such pornographic texts should be buried or effaced from view. At issue is how we use them and write against their prurient grain.

64. Dr. C. H. Stratz, De vrouwen op Java: eene gynaecologische studie (Amsterdam: Scheltema and Holkemas; Samarang: G.C.T. van Dorp, 1897).

an entirely different understanding of lying and cheating than Europeans do."[65] Gynecologically speaking, these might seem superfluous observations. But this is not only a sexual treatise on women; it is a "scientific" treatise on the aesthetics of race, on the erotics of the exotic, on Javanese women as a prototype of what makes their bodies desirous to, and their bodies and minds so distinctive from, Europeans. Stratz's description of Javanese women attends closely to skin shade, to color and quantity of hair, as he moves down from "their sleek dark hair," to the "dark dusky eyes," to the nearly hairless armpits, and to the "thick-haired mons veneris."[66]

The titillations that this passage may provoke are not unrelated to the particular kind of knowledge it holds in store. First, it celebrates the beauty of *all* Javanese women's bodies as a generic type. Second, in asserting that Javanese women of the "Hindu and Malay type . . . share many common characteristics" it underscores that whatever differences might exist between different Asian bodies, more marked (and significant) is how they differ from Europeans and how much, among them, they are timelessly the same.

But what stands out in Stratz's account is how clearly internal and skeletal body form reveals a woman's hidden racial characteristics even when her physical appearances is that of a European. Stratz's case in point is that of the distinctively Javanese pelvic shape of "a young woman, who was a fifth generation descendant of a Javanese mother and who distinguished herself by a conspicuously white, soft skin and pretty blonde hair."[67] Outward similarity masks essential difference. The contrast offered with European women's bodies are evinced in the "more spherical" shape of the skull and (in a "cursory inspection" of some twenty-five women housed in Soerabaja's women's hospital) by the measurements of the pelvis which (like the skull) is "rounder."[68] This holds as well, Stratz notes, for the "colored of all racial types" who share this "round form." The pelvis tells the inner "truth" of race and identity in ways that could not otherwise be proved or observed.

Following a centimeter fine comparison of pelvic measurements, Stratz

65. Stratz, *De vrouwen op Java* 5.
66. Stratz 6, 8.
67. Stratz 14.
68. Stratz 14.

turns back to his aesthetic concerns. He counts the "fine modelling of the trunk, shown especially in the delicate line of the dorsal muscle" as being one of the great beauties of the Javanese female body." This, he notes, is less a "racial characteristic" than due to the "total absence of a corset in the Javanese women's dress." [69] Thus, despite their small size, they can be "very elegant" and Stratz points the reader to the frontal and profile photographs of two nude young women, one only adorned with an ankle bracelet, her body positioned in a languid pose, her arms lifted and curved away from the photographer, wrapped around her neck.

Stratz confirms that "this fine modelling of the trunk" is not a "racial characteristic," noting that many European women on Java wear no corsets and if so only in the afternoons, and "therefore one finds among them as well many more beauties and also more well-kept up figures at a later age than in the high gloss (geverniste) fashion world of Europe." [70] This is a dissonant passage on several counts: one, because the dress codes of European women would seem to be beside the point, and two, few texts attribute any beauty to European women in the tropics and certainly none that might derive from their physical form. More commonly underscored is the aesthetic and emotional price that European women pay to live indolently in the tropics—the ravaging of their bodies by inactivity, cumbersome and dangerous pregnancies, and rash-producing heat. It is the tropics that bring all women closer to (their) nature.

But Stratz does not dwell on these climatic levellings. He turns back to racial characteristics, to those "finely built limbs," to the "hyperextension of the elbow joints" that one often sees in the "engravings at [the Hindu temple of] Borobodur," to the shape of the fingers, legs, feet, toes, and to the "extremely limited development of the calves," a "characteristic [that Javanese] share with all Oriental peoples." [71] Again he returns to color, to the skin tone of Javanese women, to the "blue spot" at the base of the spine and finally to a studied description of the vagina's pigment variations from the outer labia to those "smaller pigment spots lying scattered high

69. Stratz 14–15. Given that all of Stratz's models are nude, the reader would have little reason to doubt his claims, but it is a strange observation for anyone familiar with urban and rural women's dress in Java since the *setagen*, a long "abdominal sash" wound several times around the body from the pelvis to up above the waist, is the girdled part of their toilet.
70. Stratz 15.
71. Stratz 16.

in the vagina." Nowhere is Stratz on, as it were, more firmly pleasurable and knowing ground.

While chromatics and other sensory modes reign supreme in his classificatory scheme, in fact it is the *hidden* features of these women's racialized sexuality—and Stratz's "expert" gaze—to which the reader is asked to attend. Differences found on the outer surface of the body are confirmed by the special and privileged knowledge and view he shares of the deep and unique markings within it. Commenting again on the lack of hair around the clitoris, he instructs his readership to the "particularly clear" view of this in a photograph he provides. But there is nothing clear in the figure at all. And this is just the point. The reader's gaze must be studied, because there is little to see in this profile picture. We must rely on Stratz's privileged view. Our gaze is pointed inward, to that which is not visible—but with Stratz's expert help—easily imagined.

The meticulous attention paid to detail in the above contrasts sharply with what the section that follows on the gynecological illnesses among European women. There is no symmetry in form or content, no detailed descriptions of bodies, no pictures, no European women subjected to view. There is no nuanced discussion of the European women's sexual organs, no lingering over their texture and gradated hue. In this context, talking about and looking for the truth of identity in sexual organs is reserved for non-whites. For European women, there is only a list of genital pathologies and a note that despite his meager sample, when compared with European statistics, noteworthy differences are evident deriving from a tropical way of life. Rather than discussing physical form and abstracted body parts, Stratz describes what he sees as more relevant, a colonial life style for European women that compares "with the most comfortable classes in Europe."[72] Their distinctions are not defined by vaginal coloring: matters of leisure, power, and privilege determine where the difference rests. He notes that white women are surrounded by a bevy of servants who spare them hard or exerting physical labor, outside the home and within it. They have, he notes, the time to keep themselves pure and clean, bathing at least twice a day in cool water, lathering the whole body. And least we think these purifying ceremonies are confined to grown women

---

72. Stratz 20.

he adds that "daily vaginal douches . . . [for] children are an integral part of daily bodily cleansing."

Here the aesthetics is, if anything, of race, the pleasures are of purification. Unlike Stratz's earlier allusion to the beauty of some European women in the tropics, here he returns to a more conventional portrayal, of colorless bodies, cleansed of dirt, devoid of sex. The discourse is one of physical inactivity and vigilant hygiene for women and children. He notes that this "hygienic way of life" seems to contrast sharply with the striking "paleness of all European women living in the tropics" which even experts attribute to "tropical anemia." But Stratz believes in no such thing. His antiseptic ethnographic account ends with approval of an Indies dress code that affords European children freedom of movement and adult women freedom from the restricting undergarments of Europe that press on stomach and breasts.[73]

While it would be disingenuous to take Stratz's study as representative of what preoccupied all Dutch colonial medical practitioners, the aestheticization of race and the distributions of sexual desire that it invoked were neither confined to the Indies, unique to the Dutch, nor unusual among them. In fact Stratz's discourse is part of a well-honed tradition in the science of race. George Mosse dates the aestheticization of race from the late 1700s; the eroticization of race is a discourse of the Renaissance long before. Sander Gilman documents such scientific study of the unique sexuality of different races from the early 1800s. Others, such as Gilberto Freyre, continued to produce such discourses well into the twentieth century. But the "standard of beauty as a criterion of racial classification" did not produce as neat a correlation between beauty and desire, between aesthetically pleasing and racially superior populations as some commentators would lead one to expect.[74] For Javanese women could be considered both "beautiful" and "lazy," "elegant," and "deceitful," "finely-modelled," and intellectually lacking at the same time. To be physically "underdeveloped" and libidinally "oversexed" was not an oxymoron. For this was a discourse and a domain of knowledge that was productive of, and responsive to, taxonomies of power and a range of desires that articulated unevenly with the multiple hierarchies of nation, gender, race, and class.

73. Stratz 22.

74. George Mosse, *Toward the Final Solution: A History of European Racism* (Madison: U of Wisconsin P, 1985) 23.

It is not insignificant, for example, that this "gynecological study" of women on Java eroticizes some women and not others or that the section on obstetrics contains no photographs at all. Sexuality is the stronger marker of difference and what Stratz knows about. He writes that both native and European women unwisely sought the help of poorly trained native and European midwives less than skilled doctors like himself. As he put it, "the white woman on Java" was "very far behind her European sisters." In the domain of reproduction Javanese and European women would seem to be similar, but this too is not the case. For the discourse on respectable European women in the Indies is almost exclusively framed by their functional roles as mothers and wives in contrast to the discourse on native and mixed-blood women which is not.

Stratz's text is blatantly salacious, deceptively straightforward—and misleading. Based on it alone one might conclude that discourses on sexuality always took a predictable form in which colonial knowledge and power were invariably produced from the prurient sexual pleasures bestowed on those who recorded, read, and vicariously participated in it. It demands that readers rivet their attention on genitalia in the making of race, confirming the story that colonialism was that quintessential project in which desire was always about sex, that sex was always about racial power, and that both were contingent upon a particular representation of non-white women's bodies. It rehearses the proverbial story that native women were the object of the white male gaze and white women were assiduously protected from it. Even from a critical vantage point, readers are caught within its frame. It is a story about powerful subjects looking upon sexual objects, one in which sex was about power and other desires were merely deflections and projections of both.

While we should attend to such accounts, they have their limitations. As should be clear from chapters 4 and 5, the discourse of sexuality tied truth claims about persons to the truth about sex in more nuanced ways. That discourse embraced a range of other desires between mothers and children, nursemaids and their charges, European men and their Asian housemaids and between European men that spoke to a broader set of sentiments. If it is the production of desire we are after, then it is neither to Stratz's aestheticized prurience nor to the greedy gaze of French colonial postcards that we should turn. We need to situate these discourses in a wider frame, one in which desire itself is the subject, where its relationship to the colonial order of things was sometimes askew, sometimes opaque, where desire and race were mediated through other sentiments by which they were more insidiously bound.

Of Desire and Other Sentiments

These discourses on sexuality had concrete effects, as Foucault would suggest, that in turn intensified the micro-centers of colonial control: a strict control of servants, a protracted discourse on and investments in the education and rearing of European children, a century-long debate over poor white welfare, and increasingly tighter restriction on which Europeans could immigrate to the colonies and the moral standards and domestic arrangements by which they were obliged to live. Cultivation of the bourgeois self depended on a catalogue of sexual dispositions about different human kinds. This sexual taxonomy was paired with a wider set of psychological and invisible characteristics that glossed the categories of bourgeois respectability, whiteness, and true Europeans.

But sexual desires were structured by desires and discourses that were never about sex alone. Desires to "pass" as white, to have one's progeny be eligible for higher education, or the sentiment that Frantz Fanon attributes to the man of color who desires "to marry white culture . . . to grasp white civilization and dignity and make them mine" all suggest that sexual desire in colonial and postcolonial contexts has been a crucial transfer point of power, tangled with racial exclusions in complicated ways.[75] Such desires, on the one hand, may use sex as a vehicle to master a practical world (privileged schooling, well-paying jobs in the civil service, access to certain residential quarters) which was in part what being colonial and privileged was all about.

How do we untangle what is about sex and what is not? Foucault's starting point in some ways facilitates that task, but not in others. For The History of Sexuality is not a history of western desire but rather a history of how sexual desire came to be the test of how we distinguish the interior Other and know our true selves. In this perspective, the protracted colonial discourses that linked sexual passion to political subversion and managed sexuality to patriotic priorities make sense. These were discourses that secured the distinctions of individual white bodies and the privileges of a white body politic at the same time. But Foucault's account in volume 1

---

75. Fanon, Black Skin, White Masks 63.

of *The History of Sexuality* assumes that sexuality was the dominant, principal mode in which the truth of the self was expressed—a claim on which his later volumes were to cast some doubt.

What is so striking in the discourse on the sexuality of masturbating children, servants, degenerate white men, and intruders in the bourgeois home is what constitutes the threat in these trangressive moments. Sometimes sexual intimacy and precocity were at issue, but it was rarely just these. Evidence of affective ties, affective kinship, confusions and transfusions of blood and milk, sentiments of cultural belonging were as dangerous as carnal knowledge. Nor can those other sentiments be reduced to just alternative ways of talking about sexual contagion.[76] Subversions to the bourgeois order were those that threatened the cultivation of personality, what Weber once called "a certain internal and external deportement in life," that repertoire of sensibilities that were glossed as "personal character" and carefully marked the boundaries of class and race.[77] It is these alienations of affection, these moments of "cultural contagion" that cut across the dichotomies of ruler and ruled, that clarified and confused what being respectable and colonial entailed.[78] Control and release of sexual desire was one of the leitmotifs of that story, but it embodied other themes as well. Cultivation of the self at once defined the interior landscapes of "true" Europeans and the interior frontiers of the superior polities to which they were constantly reminded they rightfully belonged.

Foucault's equation of desire and power poses a problem for how we view the psychological ambivalences that colonial discourse invoked by suggesting that desire and power were always bound. Is it only an "illusion" and "vanity," as Foucault claims, to ask whether there were no desires that stood to the side of colonial power or beyond it? Were there no desires that evaded the grip of power and escaped subsumption? Or would these retreats from the norm only further substantiate a normalizing pro-

76. On contagion as a dominant metaphor in Victorian culture see Athena Vrettos, *Somatic Fictions: Imagining Illness in Victorian Culture* (Stanford: Stanford UP, 1995).

77. M. Weber, *From Max Weber: Essays in Sociology*, eds. H. H. Gerth and C. Wright Mills (London: Routledge, 1948) 426. Also see Ian Hunter's analysis of "personality as a vocation" in the making of liberal education in Mike Gane and Terry Johnson, eds., *Foucault's New Domain* (London: Routledge, 1993).

78. On the "contagious" quality of sentiment and feeling in the eighteenth century, see Adela Pinch's fine analysis of Hume's treatise on the passions in *Strange Fits of Passion: Epistemologies of Emotion, Hume to Austen* (Stanford: Stanford UP, forthcoming).

cess by which all those with claims to civility—and those who rejected it—were bound? We have evidence of some such possible evasions, but not enough. Of European men and native women who cohabited in ways that went beyond the utilitarian sexual economy of concubinage, of European men who relinquished their claims to privilege by opting instead for liminal lives on the outskirts of European society, of native mothers whose desires to stay close to their children and not give them "up" to European schools may have expressed a rejection of the bourgeois European scales of merit all together.

While it is clear that production of these desires was not indifferent to the taxonomies of rule, they did not always uphold them. We may reject, with Foucault, a notion of primordial drive but still explore a space for individual affect structured by power but not wholly subsumed by it. In thinking about the "education of desire" more broadly, we are freed up from another Foucauldian quandary; namely, that by avoiding such an intense focus on sexuality, we can avoid reproducing the very terms of the nineteenth century imperial discourse that reduced and read all desires as sexual ones.[79] This is not to suggest that an obsession with sexuality does not underwrite colonial discourses. Rather it acknowledges a wider range of transgressive sentiments and cultural blurrings that informed what was unspeakable and what was said.

If a desiring subject, as Judith Butler writes, has the philosophical aim of discovering the "entire domain of alterity," of finding "within the confines of this self the entirety of the external world," then the imagined and practical world of empire must be seen as one of the most strategic sites for realizing that aim.[80] If desire is about both externalization and mimesis as so much of the philosophical literature on desire suggests, then no political story is more relevant to the production of western desire than colonialism, itself the quintessence of a process in which the mirroring of bourgeois priorities and their mimetic subversion played a defining role. Affirmation of the bourgeois self entailed an overlapping series of discursive displacements and distinctions on which its cultivation rest. There was no bourgeois identity that was not contingent on a changing

79. Ruth Levitas draws on E. P. Thompson's use of this term to describe nineteenth-century utopian projects. I use the "education of desire," rather, as a way of understanding why parental, and specifically maternal, affection was so central to the racial and nationalist visions of the Dutch colonial state. See Ruth Levitas, The Concept of Utopia 1990.
80. Butler, Subjects of Desire ix–x.

set of Others who were at once desired and repugnant, forbidden and subservient, cast as wholly different but also the same.

That "enemy within" that Foucault traced to the defense of society and that Freud traced to the defense of the self, may have more in common when the issue of racism is in clearer view. In an imperial frame, the pyschological and political anxieties attributed to European bourgeois society draw on a common vocabulary in some striking ways—that European bourgeois self defined by its interior other, those European nation-states built on their individuated and collective "interior frontiers," and those colonial empires that were the exteriorized sites where these internal borders were threatened and clarified are not part of a different order of things. Together they articulate what has made racial discourse so central—and resilient—in defining what being bourgeois and European were and continue to be about.

Truth claims made in the discourse on European sexuality can only appear as part of the deep genealogy of a European confessional mode when the imperial coordinates of the nineteenth century are not at issue. But even for Europe it is doubtful. For if we take our cue from the lectures on race, rather than from volume 1 of The History of Sexuality, Foucault himself alerts his audience to look in a different direction. The nineteenth-century discourse on bourgeois sexuality may better be understood as a recuperation of a protracted discourse on race, for the discourse on sexuality contains many of the latter's most salient elements. That discourse on sexuality was binary and contrastive, in its nineteenth-century variant always pitting that middle-class respectable sexuality as a defense against an internal and external other that was at once essentially different but uncomfortably the same. The contaminating and contagious tropes of nineteenth-century sexual discourse were not new: they recalled and recuperated a discourse that riveted on defensive techniques for "constant purification."[81]

Foucault might be right that the explanatory *scientific* weight accorded to sexual instinct only emerged in Freud's psychoanalytic theory of the

81. We might remember from Chapter 3 how Foucault described that discourse of race in the seventeenth century as one which bifurcated society into an "upper" and a "lower" race with the latter representing the "reappearances of its own past" (DS:54), reminding us of Rawick's notion that Englishmen in the seventeenth century saw West Africans as a "pornography of their former life." But Rawick's account is, as we saw, indebted to Freud's notion of repression, not to Foucault.

nineteenth century, but its genealogical antecedents go back much further still.[82] Assessments of sexual proclivity and racial membership were joined much earlier in a discourse that conferred the right to live in a certain way on those with the cultural competencies to exercise freedom, with the cultivated sensibilities to understand the limits of liberty, and with the moral strength to be untempted by lust and leisure. Sexual excess and misguided sentiments characterized those who were more fit to be slaves, indentured workers and the laboring under class or, like creoles and Indos in the Indies, unfit to rule an imperial world. Domesticated sexuality and managed sensibilities were endowments of those who stood above, and labelled, those troubled categories.

The point is not to reduce the entire discourse that coupled the truth of the self and the truth about one's sexual desire to a discursive variation on the discourse of race; but rather to suggest that the production and distribution of desires in the nineteenth-century discourse on sexuality were filtered through—and perhaps even patterned by—an earlier set of discourses and practices that figured prominently in imperial technologies of rule. Civilization could be defended against trangression by invoking the reasoned logic of race. Foucault would agree with this general point. There was no unitary bourgeois self already formed, no core to secure, no "truth" lodged in one's sexual identity. That "self," that "core," that "moral essence" that Fichte and colonial lawyers like Nederburgh sought to identify was one that Europe's external and internal "others" played a major part in making.[83]

In locating the power of the discourse of sexuality in the affirmation of the bourgeois self, Foucault shortcircuited the discursive and practical field of empire in which Western notions of self and other were worked out for centuries and continue to be drawn. Race comes late into Fou-

82. Sander Gilman's recent work on Freud and race, where he argues that Freud's theories of sexual instinct were responsive to a common and earlier racial discourse that pathologized the sexual instincts of Jews, could add further credence to my claim. Gilman holds that Freud generalized a sexual pathology that had been discursively construed as a predisposition of Jews and made it into one of civilization, allowing Freud to reformulate "the illness attributed to the Jew's body [as] the disease of all human beings." Freud, Race and Gender 1993: 90–91. Also see Marianna Torgovnick's Gone Primitive (Chicago: Chicago UP, 1990), which situates Freud's analysis of sexuality and his fascination with the primitive in a wider Western discourse.
83. Stratz, De vrouwen op Java 18.

cault's story in *The History of Sexuality*, not basic to its grammar, where—in the lectures—he seems to suggest it belonged. One could argue that the history of Western sexuality must be located in the production of historical Others, in the broader force field of empire where technologies of sex, self, and power were defined as "European" and "Western," as they were refracted and remade.

Epilogue

Critique is the art of reflective insolence [1]

No other contemporary cultural critic called on his readers so explicitly as did Foucault to use his work, go beyond it, and as he once put it, allow it to "self-destruct." In that spirit, I have drawn on him extensively but also sought to identify what he could not and did not do. I have tried to steer a course that neither assumes the universal applicability of his insights nor rejects those insights because they do not conform to particularistic notions of what constitutes "real" social history. My course instead has been to appreciate the ways in which Foucault's understanding of bio-power shaped how he saw the relationship between the discourses of sexuality and race and thus between bourgeois Europe and its imperial order. How we render those insights is a complicated task. Part of the difficulty, as we have seen, is that while Foucault's analysis of the discourses of sexuality entailed racism as a tactic within it, his analysis of racism in his lectures was less explicitly linked to the history of sexuality. Part of the problem too is that while Foucault's history of nineteenth-century bourgeois sexuality forcefully targeted what he saw as the fiction of sexual liberation in post-1968 left politics, his analysis of the genealogy of racism had little resonance as an effective history of racism's enduring presence in the fabric of European society itself. A French post-world war II episteme defined his understanding of racism in some predictable ways. His

1. Michel Foucault, "Qu'est-ce que la critique? (Critique et Aufklarung)," *Bulletin de la Société française de philosphie* 84.2 (April–June 1990): 35–63, 39, quoted in Didier Eribon, *Michel Foucault et ses contemporains* (Paris: Gallimard, 1994) 67, who notes that this text unfortunately is not included in *Dits et Ecrits*.

central reference for racism was still that of the holocaust and the Nazi state, not the discourses and dislocations of decolonization that, in the last two decades, have transfigured the face of Europe, the United States, and those who speak through and against racial politics within them.

Where Foucault was predictably constrained on some counts, he was not on others. How contemporary cultural studies, and colonial studies in particular, has come to understand colonial discourse and diasporas has in no small measure been influenced by him. But I have suggested that a deeper engagement with his specific genealogies of race and sexuality might help us rethink our own. His attention to the intimate ties between biopower and the discourse of race, to the wide distribution of state racisms, to racial discourse as part of—but not reducible to—an effect of capitalist exigencies are analytic openings we have yet to explore. Foucault's counter-intuitive insight that the discourse of race first appeared, not as a discourse of dominance, but as a *contre-histoire* deserves our attention. We might remember from his 1976 lectures that the vacillating quality of racial discourse, the fact that it always combined subjugated and erudite knowledge, accounts not only for the quixotic shifts in the political projects that discourse once served; tracking the relationship between subjugated and erudite knowledge is a key to the very method of genealogy. In re-viewing *The History of Sexuality* through the prism of empire, I have sought to understand how his implicit historical strategies and readings might prompt us to review our own analytic frame and reassess what sorts of genealogies of racism might speak to a history of the present.

There are several possible ways one might follow a Foucauldian impulse to conclude a book such as this. One could, as I have suggested, look at how Foucault's work on sexuality and race prompts a rethinking of colonial studies. But there is another sort of question: why undertake colonial studies at all, and what accounts for the enormous amount of intellectual energy invested in it today? Most of what follows focuses more on the former, but I first pose the latter on the premise that the answers to it are at once obvious and elusive. Colonial studies in the 1990s is clearly a charged and densely occupied field, signaling new political engagements and critical spaces. But it may also speak to more conservative agendas and political interests at the same time.

What issues are being expressed and spoken through the contemporary study of colonialism and race? Can we account for the resurgence of interest in these topics as the response and lead of postcolonial intellectuals now positioned to interrogate official wisdom about the colonial past, as they create and verify subjugated knowledges long repressed? Or does that resurgence also signal a verbose response to the crisis and anxieties of securing bourgeois identity in a rapidly shifting transcultural world in which "core" and "periphery" no longer look different in familiar ways or even map on to the same geopolitical entities? Are both of these critical responses to the resurgence of racism's opaque and virulent forms today? How do we tell the difference in a field that has become so diffuse. For a subject that has come into vogue across such a wide range of disciplines, how do we tell the difference between a reappraisal of the colonial order of things as a politically engaged strategy and one that is a retreat from the political exigencies of the present, scholarship at a safe distance, a voyeurism of the past?

More broadly framed, what range of statements characterize the contemporary discourse on race? What explains the incessant search for racism's originary moment? What truth-claims about modernity and the post-colonial condition are lodged in the wide spectrum of stories constructed about the imperial history of race? Do the contemporary anti-racist critiques offered on racial thinking, racial theory, racial formations, racism as ideology and racism as social practice in fact subvert those categories or, as Pierre-Andre Taguieff has argued, serve in some ways to shore them up?[2] Does the contemporary celebration of the social construction-ist view of race, in which I share, deter us from investigating possible psychological and cognitive mappings of minds that make us susceptible to seeing human kinds in essentialist terms?[3]

I pose these questions, not because I can answer them here but because I think they should be collectively addressed. Some scholars have tried to do so.[4] Nicholas Thomas for one argues that in "anti-colonial critique, it

2. See Pierre-Andre Taguieff, *La force du préjugé: essai sur le racisme et ses doubles* (Paris: La Decouvert, 1988), especially chapter 10 "De l'antiracisme: type idéal, corruption idéologique, effets pervers" where he argues that antiracist discourse is a "hypermoral vision of the world" that at once prescribes to "la norme differentialiste" ("the right to be different") and "la norme mélangiste," combining a "heterophilic respect for belonging to communities of origin *and the mixophile* obligation of generalized racial mixing" (356).

3. See Lawrence Hirschfeld, *Race in the Making: Culture, Cognition and the Child's Construction of Human Kinds* (Cambridge: MIT Press, forthcoming), where he argues that "racial thinking is parasitical on a domain-specific competence for perceiving and reasoning about human kinds."

4. See, among others, Nicholas Dirk's lucid introduction to *Culture and Colonialism* (Ann Arbor: U of Michigan P, 1992) 1–25; Dipesh Chakrabarty's "Postcoloniality and the Artifice of History:

is the similarity of past and present that defamiliarizes the here and now and subverts the sense of historical progress."[5] But the quest for similarity may underwrite other purposes: colonialism has long served as a metaphor for a wide range of dominations, collapsing the specific hierarchies of time and place into a seamless whole. In this scenario, "to colonize" is an evocative and active verb accounting for a range of inequities and exclusions—that may have little to do with colonialism at all. As a morality tale of the present the metaphor of colonialism has enormous force but it can also eclipse how varied the subjects are created by different colonialisms. But ferreting out the stark *differences* between "then and now" is not much better. Frederick Cooper and I elsewhere have discussed the emergence of a post-colonial stance that often assumes a coherent story, a shared legacy of what colonialism has meant and continues to mean for those whose lives and labors have been enlisted in it.[6]

Whether emphasis is on the continuity between these moments or on the abrupt rupture that decolonization presents, nothing is gained by flattening colonial history into a neat story of colonizers pitted against the colonized. The reification of a colonial moment of binary oppositions may speak more to contemporary political agendas than to ambiguous colonial realities. For it often rests on making the case that the world today is infinitely more complicated, more fragmented and more blurred.[7] We need to think through not only why colonial history appears as manichean but also why so much historiography has invested (and continues to invest) in that myth as well. "Strategic essentialism" may represent the *contre-histoire* in racial discourse, the form in which subjugated knowledges make their space. That may be its political virtue. But as a political strategy for rewriting histories that reflect both the fixity *and* fluidity of racial categories, that attend to how people reworked and contested the boundaries of taxonomic colonial states, it is, if not untenable, at least problematic.

There may be a more fruitful tack to take: not to ask whether colonial-

---

Who Speaks for "Indian" Pasts?" *Representations* 37 (Winter 1992): 1–26; and "Colonial Discourse and Post-Colonial Theory: An Introduction," in Patrick Williams and Laura Chrisman, eds., *Colonial Discourse and Post-Colonial Theory* (New York: Columbia UP, 1994) 1–20.

5. Nicholas Thomas, *Colonialism's Culture: Anthropology, Travel and Government* (Princeton: Princeton UP, 1994) 21.

6. See our introduction to *Tensions of Empire: Colonial Cultures in a Bourgeois World* (forthcoming).

7. Also see Anne McClintock, "The Angel of Progress: Pitfalls of the Term "Post-Colonialism," *Social Text* 31-32 (1990): 84–98.

ism can speak to the inequities of today (stressing similarity) or whether the "creolization" and hybrid identities that colonialism spawned clarify a distinctive postmodern moment (stressing difference). We might instead ask a question similar to Foucault's: how the polyvalent discourses on race and their effects might better be viewed as complex processes of rupture and recuperation? At the end of chapter 3, I raised the possibility that an understanding of this tension between rupture and recovery might help clarify why racisms have so often appeared as both new and renewed at the same time. While Foucault identified the fact of that tension, his refusal to draw on political economy (it being, for him, a nineteenth-century relic, a positivist epistemic trace) sharply circumscribed the sorts of power relations he saw at play. It is for us to work out how these discourses are historically layered, what new planes of earlier discourses are exposed in new political contexts, how discursive and non-discursive practices on a global terrain reconfigure the truth-claims that relate individual bodies to the social body and thus how this recuperative process has transformed the socio-economics and the sexual politics of race.

If the discourses on racisms gain their force from their "polyvalent mobilities," from the "promiscuous" range of progressive and conservative projects that they can express, then students of colonial and contemporary racism have a daunting task. Take one of the most charged discursive sites in the U.S. discourse on race: the relationship between race and poverty. How can those with opposing political positions on this issue frequently utter the same statement: namely, that "Blacks are poor because they are black"—and mean totally different things? Self-proclaimed racists might say "Blacks are poor because they are black" and mean that they are poor because they are racially inferior. Anti-racist critics might say "Blacks are poor because they/we are black" and mean that Blacks are poor because they have been labelled as black. But the statement might also serve those who no longer see race as the "real" issue. Here the statement "Blacks are poor because they/we are black" has other implications and effects. A prior history of racist oppression (now in the past) has made Blacks a distinct and "objectively" different population (defined by higher rates of school attrition, welfare recipience and joblessness) thus explaining their poverty.

One could write off this ambiguity with the argument that language is always polysemic, but that would be to take the convergence as fortuitous and to miss something perhaps more distinctive in the contemporary discourse on race. It is not only that the same statement can have different meanings, but that opposing statements can mean the same thing. Again the statements "Blacks are poor because they are black" or "Blacks are not poor because they are black" are both part of the rhetoric of the conservative right: the first could imply that Blacks are poor because of a familiar set of essential characteristics attributed to them while the second, its ostensible inverse, could "say" the same thing. Blacks are not oppressed because of race or racism. "Nothing is keeping them down but themselves." They have not seized the opportunities available to them.

Take another example of contemporary discourses on race: in March 1995, the French National Consultative Commission on the Rights of Man (CNCDH) published a report declaring that 69 percent of the respondents to its poll (based on a sample of 1,012 persons) acknowledged/confessed ("s'avouent") themselves to be racist ("rather racist," "a little racist," "not very racist").[8] Only 31 percent declared themselves "not racist at all." The figures are somewhat startling, but more so is the fact of making such an admission (to pollists on human rights, no less) and what such a poll is supposed to measure. What does such a confession mean, if anything, in French politics today? Does admitting to being a racist make one more firmly and clearly French? Is the truth of the French self no longer lodged only in one's sexual desires as Foucault argued, but in the particular kind of patriotic or generic racist one admits to be?

The poll is disturbing on other counts: in response to a question concerning "personal sentiments" toward other groups and minorities 85 percent of those polled felt a "sympathie" (liking) for southern Europeans and only 65 percent for Jews. Among those considered "moins sympathique" (less likeable) 47 percent named Maghrebins and 49 percent named homosexuals.[9] Why the category of homosexual in a poll on race? What is more unsettling here, the categories of the poll, the size of the sample (reported in the conservative daily, Le Figaro, under the frontpage headline, "The French admit themselves to be racists"), the politically strategic timing of its publication, or the responses themselves? Why was it only Le Figaro and not the other major dailies, Le Monde or the left/liberal Libération, that made so much of the statistics?

In fact, Libération on the same day, and Le Monde two days later, chose to

---

8. "Sondage: les Français s'avouent racistes," Le Figaro, 22 March 1995, 1.
9. "Racisme: l'état de la France," Le Figaro, 22 March 1995, 11.

report another major two-year survey, not on racism, but on the extent of assimilation among immigrants in France carried out by the National Institute for Demographic Study (INED). As Le Monde noted, in the hypocritical name of equality and non-discrimination, "politically correct" national survey research had always recognized only two categories: those who were French and those who were foreigners, with no distinctions made between those of different origin, cultural background, or ethnic group.[10] Le Monde applauded the new survey's debunking of such a fictitious dichotomy and noted that while the rhetoric of the French state might have backed such a fiction, the practices of the state's local agents do not. Police reports frequently refer to "individuals of the North African type" without acknowledging how often those detained are of French nationality: city mayors gather statistics on "foreigners" but usually only include those inhabitants of color, rarely those who are considered white.

Just as striking is how much both Le Monde and Libération underscored the survey's "scientific" accuracy. In the face of the extreme right's inflationary rhetoric about the threatening flood of black immigrants, Libération saw hope in the fact that this first survey of its kind provides a "very precise photograph" of the extent of integration.[11] Both papers suggested that the survey's scientific rigor would, as Le Monde put it, make it harder now "in good faith" to confuse the categories of Maghrebin and Muslim, or African and polygamist. It would also discourage a discourse like that of the former Prime Minister Michel Rocard who branded immigrants over the last twenty years as "the wretched of the earth," and rectify that picture by portraying them for what many were, urbanites long well-educated in their countries of origin.

What do these discourses of left, right, and middle say, and do they even divide along these lines? Does the discourse of race, and its new high-tech survey apparatus confer new effects because it is so assiduously recorded, quantified, and, most importantly, confessed? Writing from the U.S. one cannot help but be struck by the increasing convergence between the conservative rhetorics of the U.S. and France. The New York Times several weeks later featured a review of Alien Nation: Common Sense about America's

10. "L'immigration sans naïveté ni démagogie," Le Monde, 24 March 1995: 1, 16.
11. "Immigrés: comment march l'integration [première grande enquête sur 13,000 immigrés français et leurs enfants]," Libération, 22 March 1995, no. 4305, 1, 4.

Immigration Disaster, written by Peter Brimelow (senior editor of *Forbes* and *National Review*).[12] Entitled "Too many foreigners," the review notes that anti-immigration is, in Brimelow's popular view, "a defense of the republic," or, as Foucault might have put it, a defense of society against itself. And like for Foucault, it is less those still external to the social body that are at issue, but those who put a moral and economic "drain" upon society and who are already within its fold.

One might argue that all of these statements are familiar to students of colonial history and represent a continuing and insidious discourse of nineteenth-century racism. But I would question whether there is not a new logic that underwrites the ambiguity of this discourse and the political field in which it is framed. To say that the discourses of racism are promiscuous and polyvalent does not mean that we should expect them to remain consistently polyvalent along the same axes and about the same things. How we subvert this discourse is not merely a matter of under-covering ambiguous meanings. At least part of the task is to figure out what sorts of knowledge racial thinking feeds off and invokes. How does state racism manufacture both consent and common sense? In what ways does it recuperate earlier forms of sedimented knowledge as it calls on new ones today?

Indiscreet Jewels and the Epistemologies of Sex and Race

In volume 1 of *The History of Sexuality*, Foucault described his aim as an effort "to transcribe into history the fable of *Les Bijoux Indiscrets*" (The Indiscreet Jewels), Denis Diderot's libertine novel of 1748 for which he was imprisoned a year later (HS:77).[13] It is an extraordinary novel in which women's genitalia literally speak the secrets and truth of society and society reveals itself in the voice of womens' jewels, their sex. Some critics have held that the novel is a *roman à clé*, with the central characters Mangogul and Mirzoza representing Louis XV and Madame de Pompadour, and thus that it is a scathing critique of monarchical power. Whether or not that is the case (and it is not a point Foucault notes), what is significant is that Mangogul

12. Nicholas Lemann, "Too Many Foreigners," *New York Times Book Review*, 16 April 1995, 3.
13. See the English-language edition of *The Indiscreet Jewels* with a foreword by Aram Vartanian (New York: Marsilo, 1993).

and Mirzoza are not just erotic creatures—they are highly exotic as well. They are bedecked *à la turque*, rulers of an imaginary Oriental kingdom that is possibly Ottoman, maybe the Congo, but is definitely not France.

For Foucault, *Les Bijoux Indiscrets* served one purpose: it captured the absurdity of what is emblematic in "Occidental" society today, "our society" that wears "among its many emblems," that "of the talking sex" (HS:77). The orientalist magic embodied in these indiscreet jewels and the will to knowledge that this magic served—in Foucault's account—are displaced. Diderot's critique of ostentatious and decadent display may be directed at Louis XIV or XV, but oriental despotism is what drives his argument. The total contempt that the Sultan Mangogul has for those who may find themselves dishonored and deceived when the sex of women speak may target French absolutism, but it is a given, imperious Oriental Other through which that critique is conveyed. The truth is spoken by that loquacious jewel of sex, but it is not any sex that speaks—only a gendered exoticized version. The will to know the truth of ourselves is in sex, but not in it alone. The discourses of sexuality are racialized ways of knowing that relate somatic signs to hidden truths.

Periodizing racisms is so problematic because racisms are not, and never have been, about race alone. Racisms are never pure and unencumbered; they are, and remain, overdetermined. Racisms have been part of the consolidation of bourgeois projects, the forming of national states and the uncertain cultivation of identities forged around what Stuart Hall has called these "structures of dominance." They responded to the pervasive terror of, and attempt to contain and control, the problem of class difference at the same time that class and race achieved their distinct ontological status. Racisms have coincided with the decline of absolutism and the unmooring of persons from the naturalized hierarchies in which they were ruled and did the ruling. They marked the emergence of a new kind of *contre-histoire* and new forms of disciplinary and regulatory power that replaced that of sovereignty. Not least as a technology of the state, state racism was and remains dependent on biopower in its modern form. To identify which of these definitively explains racism's originary moment is a moot point and is, as Foucault rightly suggests, the wrong question. We need to understand that racial discourses, like those of the nation, have derived force from a "polyvalent mobility," from the density of discourses they harness, from the multiple economic interests they serve, from the subjugated knowledges they contain, from the sedimented forms of knowledge that they bring into play.

The relationship between knowledge production and racism has been a well-researched subject for some time, but there is another sense in which I want to pursue it here. While we know that racial theories have been built on and engendered a range of "scientific" subdisciplines—from Lamarckianism to Social Darwinism, eugenics, degeneracy theory, anthropology, philology, and social psychology—we have not really interrogated the epistemic principles, the ways of knowing—on which racisms rely. Folk and scientific theories of race have rarely, if ever, been about somatics alone.[14] What is so striking as we turn to look at the epistemic principles that shaped nineteenth-century enquiries into race and sexuality is that both were founded on criteria for truth that addressed the invisible coordinates of race by appealing to both visual and verbal forms of knowledge at the same time.

Theories of race have combined the visuality of the gaze and the invisibility of race's most telling ontological moment. It is the linkage between them that I think should be stressed. In *The Order of Things* (where the discourse of race does not figure), Foucault identifies this knowledge based on the invisible as a new knowledge invented at the turn of the nineteenth century.[15] It was based on "great hidden forces" where things would now be "inescapably grouped by the vigour that is hidden down below, in those depths" (OT:251). The resonance with racial thinking is hard to miss. Racism is not only a "visual ideology" where the visible and somatic confirms the "truth" of the self. Euro-American racial thinking related the visual markers of race to the protean hidden properties of different human kinds. Nineteenth-century bourgeois orders were predicated on these forms of knowledge that linked the visible, physiological attributes of national, class, and sexual Others to what was secreted in their depths—

14. Barbara Fields has made this point particularly well: "It is ideological context that tells people which details to notice, which to ignore, and which to take for granted in translating the world around them into ideas about the world." See "Ideology and Race in American History," *Region, Race and Reconstruction*, eds. J. Morgan Kousser and James M. McPherson (New York, 1982) 146.
15. On Foucault's analysis of ocular vs. discursive technologies of power see Martin Jay's thoughtful discussion in "In the empire of the Gaze: Foucault and the Denigration of Vision in Twentieth-Century French Thought," in David Couzens Hoy, ed., *Foucault: A Critical Reader* (Oxford: Blackwell, 1986) 175–203.

and none of these could be known without also designating the psychological dispositions and sensibilities that defined who and what was *echte*
European.

It is this combined palpability and intangibility that makes race slip
through reason and rationality. For it, like nationalism, is located in "invisible ties" and hidden truths, unspoken assumptions about morality
and character. Invoked as common sense knowledge, these hidden truths
are rarely identifiable; but because they are hidden they can be explicitly
enumerated by those with expert medical, psychological, and pedagogic
knowledge—and just as quickly regrouped and subject to change. If the
truth of ourselves has been construed to reside in our deep sexual desires, and it is race that has been construed to differentiate who has what
desires, then the sorts of knowledge produced about the bourgeois self
in a European imperial world must be seen in a grid of intelligibility that
includes both.

In some ways, it is Foucault who helps us look in that direction. One
crucial development he prompts us to explore is the rise of state racism.
While his own genealogy centered on the internal dynamics of European
states, ours need not. Frederick Cooper and I have argued for some time
that despite the amount of work devoted to the racist principles of colonial policy, the nature and specificity of the colonial state has been largely
ignored.[16] But if racism is an intimate part of the strategies of the biopolitical normalizing state, as Foucault argued, then no historical context is
more relevant to its examination than the rapidly expanded state and quasi-
state institutions to which colonial settlement gave rise. While we know
something about that *cordon sanitaire* of medical discourse and colonial administrative practice that partitioned space and segregated populations,
we have not explicitly considered colonial states as biopolitical ones.

However, that project is in some ways already implicit in the sort of
histories that students of colonialism have begun to undertake. In exam-
ining how strategies for the defense of a respectable European bourgeois
self and the defense of a colonizing society collided and converged, we
have turned to question not only the civilities that all whites were suppose to share, but the "microphysics" of their production—why managed
sexuality and guided sentiments were crucial to them.

16. See Ann Laura Stoler and Frederick Cooper, "Between Metropole and Colony: Rethinking a
Research Agenda," in *Tensions of Empire: Colonial Cultures in a Bourgeois World.*

In pursuing the "microphysics" of those sites of power on which Foucault only touched—such as those discourses on, and practices that surrounded, the sexualization of children and masturbation discussed in chapter 5—the contingency between the cultivation of the bourgeois self and the genealogy of racial discourse come into sharper view. We cannot understand the work of racial discourse—and why children's sensibilities and adult's sentiments were so central to it—without attending to the ways in which the cultivation of "character," personality and the cultural competencies by which they were marked figured in the making of race.

Nor were these concerns only implied. Colonial agents of state and quasi-state institutions, as we have seen, debated issues of milieu, habitus and the shaping of sentiment with studied care. Students of colonialism have tended to focus more on rationality, reason, and progress as the dominant fictions legitimating European rule. But the tight web that allowed gender ideology and class culture to serve in policing the boundaries of race were as contingent on the assessment of other mental states, on evaluations of the capacity for affection, on mothering styles, on the mapping of moral environments. In this regard it is no accident that those discourses on nation and citizenship articulated so strongly with those on race. Both clarified the national, enforced class distinctions and affirmed the fiction of a North European centered *homo europeaus* at the same time. Both invoked an internal enemy. And both attempted to designate those interior frontiers that would guard bourgeois society's boundaries—and defend those it was feverishly making.[17]

Foucault offers a genealogy of racism with "Europe" as an unproblematic entity in a way that I have repeatedly questioned here. But my challenge to chronology and geography has served to make a more important point: that this fixed and firm European bourgeois order of the nineteenth century was one that forged its changing and porous parameters around the biopolitics of race. Biopower may have been a uniquely bourgeois form of modern power, but it was also an inherently imperial one.

17. Michael Taussig makes a related point in *Mimesis and Alterity: A Particular History of the Senses* (New York: Routledge, 1993):

> Rather than thinking of the border as the farthermost extension of an essential identity spreading out from a core, [we should] think instead of the border itself as that core . . . identity acquires its satisfying solidity because of the effervescence of the continuously sexualized border, because of the turbulent forces, sexual and spiritual, that the border not so much contains as emits." (151)

In 1976, in an interview with the editors of the French geography review, Herodote, Foucault was pointedly asked how he could so meticulously
periodize history and remain so sloppy about place: why the constant deployment of geographic metaphors without specifying the populations,
the places, the territories to which generalizations applied?[18] Foucault was
open to the criticism and somewhat more contrite than one might expect.
But more interesting are the issues his response addressed:

> If I . . . allow the frontier to wander about, sometimes over the whole
> of the West, that's because the documentation I was using extends
> in part outside France, and also because in order to grasp a specifi-
> cally French phenomenon I *was often obligated to look at something that
> happened elsewhere in a more explicit form that antedated or served as a model for
> what took place in France.* This enabled me—allowing for local and re-
> gional variations—to situate these French phenomena in the context
> of Anglo-Saxon, Spanish, Italian and other societies. I don't specify
> the space of reference more narrowly than that since it would be as
> warranted to say "I am speaking only of France" as to say "I am talking
> about all of Europe." *There is indeed a task to be done of making the space in
> question precise, saying where a certain process stops, what are the limits beyond
> which one could say "something different happens"*—though this would have to be a
> *collective undertaking.* (PK:67–68, emphasis added)

It has become one. But this collective project has turned in a somewhat
different direction than the one Foucault might have pursued. It has come
to question precisely "the models" on which the "French" and other
European cases were based, the colonial regimes of power/knowledge
that possibly "antedated" phenomena that later occurred and appeared as
quintessentially "European" in England, The Netherlands, or France.

We need not imagine that European culture was invented in the colonies or that imperial forms of power always prefigured metropolitan
ones. The point is to register explicitly that what appeared as distinctively
French, Dutch, or generically European in the late nineteenth century

18. The interviewer from Herodote noted:
   Your domains of reference are alternately Christendom, the Western World, Northern Europe
   and France, without these spaces of reference ever really being justified or even precisely
   specified. . . . You accord a de facto privilege to the factor of time, at the cost of nebulous or
   nomadic spatial demarcations whose uncertainty is in contrast with your care in marking off
   sections of time, periods and ages. (Power/Knowledge, Questions on Geography, 1977, 67)

were sometimes cultural and political configurations honed and worked through the politics of empire earlier. It is this insight that allows us to question the relationship between the language of class and the language of race in new ways. Both derived from a long genealogy of exclusions, a set of social taxonomies that placed these classifications of social kinds in a broader imperial field of calibrated and contingent dominations. Those subjected to these taxonomies "at home" and "abroad" were made at once objects and particular kinds of subjects in a philanthropic civilizing mission that defined their place. But that mission also shaped the sexual and racial coordinates, the boundaries at the core of what bourgeois morality and respectability were to be exclude and contain.

It is within this wider analytic frame that colonial studies has challenged the bracketed domains of European history and what counts as Europe itself. It is Foucault's example of "reflective insolence" that has prompted some of those new directions. That same example should prompt us to, as Wittgenstein put it, "pull up the ladder"—a gesture that would be in keeping with Foucault's impulse to fold back on what he did, rework old concepts and abandon others, as he pushed his project further. It seems fitting that we should acknowledge our debt with respectful and reflective insolence toward what Foucault so stunningly pursued—and what he categorically chose not to explore.[19]

19. The last paragraph of the *Tractatus* reads:

My propositions serve as elucidations in the following way: anyone who understands me eventually recognizes them as nonsensical, when he has used them—as steps—to climb up beyond them. (He must, so to speak, throw away the ladder after he has climbed up it.) He must transcend these propositions, and then he will see the world aright.

Ludwig Wittgenstein, *Tractatus Logico-Philosphicus* (Altantic Highlands, N.J.: Humanities Press, 1961) 74.

Bibliography

(N.B. Included here are some works on Foucault that were consulted but not referenced in the text)

Abor, Raoul. *Des Reconnaissance Frauduleuses d'Enfants Naturels en Indochine*. Hanoi: Imprimerie Tonkinoise, 1917.

Adams, Julia. "The Familial State: Elite Family Practices and State-making in the Early Modern Netherlands." *Theory and Society* 23(Summer 1994): 505–539.

Ahmad, Aijaz. *In Theory: Class, Nation, Literatures*. London: Verso, 1992.

Alatas, Syed. *The Myth of the Lazy Native: A Study of the Image of the Malays, Filipinos and Javanese from the 16th to the 20th Century and its Function in the Ideology of Colonial Capitalism*. London: Cass, 1977.

Allen, Ann Tylor. "Gardens of Children: Gardens of God: Kindergartens and Daycare Centers in 19th Century Germany." *Journal of Social History* 19 (1986): 433–50.

Alloula, Malek. *Colonial Harem*. Minneapolis: U of Minnesota P, 1986.

Amiel, Charles. "La 'pureté de sang' en Espagne" *Etudes inter-ethniques* 6 (1983): 28–45.

Anderson, Benedict. "Fax Nationalism" manuscript, nd.

——. *Imagined Communities*. London: Verso, 1983.

Arendt, Hannah. *The Origins of Totalitarianism*. New York: Harcourt and Brace, 1948.

Aries, Philippe. *Centuries of Childhood: A Social History of Family Life*. New York: Knopf, 1962.

Armstrong, Nancy. *Desire and Domestic Fiction: A Political History of the Novel*. London: Oxford, 1987.

Armstrong, Timothy J. *Michel Foucault Philosopher*. New York: Routledge, 1992.

Arnold, David. "European Orphans and Vagrants in India in the Nineteenth Century." *Journal of Imperial and Commonwealth History* 7.2 (January 1979): 104–27.

Asad, Talal. *Anthropology and the Colonial Encounter*. New York: Humanities Press, 1973.

Balibar, Etienne. "Paradoxes of Universality." *Anatomy of Racism*. Ed. David Goldberg. Minneapolis: U of Minnesota P, 1990.

——. "Foucault et Marx: L'enjeu du nominalisme." *Michel Foucault: Philosphe*. Paris: Seuil, 1989.

——. *Masses, Classes, Ideas*. London: Routledge, 1994.

Ballhatchet, Kenneth. *Race, Sex and Class under the Raj: Imperial Attitudes and Policies and their Critics*. New York: St. Martin's Press, 1980.

De Banier, 9 November 1926, 1.

Banton, Michael. *The Idea of Race.* London: Tavistock, 1977.

Barzun, Jacques. *The French Race: Theories of its Origins and Their Social and Political Implications Prior to the Revolution.* New York: Kennikat Press, 1932.

Baudin, D. C. M. *Het Indische Leven.* 1927. 's-Gravenhage: H.P. Leopolds, 1941.

Baudrillard, Jean. *Forget Foucault.* New York: Semiotext, 1977.

Bauman, Zygmunt. *Modernity and the Holocaust.* Ithaca: Cornell UP, 1989.

Beekman, E. M. "The Passatist: Louis Couperus' Interpretation of Dutch Colonialism." *Indonesia* 37 (1984): 59–76.

Behdad, Ali. *Belated Travelers: Orientalism in the Age of Colonial Dissolution.* Durham: Duke UP, 1994.

Beidelman, T. O. *Colonial Evangelism.* Bloomington: Indiana UP, 1982.

Berger, Mark T. Review of Hyam, "Empire and Sexual Opportunity." *Journal of Imperial and Commonwealth History* 17.2 (1988): 83–89

Berlant, Lauren. *The Anatomy of a National Fantasy: Hawthorne, Utopia and Everyday Life.* Chicago: Chicago UP, 1991.

Berreman, Gerald. *The Politics of Truth: Essays in Critical Anthropology.* New Delhi: South Asian Publishers, 1981.

Bertling, C. T. "De zorg voor het adatlooze kind." *Koloniale Studien* 15 (1931): 790–844.

Bhabha, Homi. "The Other Question." *Screen* 24.6 (November 1983): 18–36.

———. "Remembering Fanon: Self, Psyche and the Colonial Condition." *Colonial Discourse and Post-Colonial Theory.* Eds. Patrick Williams and Laura Chrisman. New York: Columbia UP, 1994 (originally published in 1986 as a Foreword to the republication of *Black Skin, White Masks*).

———. *The Location of Culture.* London: Routledge, 1994.

Biddis, Michael. *The Age of the Masses: Ideas and Society in Europe Since 1870.* London: Penguin, 1977.

Björgo, Tore and Rob Witte. *Racist Violence in Europe.* London: St. Martin's Press, 1993.

Bock, Gisela and Pat Thane, eds. *Maternity and Gender Policies: Women and the Rise of the European Welfare States 1880s–1950s.* London: Routledge, 1991.

Boogaart, Ernest van den. "Colour Prejudice and the Yardstick of Civility: The Initial Dutch Confrontation with Black Africans, 1590-1635." *Racism and Colonialism.* Ed. Robert Ross. Leiden: Martinus Nijhoff, 1982.

Borges, Dain. " 'Puffy, Ugly, Slothful and Inert': Degeneration in Brazilian Social Thought, 1880–1940." *Journal of Latin American Studies* (1993) 25:235–56.

Bourdieu, Pierre. *Distinction: A Social Critique of the Judgement of Taste.* Cambridge: Harvard UP, 1984.

———. *Outline of a Theory of Practice.* Cambridge: Cambridge UP, 1977.

Boxer, C. R. *The Dutch Seaborne Empire 1600–1800.* London: Hutchinson, 1965.

———. *The Portuguese Seaborne Empire.* New York: Alfred Knopf, 1969.

Bracken, Harry. "Essence, Accident and Race" *Hermathena* 116 (Winter 1973): 81–96.

Braconier, A. de. *Kindercriminaliteit en de verzorging van misdadig aangelegde en verwaarloosde minderjarigen in Nederlandsch-Indie.* Baarn: Hollandia, 1918.

———. "Het Kazerne-Concubinaat in Ned-Indie." *Vragen van den Dag* 28 (1913): 974–95.

Breman, Jan, ed. *Imperial Monkey Business: Racial Supremacy in Social Darwinist Theory and Colonial Practice.* Amsterdam: VU UP, 1990.

Brenner, Neil. "Foucault's New Functionalism." *Theory and Society* 23 (forthcoming).

Brugmans, Izaak Johannes. *Gescheidenis van het Onderwijs in Nederlandsch-Indie.* Groningen: J.B. Wolters, 1938.

Buker, Eloise. "Hidden Desires and Missing Persons: A Feminist Deconstruction of Sexuality." *Western Political Quarterly* 43 (1990): 811–32.

Burnett, Frances Hodgson. *The Secret Garden.* 1910. London: Purnell, 1975.

Buruma, Ian. "Revenge in the Indies." *New York Review of Books* August 11, 1994: 30–32.

Butcher, John. *The British in Malaya, 1880–1914.* Kuala Lumpur: Oxford UP, 1979.

Butler, Judith. *Gender Trouble.* London: Routledge, 1990.

——— . *Subjects of Desire: Hegelian Reflections in Twentieth-Century France.* New York: Columbia UP, 1987.

Buur, Dorothée. *Indische Jeugdliteratuur: Geannoteerde Bibliografie van Jeugdboeken over Nederlands-Indie en Indonesie, 1825–1991.* Leiden: KITLV, 1992.

Canny, Nicholas and Anthony Pagden, eds. *Colonial Identity in the Atlantic World, 1500–1800.* Princeton: Princeton UP, 1987.

Caplan, Pat, ed. *The Cultural Construction of Sexuality.* London: Tavistock, 1987.

Caputo, John and Mark Yount, eds. *Foucault and the Critique of Institutions.* University Park, Pennsylvania: The Pennslyvania State UP, 1993.

Chakrabarty, Dipesh. "Postcoloniality and the Artifice of History: Who Speaks for "Indian" Pasts?" *Representations* 37 (Winter 1992): 1–26.

Chatterjee, Partha. *The Nation and Its Fragments.* Princeton: Princeton UP, 1993.

Chaudhuri, Nupur. "Memsahibs and Motherhood in Nineteenth-Century Colonial India." *Victorian Studies* 31.4 (1988): 517–36.

Chaudhuri, Nupur and Margaret Strobel, eds. *Western Women and Imperialism: Complicity and Resistance.* Bloomington: Indiana UP, 1992.

Chijs, Mr. J. A. van der. Nederlandsche-Indisch Plakaatboek, 1602–1811, Part I, 1602–1642, Batavia: Landsdrukkerij, 1885. 461–65.

Chivas-Baron, C. *La femme française aux colonies.* Paris: Larose, 1929.

Clerkx, Lily. *Moeders, kinderen en kinderopvang: veranderingen in de kinderopvang in Nederland.* Nijmegen: SUN, 1981.

——— . "De kinderjuffrouw. Opvoedster en dienstbode tussen ouders en kinderen." *Sociologisch Tijdschrift* 10.4 (1984): 671–715.

Clifford, James. *The Predicament of Culture.* Cambridge: Harvard UP, 1988.

Coetzee, J. M. "Blood, Flaw, Taint, Degeneration: The Case of Sarah Gertrude Millin." *English Studies in Africa* 23.1 (1980): 41–58.

Cohn, Bernard. "Past in the Present: As Museum of Mankind." *An Anthropologist among the Historians and Other Essays.* Delhi: Oxford UP, 1987.

——— . "The Census, Social Structure and Objectification in South Asia" *An Anthropologist among the Historians and Other Essays.* Delhi: Oxford UP, 1987.

——— . "The Peoples of India: From the Picturesque to the Museum of Mankind." n.d.

Comaroff, Jean. *Body of Power, Spirit of Resistance: The Culture and History of a South African People.* Chicago: Chicago UP, 1985.

Comaroff, Jean and John Comaroff. *Ethnography and the Historical Imagination.* Boulder: Westview Press, 1992.

——— . "Home-Made Hegemony: Modernity, Domesticity, and Colonialism in South Africa." *African Encounters with Domesticity.* Ed. Karen Hansen. New Brunswick: Rutgers UP, 1992.

——— . *Of Revelation and Revolution.* Chicago: Chicago UP, 1991.

Comaroff, John. "Images of Empire, Contests of Conscience: Models of Colonial Domination in South Africa." *American Ethnologist* 16.4 (1989): 661–85.

Cooper, Frederick and Ann Laura Stoler. *Tensions of Empire: Colonial Cultures in a Bourgeois World.* Berkeley: U of California P, forthcoming.

Coronil, Fernando. "Beyond Occidentalism: Toward Non-Imperial Geohistorical Categories," *Cultural Anthropology*, forthcoming.

Costa, Emilia Viotti da. *The Brazilian Empire: Myths and Histories.* Chicago: U of Chicago P, 1985.

Cott, Nancy. "Notes Toward an Interpretation of Antebellum Childrearing." *Psychohistory Review* 7.4 (1973): 20.

Couperus, Louis. *The Hidden Force: A Story of Modern Java.* New York: Dodd, Mead and Company, 1924.

Curtin, Philip D. *Death by Migration: Europe's Encounter with the Tropical World in the Nineteenth Century.* New York: Cambridge UP, 1989.

David, F. James. *Who is Black? One Nation's Definition.* University Park: Pennsylvania State UP, 1991.

Davidson, Arnold. "Sex and the Emergence of Sexuality." *Critical Inquiry* 17 (1987): 16–48.

Davin, Anna. "Motherhood and Imperialism." *History Workshop* 5 (1978): 9–57.

Deleuze, Gilles. *Foucault.* Minneapolis: U of Minnesota P, 1986.

Deleuze, Gilles and Felix Guattari. *Anti-Oedipus: Capitalism and Schizoprenia.* Minneapolis: U of Minnesota P, 1983.

Demause, Lloyd. "The Evolution of Childhood." *History of Childhood Quarterly: The Journal of Psychohistory* 1 (1974): 536.

DeWit, C. H. E. *De Strijd tussen Aristocratie en Democratie in Nederland, 1780–1848.* Heerlen: Winants, 1965.

Diawara, Manthia. "Reading Africa through Foucault: Mudimbe's Reaffirmation of the Subject." *October* 55 (1990): 79–92.

Diderot, Denis. *The Indiscreet Jewels.* 1748. New York: Marsilio, 1993.

Dikötter, Frank. *The Discourse of Race in Modern China.* Stanford: Stanford UP, 1992.

Dirks, Nicholas, ed. *Colonialism and Culture.* Ann Arbor: U of Michigan P, 1991.

——— . "Introduction: Colonialism and Culture." *Colonialism and Culture.* Ed. Nicholas Dirks. Ann Arbor: U of Michigan P, 1991.

Dirks, Nicholas B. *The Hollow Crown: Ethnohistory of an Indian Kingdom.* Cambridge: Cambridge UP, 1987.

Dirks, Nicholas B., Geoff Eley, Sherry B. Ortner, eds. *Culture/Power/History: A Reader in Contemporary Social Theory.* Princeton: Princeton UP, 1993.

Dominquez, Virginia. *White by Definition: Social Classification in Creole Louisiana.* New Brunswick, N.J.: Rutgers UP, 1986.

Donzelot, Jacques. *The Policing of Families.* New York: Random House, 1979.

Dreyfus, Herbert and Paul Rabinow. *Michel Foucault: Beyond Structuralism and Hermeneutics.* Chicago: Chicago UP, 1983.

Drinnon, Richard. *Facing West: The Metaphysics of Indian-Hating and Empire-Building.* Minneapolis: U of Minnesota P, 1980.

Ducimus. "Het prostitutie-vraagstuk in het Indische leger." *Indisch Militair Tijdschrift* 1–6 (1902): 188–212 and 318–28.

Eley, Geoff. "Scholarship Serving the Nazi State I; Studying the East." *Ethnic and Racial Studies* 12.4 (1989): 576.

———. "Liberalism, Europe, and the Bourgeoisie" in *The German Bourgeoisie*. Eds. David Blackburn and Richard Evans. London: Routledge, 1991: 293–317.

Elias, Norbert. *Power and Civility*. 1939. New York: Pantheon, 1982.

Engelstein, Laura. "Combined Underdevelopment: Discipline and the Law in Imperial and Soviet Russia." *American Historical Review* 98.2 (April 1993): 338–63.

Eribon, Didier. *Michel Foucault*. Cambridge: Harvard UP, 1991.

———. *Michel Foucault et ses contemporains*. Paris: Gallimard, 1994.

Eyk, W. van. *Het openbaar lager ondwerijs voor Europeanen in Nederlandsch-Indie*. Deventer: Hulscher, 1870.

Ezell, Margaret. "John Locke's Images of Childhood." *Eighteenth-Century Studies* 17 (Winter '83/ '84): 139–55.

Fairchilds, Cissie. *Domestic Enemies: Servants and their Masters in Old Regime France*. Baltimore: Johns Hopkins UP, 1984.

Fanon, Franz. *Black Skin, White Masks*. New York: Grove, 1967.

———. *The Wretched of the Earth*. New York: Grove, 1963.

Fasseur, Cees. "De 'adeldom' van de huid: De role van de Indische Nederlander in het Nederlands-Indisch bestuur." *Sporen van een Indische Verleden* (1600–1942). Ed. Wim Willem. Leiden: Rijkuniverseiteit, 1992.

———. "Cornerstone and Stumbling Block: Racial Classification and the Late Colonial State in Indonesia." *The Late Colonial State in Indonesia: Political and economic foundations of the Netherlands Indies 1880–1942*. Ed. Robert Cribb. Leiden: KITLV, 1994: 31–56.

———. *De Indologen: Ambtenaren voor de Oost, 1825-1950*. Amsterdam: Bert Bakker, 1993.

Fields, Barbara J. "Ideology and Race in American History." *Region, Race, and Reconstruction*. Ed. J. Morgan Kousser and James M. McPherson. New York, 1982: 143–77.

Fields, Karen E. *Revival and Rebellion in Colonial Central Africa*. Princeton: Princeton UP, 1985.

Finas, Lucette. "Michel Foucault: Les Rapport de pouvoir passent a l'interieur des corps." *La Quinzaine Litterature* 247 (1977): 4–6.

Flandrin, Jean-Louis. *Familles: Parenté, Maison, Sexualité dans l'ancienne société*. Paris: Hachette, 1976.

Foucault, Michel. "About the Concept of the 'Dangerous Individual' in 19th Century Legal Psychiatry." *International Journal of Law and Psychiatry* I (1978): 1–18.

———. *The Archaeology of Knowledge*. New York: Pantheon, 1972.

———. *Birth of the Clinic: An Archaeology of Medical Perception*. New York: Vintage, 1973.

———. *The Care of the Self. The History of Sexuality, Volume 3*. New York: Random House, 1988.

———. *Difendere la societa*. Florence: Ponte alle Grazie, 1990.

———. *Discipline and Punish: The Birth of the Prison*. New York: Vintage, 1979.

———. "Faire vivre et laisser mourir: la naissance du racisme." *Les Temps Modernes* (February 1991): 37–61.

———. *Folie et Déraison: Historie de la Folie à l'âge classique*. Paris: Plon, 1961.

———. *Foucault Live*. New York: Semiotext(e), 1989.

———. *History of Sexuality*. New York: Vintage Books, 1985.

———. *Language, Counter-Memory, Practice: Selected Essays and Interviews*. Ed. Donald Bouchard. Ithaca: Cornell UP, 1977.

———. "La Loi du Pudeur." *Recherches* 37 (April 1976): 77–78.

———. "Non au sexe roi." *Nouvel Observateur* 644 (1977): 93–94, 98–100, 105, 111, 124, 130 (interview with Bernard-Henri Levy).

———. *The Order of Things: An Archaeology of the Human Sciences.* London: Tavistock, 1970.

———. "Qu'est-ce que la critique? (Critique et Aufklarung)" *Bulletin de la Societe Francaise de Philosophie* 84.2 (April–June 1990): 35–63.

———. *Power/Knowledge: Selected Interviews and Other Writings, 1972–1977.* Ed. Colin Gordon. New York: Pantheon, 1977.

———. "Préface à la trangression." *Critique* 75 (1963): 751–69.

———. *Remarks on Marx.* New York: Semiotext(e), 1991.

———. *Resumé des cours: 1970–1982.* Paris: Julliard, 1984.

———. *La volonté de savoir.* Paris: Gallimard, 1976.

———. *The Uses of Pleasure: The History of Sexuality, Volume Two.* New York: Pantheon, 1985.

——— and Richard Sennett. "Sexuality and Solitude." *Humanities in Review* 1 (1982): 3–21.

Fraser, Nancy. *Unruly Practices: Power, Discourse and Gender in Contemporary Social Theory.* Minneapolis: U of Minnesota P, 1989.

Fraser, Nancy and Linda Gordon. "A Genealogy of Dependency: Tracing a Keyword of the U.S. Welfare State." *Signs* 19 (1994): 309–36.

Fredrickson, George. *The Black Image in the White Mind: The Debate on Afro-American Character and Destiny, 1817–1914.* New York: Harper and Row, 1972.

———. *White Supremacy: A Comparative Study in American and South African History.* Oxford: Oxford UP, 1981.

Freyre, Gilberto. *The Masters and the Slaves.* New York: Knopf, 1946.

Friedman, Elizabeth. *Colonialism and After: An Algerian Jewish Community.* South Hadley, MA: Bergin and Garvey, 1988.

Freud, Sigmund. *Introductory Lectures on Psycho-Analysis.* New York: Norton, 1966.

———. *Civilization and Its Discontents.* New York: Norton, 1961.

Furet Francois and Mona Ozouf. "Deux legimitations historiques de la societé française au XVIII siècle: Mably et Boulainvilliers." *L'Atelier de l'histoire.* Paris: Flammarion, 1982: 165–83.

Fuss, Diana. "Interior Colonies: Frantz Fanon and the Politics of Identification." *Diacritics* 24.2–3 (1994): 20–42.

Gaastra, F. S. "The Independent Fiscaals of the VOC, 1689–1719." *All of One Company: the VOC in Biographical Perspective.* Utrecht: Hes, 1986.

Gann, L. H. and Peter Duignan. *The Rulers of British Africa, 1870–1914.* Stanford: Stanford UP, 1978.

Gates, Henry Louis, Jr., ed. *"Race", Writing, and Difference.* Chicago: U of Chicago P, 1986.

Gathorne-Hardy, Jonathan. *The Rise and Fall of the British Nanny.* London: Hodder and Stoughton, 1972.

Gay, Peter. *The Cultivation of Hatred: The Bourgeois Experience, Victoria to Freud.* New York: Norton, 1993.

Geertz, Clifford. "Stir Crazy." Rev. of *Discipline and Punish* by Michel Foucault. *New York Review of Books* 28 January 1978: 3–4, 6.

Geertz, Hildred. *The Javanese Family: A Study of Kinship and Socialization.* New York: Free Press of Glencoe, 1961.

Genovese, Eugene D. *Roll Jordan Roll: The World the Slaves Made.* New York: Pantheon, 1974.

George, Rosemary. "Homes in the Empire, Empires in the Home." *Cultural Critique* (Winter 1993–94): 95–127.

Geuns, A. de. "Moeten onze kinderen naar Holland?" *'t Onderwijs* 36 (15 September 1906): 420.

Geuns, M. van. "De karaktervorming der Indo's." *Weekblad voor Indie* 11 December 1904, 2.

Gilman, Sander. "Black Bodies, White Bodies." *Race, Writing and Difference.* Ed. Henry Louis Gates, Jr. Chicago, U of Chicago P, 1986.

——— . *Difference and Pathology: Stereotypes of Sexuality, Race, and Madness.* Ithaca: Cornell UP, 1985.

——— . *Freud, Race and Gender.* Princeton: Princeton UP, 1993.

Goldberg, David. *Racist Culture: Philosophy and the Politics of Meaning.* Oxford: Blackwell, 1993.

Goldberg, Jonathan. *Sodometries: Renaissance Texts, Modern Sexualities.* Stanford: Stanford UP, 1992.

Gordon, Colin. 1986. "The Soul of the Citizen: Max Weber and Michel Foucault on Rationality and Government." *Max Weber: Rationality and Modernity.* Eds. Sam Whimster and Scott Lash. London: 293–316.

——— . "Histoire de la folie: An Unknown Book by Michel Foucault." *History of the Human Sciences* 3.1 (February 1990): 3–26 (and Responses to Colin Gordon's paper: 27–68).

——— , ed. *The Foucault Effect: Studies in Governmentality.* Chicago: Chicago UP, 1991.

Gordon, Linda. *Woman's Body, Woman's Right: A Social History of Birth Control in America.* New York: Grossman, 1976.

Gouda, Frances. "The Gendered Rhetoric of Colonialism and Anti-Colonialism in Twentieth-Century Indonesia." *Indonesia* 55 (April 1993): 1–22.

——— . *Poverty and Political Culture: The Rhetoric of Social Welfare in the Netherlands and France, 1815–1854.* Lanham, MD: Rowen and Littlefield, 1995.

Green, Michelle. *The Dream at the End of the World: Paul Bowles and the Literary Renegades in Tangiers.* New York: Harper, 1992.

Grigg, Kenneth. " 'All Roads Lead to Rome': the Role of the Nursemaid in Freud's Dreams." *Journal of American Pyschoanalytic Association* 21 (1973): 108–126.

Grimshaw, Patricia. *Paths of Duty: American Missionary Wives in Nineteenth-Century Hawaii.* Honolulu: U of Hawaii P, 1989.

Guha, Ranjait and Gayatri Chakravorty Spivak, eds. *Selected Subaltern Studies.* New York: Oxford UP, 1988.

Groot, Joanna de. " 'Sex' and 'Race': the Construction of Language and Image in the Nineteenth Century." *Sexuality and Subordination.* Eds. Susan Mendus and Jane Rendall. London: Routledge, 1989.

Guillaumin, Collette. "The Idea of Race and its Elevation to Autonomous Scientific and Legal Status." *Sociological Theories: Race and Colonialism.* Paris: UNESCO, 1980.

Gunning, H. C. H. "Het Woningvraagstuk." *Koloniale Studien* 2 (1918): 109–126.

Guy, Donna J. " 'White Slavery,' Citizenship and Nationality in Argentia." *Nationalisms and Sexualities.* Eds. Andrew Parker, Mary Russo, Doris Sommer and Patricia Yaeger. New York: Routledge: 201–17.

Habermas, Jurgen. *The Philosophical Discourse of Modernity: Twelve Lectures.* Cambridge: MIT Press, 1990.

Hacking, Ian. "The Looping Effects of Human Kinds." Fondation Fyssen Conference, Paris, 7–11 January 1993.

Hall, Catherine. *White, Male and Middle-Class: Explorations in Feminism and History.* London: Polity Press, 1992.

Hall, Stuart. "Race, Articulation and Societies Structured in Dominance." *Sociological Theories: Race and Colonialism*. Paris: UNESCO, 1980.

Hay, Denys. *Europe: The Emergence of an Idea*. Edinburgh: Edinburgh UP, 1957.

Henny, Taco. *Verslag van het Verhandelde in de Bijeenkomsten der Nederlandsch-Indische Juristen-Vereeniging*. Batavia, 1887.

Hesselink, Liesbeth. "Prostitution: the Necessary Evil." *Indonesian Women in Focus*. Eds. Elsbeth Locher-Scholten and Anke Niehof. Dordrecht, Holland: Foris, 1987.

Hilgers, Th. J. A. en H. Douma. *De Indische Lagere School*. Weltevreden: Visser, 1908.

Hirschfeld, Lawrence. "Do Children Have a Theory of Race?" *Cognition* 54 (1995): 209–252.

——— . *Race in the Making: Cognition, Culture and the Child's Construction of Human Kinds*. Cambridge: MIT Press (in press).

Hobsbawm, Eric. *The Age of Capital: 1845–1878*. New York: Scribner, 1975.

Holt, Thomas C. *The Problem of Freedom: Race, Labor, and Politics in Jamaica and Britain, 1832–1938*. Baltimore: Johns Hopkins UP, 1992.

Horst, D. W. "Opvoeding en onderwijs van kinderen van Europeanen en Indo-Europeanen in Indie." *Indische Gids* 2 (1900): 989.

Hoy, David Couzens, ed. *Foucault: A Critical Readers*. Oxford: Blackwell, 1986.

Hughes, Robert. *The Fatal Shore*. New York: Knopf, 1987.

Hunt, Lynn. *The Family Romance of the French Revolution*. Berkeley: U of California P, 1992.

Hunt, Nancy Rose. " 'Le bébé en brousse': European Women, African Birth Spacing and Colonial Intervention in Breastfeeding in the Belgian Congo." *International Journal of African Historical Studies* 21.3 (1988): 401–32.

Hunter, Ian. "Personality as a Vocation: The Political Rationality of the Humanities." *Foucault's New Domains*. Eds. Gane, Mike and Terry Johnson. London: Routledge, 1993.

Hussain, Athar. "Foucault's History of Sexuality." *M/F* 5 (1981): 169–91.

Hyam, Ronald. *Empire and Sexuality: The British Experience*. Manchester: Manchester UP, 1990.

Hymes, Dell, ed. *Reinventing Anthropology*. New York: Random House, 1969.

"Iets over kinderopvoeding in Indie." *Indie* 3.52 (March, 1920): 847.

Ileto, Reynaldo. *Pasyon and Revolution: Popular Movements in the Philippines, 1840–1910*. Quezon City: Ateneo de Manila UP, 1979.

Ingelson, John. "Prostitution in Colonial Java." *Nineteenth and Twentieth Century Indonesia: Essays in Honour of Professor J. D. Legge*. Clayton, Victoria: Monash UP, 1986: 123–40.

Jameson, Fredric. "Modernism and Imperialism." *Nationalism, Colonialism and Literature*. 1990. Minneapolis: U of Minnesota P, 1990: 43–68.

JanMohamed, Abdul R. "Sexuality on/of the Racial Border: Foucault, Wright and the Articulation of 'Racialized Sexuality.' " *Discourses of Sexuality*. Ed. Donna Stanton. Ann Arbor: U of Michigan P, 1992.

Jay, Martin. *Adorno*. Cambridge: Harvard UP, 1984.

——— . "In the Empire of the Gaze: Foucault and the Denigration of Vision in Twentieth-Century French Thought." *Foucault: A Critical Reader*. Ed. David Couzens Hoy. Oxford: Blackwell, 1986: 175–203.

——— . *Force-Fields: Between Intellectual History and Cultural Critique*. London: Routledge, 1993.

Johnson, David. "Aspects of a Liberal Education: Late Nineteenth-Century Attitudes to Race, from Cambridge to the Cape Colony." *History Workshop Journal* 36 (1993): 162–182.

Jolly, Margaret. "Foucault goes Troppo" Rev. of *Knowledge and Power in a South Pacific Society* by L. Lindstrom. *The Journal of Pacific History* 27.2 (1992): 237–43.

———. "Colonizing Women: The Maternal Body and Empire." *Feminism and the Politics of Difference.* Eds. Sneja Gunew and Anna Yeatman. Boulder: Westview Press, 1993: 113–27.

Jordan, Winthrop D. *White over Black: American Attitudes toward the Negro, 1550–1812.* Chapel Hill: U of North Carolina P, 1968.

Jouanna, Arlette. *L'idée de race en France au XVIᵉ siècle et an début du XVIIᵉ siècle: 1498–1614.* Lille: Atelier réproduction des theses, 1976.

Kamen, Henry. *Inquisition and Society in Spain in the Sixteenth and Seventeenth Centuries.* Bloomington: Indiana UP, 1985.

Kang, L. Hyun-Yi. "The Desiring of Asian Female Bodies: Interracial Romance and Cinematic Subjection." *Visual Anthropology Review* 9.1 (Spring 1993): 5–21.

Kelly, John. *A Politics of Virtue: Hinduism, Sexuality, and Countercolonial Discourse in Fiji.* Chicago: U of Chicago P, 1991.

Kern, R. A. "De kontoleurs en 't concubinaat." *Tijdschrift voor het Binnenlandsch Bestuur* (1904) 28.1–6: 250–52.

Kevles, Daniel. *In the Name of Eugenics: Genetics and the Uses of Human Heredity.* Berkeley: U of California P, 1985.

Kiernan, Victor. *The Lords of Human Kind.* London: Wiedenfeld and Nicolson, 1969.

Kincaid, James. *Child-Loving: The Erotic Child and Victorian Culture.* New York: Routledge, 1992.

Knaap, Otto van. "De Verindisching van ons Nederlandsche." *De Indische Gids* (1902): 1871–72.

Knapman, Claudia. *White Women in Fiji, 1835–1930: The Ruin of Empire?.* Boston: Allen and Unwin, 1986.

Kohlbrugge, J. F. "Het Indische kind en zijne karaktervorming." *Blikken in het zielenleven van den Javaan en zijner overheerschers.* Leiden: Brill, 1907.

Kohlbrugge, J. F. "Prostitutie in Nederlandsche-Indie." *Indisch Genootschap* 19 (February 1901): 26–28.

Koontz, Claudia. *Mothers in the Fatherland: Women, the Family, and Nazi Politics.* New York: St. Martin's Press, 1987.

Koot, W. D. "Het Concubinaat." (no publisher), 1905.

Koven, Seth and Sonya Michel, eds. *Mothers of a New World: Maternalist Politics and the Origins of Welfare States.* London: Routledge, 1993.

Krafft-Ebing, Richard von. *Psychopathia Sexualis: mit besonderer Berucksichtigung der contraren Sexualemfindung. Eine Klinisch-Forensische Studie.* Stuttgart: F. Enke, 1892.

Kristeva, Julia. *Strangers to Ourselves.* New York: Columbia UP, 1991.

Kritzman, Lawrence D., ed. *Michel Foucault: Politics, Philosophy, Culture. Interviews and Other Writings, 1977–1984.* New York: Routledge, 1990.

Kruithof, Bernard. "De deugdzame natie: het burgerlijk beschavingsoffensief van de Maatschappij tot Nut van 't Algemeen tussen 1784 en 1860." *Symposion* 2.1 (1980): 22–37.

Kurzweil, Edith. "Michel Foucault's History of Sexuality as Interpreted by Feminists and Marxists." *Social Research* 53.4 (Winter 1986): 647–63.

LaCapra, Dominick. *Soundings in Critical Theory.* Ithaca: Cornell UP, 1989.

Laqueur, Tom. *Making Sex: Body and Gender from the Greeks to Freud.* Cambridge: Harvard UP, 1990.

Lash, Scott. "Genealogy and the Body: Foucault/Deleuze/Nietzsche." *Theory, Culture, Society* 2.2 (1984): 1–17.

Lauretis, Teresa de. *Technologies of Gender*. Bloomington: Indiana UP, 1987.

Lavrin, Asuncion, ed. *Sexuality and Marriage in Colonial Latin America*. Lincoln: U of Nebraska P, 1989.

Lebow, Richard. *White Britain and Black Ireland: The Influence of Stereotypes on Colonial Policy*. Philadelphia: Institute for the Study of Human Issues, 1976.

LeClerc, Gerard. *Anthropologie et Colonialisme: Essai sur l'Histoire de l'Africanisme*. Paris: Fayard, 1972.

Lees, Lynn Hollen. *Exiles of Erin: Irish Migrants in Victorian London*. Ithaca: Cornell UP, 1979.

Lenders, Jan. *De Burgers en de Volksschool: Culturele en mentale achtergronden van een onderwijshervorming, Nederland 1780–1850*. Den Haag: SUN, 1988.

Lévi-Strauss, Claude. *The Savage Mind*. London: Weidenfeld and Nicolson, 1966.

Levitas, Ruth. *The Concept of Utopia*. New York: Philip Allan, 1990.

Lilla, Mark. "A Taste of Pain: Michael Foucault and the Outer Reaches of Human Experience." *Times Literary Supplement* 26 March 1993: 3–4.

Lindstrom, Lamont. *Knowledge and Power in a South Pacific Society*. Washington, D.C.: Smithsonian Institution Press, 1990.

Locke, John. *Some Thoughts concerning Education*. 1693. Menston, England: Scolar Press, 1970.

Lorimer, Douglas. *Colour, Class and the Victorians*. Leicester: Leicester UP, 1978.

Lowe, Lisa. *Critical Terrains: French and British Orientalisms*. Ithaca: Cornell UP, 1991.

Macey, David. *The Lives of Michel Foucault*. New York: Pantheon, 1993.

Maheed, Javed. *Ungoverned Imaginings: James Mill's The History of British India and Orientalism*. Oxford: Clarendon Press, 1992.

Mahon, Michael. *Foucault's Nietzschean Genealogy: Truth, Power and the Subject*. Binghamton: SUNY Press, 1992.

Malleret, Louis. *L'exotisme indochinois dans la littérature française*. Paris: Larose, 1936.

Mannoni, Octavio. *Prospero et Caliban: Pyschologie de la Colonisation*. Paris: Seuil, 1950.

Marcuse, Herbert. *Eros and Civilization: A Philosophical Inquiry into Freud*. New York: Vintage, 1962.

Marks, Shula. "History, the Nation and Empire: Sniping from the Periphery." *History Workshop Journal* 29 (1990): 111–19.

Marle, A. Van. "De group der Europeanen in Nederlands-Indie." *Indonesia* 5.2 (1952): 77–121; 5.3 (1952): 314–41; 5.5 (1952): 481–507.

Martin, Biddy. "Feminism, Criticism, and Foucault." *New German Critique* 27 (Fall 1987): 3–30.

Martinez-Alier, Verena. *Marriage, Class and Colour in 19th century Cuba: A Study of Racial Attitudes and Sexual Values in a Slave Society*. London: Cambridge UP, 1974.

Marvick, Elizabeth Wirth. "Nature versus Nurture: Patterns and Trends in Seventeenth Century French Child-Rearing." *The History of Childhood*. Ed. Lloyd DeMause. New York: Psychohistory Press, 1974.

Mason, Philip. *The Birth of a Dilemma: The Conquest and Settlement of Rhodesia*. London: Oxford UP, 1958.

Masson, Jeffrey. *The Assault on Truth*. New York: Farrar, Straus and Giroux, 1984.

Mastenbroek, Willem. *De Historische Ontwikkeling van de Staatsrechtelijke Indeeling der Bevolking van Nederlandsch-Indie*. Wageningen: Veenman, 1934.

Mayhew, Henry. *London Labour and the London Poor, 1851*. New York: Penguin, 1985.

McClintock, Anne. "The Angel of Progress: Pitfalls of the Term 'Post-Colonialism.'" *Social Text* 31–32: 84–98.

McHoul, Alec. "The Getting of Sexuality: Foucault, Garfinkel and the Analysis of Sexual Discourse." *Theory, Culture and Society* 3.2 (1986): 65–79.

McNay, Lois. *Foucault Feminism*. Boston: Northeastern UP, 1992.

Megill, Allan. "Foucault, Structuralism, and the End of History." *Journal of Modern History* 51 (September 1979): 451–503.

——. *Prophets of Extremity: Nietzsche, Heidegger, Foucault, Derrida*. Berkeley: U of California P, 1987.

——. "The Reception of Foucault by Historians." *Journal of the History of Ideas* 48 (1987): 117–141.

Mehta, Uday. *The Anxiety of Freedom: Imagination and Individuality in Locke's Political Thought*. Ithaca: Cornell UP, 1992.

——. "Liberal Strategies of Exclusion." *Politics and Society* 18.4 (Dec. 1990): 427–54.

Mellman, Billie. *Women's Orients: English Women and the Middle East, 1718–1918: Sexuality, Religion and Work*. Ann Arbor: The U of Michigan P, 1992.

Memmi, Albert. *Portrait du colonisé*. Paris: Payot, 1957.

Merquior, J. G. *Foucault*. Berkeley: U of California P, 1985.

——. *Michel Foucault: Philosophe*. Paris: Seuil, 1989.

Miles, Robert. "Marxism versus the 'Sociology of Race Relations?'" *Ethnic and Racial Studies* 7.2 (1984): 217–37.

Mill, James. *The History of British India*. 6 vols. 6th ed. London: James Madden, 1858.

Miller, James. *The Passion of Michel Foucault*. New York: Simon and Schuster, 1993.

Mills, Sara. *Discourses of Differences: An Analysis of Women's Travel Writing and Colonialism*. London: Routledge, 1991.

Ming, Hanneke. "Barracks-Concubinage in the Indies, 1887–1920." *Indonesia* 35 (1983): 65–93.

Mintz, Sidney. *Sweetness and Power: The Place of Sugar in Modern History*. New York: Viking, 1985.

Mitchell, Timothy. *Colonising Egypt*. Berkeley: U of California P, 1991.

Morgan, Edmund. *American Slavery: American Freedom: The Ordeal of Colonial Virginia*. New York: Norton, 1975.

Morner, Magnus. *Race Mixture in the History of Latin America*. Boston: Little, Brown and Company, 1967.

Mosse, George. *Nationalism and Sexuality*. Madison: U of Wisconsin P, 1985.

Mosse, George. *Toward the Final Solution: A History of European Racism*. Madison: U of Wisconsin P, 1978.

Nandy, Ashis. *The Intimate Enemy: Loss and Recovery of Self under Colonialism*. New York: Oxford UP, 1983.

Nederburgh. J. A. *Wet en Adat*. Batavia: Kloff, 1898.

Newman, Karen. "'And Wash the Ethiop White': Femininity and the Monstrous in *Othello*." *Shakespeare Reproduced: The Text in History and Ideology*. Eds. Jean E. Howard and Marion F. O'Connor. New York: Methuen, 1987: 142–62.

Newton, Judith. "History as Usual: Feminism and the New Historicism." *Cultural Critique* (Spring 1988): 87–121.

Niel, Robert van. *Java Under the Cultivation System*. Leiden: KITLV, 1992.

Noordman, Jan. *Om de Kwaliteit van het nageslacht: Eugentica in Nederland, 1900–1950*. Nijmegen: SUN, 1989.

O'Farrell, Claire. *Foucault: Historian or Philosopher*. London: Macmillan, 1989.

Omi, Michael and Howard Winant. *Racial Formation in the United States: From the 1960s to the 1990s*. London: Routledge, 1994.

Ong, Aihwa. *Spirits of Resistance and Capitalist Discipline*. Binghamton: SUNY Press, 1987.

"Ons Pauperisme." *Mededeelingen der Vereeniging "Soeria Soemirat"* 2 (1892).

Onselen, Charles van. "Prostitutes and Proletarians, 1886-1914." *Studies in the Social and Economic History of the Witwatersrand*. Volume I: New Babylon. New York: Longman, 1982.

——. "Race and Class in the South African Countryside: Cultural Osmosis and Social Relations in the Sharecropping Economy of the South-western Transvaal, 1900–1950." *American Historical Review* (1990): 99–123.

Outram, Derinda. *The Body and the French Revolution: Sex, Class and Political Culture*. New Haven: Yale UP, 1989.

Padgug, Robert. "Sexual Matters: On Conceptualizing Sexuality in History." *Passion and Power: Sexuality in History*. Eds. Kathy Peiss and Christina Simmons with Robert Padgug. Philadelphia: Temple UP, 1989.

Pagliaro, Harold, ed. *Racism in the Eighteenth Century*. Cleveland: Case Western Reserve UP, 1973.

Pagter, L. de. *Het Sexuelle in de Opvoeding: een ernstig woord aan moeders en vaders*. Jogjakarta: Buning, 1901.

Pasquino, Pasquale. "Michel Foucault, 1926–84: The Will to Knowledge." *Economy and Society* 15.1 (1986): 98.

——. "Political Theory of War and Peace: Foucault and the History of Modern Political Theory." *Economy and Society* 22.1 (February 1993): 76–88.

Pateman, Carole. *The Sexual Contract*. Stanford: Stanford UP, 1988.

Het Pauperisme Commissie. *Het Pauperisme onder de Europeanen in Nederlandsch-Indie. Deerde Gedeelte. Kleine Landbouw*. Batavia: Landsdrukkerij, 1901.

Paxton, Nancy. "Mobilizing Chivalry: Rape in British Novels about the Indian Uprising of 1857." *Victorian Studies* (Fall 1992): 1–30.

Pedersen, Susan. "Gender, Welfare, and Citizenship in Britain during the Great War." *American Historical Review* 95.4 (1990): 983–1006.

——. "National Bodies, Unspeakable Acts: The Sexual Politics of Colonial Policymaking." *Journal of Modern History* 63 (1991): 647–80.

Pick, Daniel. *The Faces of Degeneration: A European Disorder, c.1848–c.1918*. New York: Cambridge, 1989.

Pigeaud, J..J. *Iets over kinderopvoeding: raadgevingen voor moeders in Indie*. Samarang: G.C.T. van Dorp & Co., 1898.

Pinch, Adela. *Strange Fits of Passion: Epistemologies of Emotion, Hume to Austen*. Stanford: Stanford UP, forthcoming.

Pluchon, Pierre. *Nègres et juifs au XVIIIe siècle: Le racisme au siècle des Lumières*. Paris: Tallandier, 1984.

Pocock, J. G. A. *The Ancient Constitution and the Feudal Law: A Study of English Historical Thought in the Seventeenth Century*. Cambridge: Cambridge UP, 1957.

Poliakov, Leon. *The Aryan Myth: A History of Racist and Nationalist Ideas in Europe*. London: Heineman, 1974.

Pollis, Carol A. 1987. "The Apparatus of Sexuality: Reflections on Foucault's Contributions to the Study of Sex in History." *Adversaria* 23.3 (1987): 401–14.

Porter, Roy. "Is Foucault Useful for Understanding Eighteenth and Nineteenth Century Sexuality?" *Contention* 1 (1991): 61–82.

Poster, Mark. *Foucault, Marxism and History: Mode of Production vs. Mode of Information.* Cambridge: Polity Press, 1984.

Pratt, Mary Louise. *Imperial Eyes: Travel Writing and Transculturation.* London: Routledge, 1992.

Price, Grenfell. *White Settlers in the Tropics.* New York: American Geographical Society, 1939.

Prins, W. F. "De Bevolkingsgroepen in het Nederlandsch-Indische Recht." *Koloniale Studien* 17 (1933): 677.

Rabinow, Paul. *French Modern: Norms and Forms of the Social Environment.* Cambridge: MIT Press, 1989.

Rafael, Vincente. *Contracting Colonialism.* Ithaca: Cornell UP, 1988.

———. "Colonial Domesticity: White Women and United States Rule in the Philippines." Unpublished manuscript, n.d.

Rajchman, John. *Michel Foucault: The Freedom of Philosphy.* New York: Columbia UP, 1985.

———. *Truth and Eros: Foucault, Lacan, and the Question of Ethics.* New York: Routledge, 1991.

Ragussis, Michael. "The Birth of a Nation in Victorian Culture: The Spanish Inquisition, the Converted Daughter, and the 'Secret Race.'" *Critical Inquiry* 20 (Spring 1994): 477–508.

Ramazanoglu, Caroline, ed. *Up against Foucault: Exploration of Some Tensions between Foucault and Feminism.* London: Routledge, 1993.

Rawick, George. *The American Slave: A Composite Autobiography.* Westport, CN: Greenwood Publishing Co., 1972.

Rebours, Marie Anel Le. *Avis aux mères qui veulent nourir leurs enfants.* Paris, 1767.

Regt, Ali de. "Arbeiders, burgers and boeren: gezinsleven in de negentiende eeuw." *Familie, Huwelijk en gezin in west-Europa.* Ed. Ton Swaan. Boom: Open Universiteit, 1993.

———. *Arbeidersgezinnen en beschavingsarbeid.* Boom: Amsterdam, 1984.

Rex, John. "The Theory of Race Relations—A Weberian Approach." *Sociological Theories: Race and Colonialism.* Paris: UNESCO, 1980.

Ridley, Hugh. *Images of Imperial Rule.* London: St. Martin's Press, 1983.

Righart, Hans. "Moraliseringoffensief in Nederland in de periode 1850–1880." *Vijf Eeuwen van Gezinsleven.* Eds. H. Peeters, et. al. Nijmegen: SUN, 1986.

Rioux, J.-P. and J.-F. Sirinelli, eds. *La Guerre d'Algérie et les intellectuels français.* Paris: Editions Complexe, 1991.

Ritter, W. L. *De Europeanen in Nederlandsche Indie.* Leyden: Sythoff, 1856.

Robbins, Bruce. *The Servant's Hand.* Durham: Duke UP, 1993.

Roediger, David. *Wages of Whiteness.* London: Verso, 1991.

Rogin, Michael. "Liberal Society and the Indian Question." *Politics and Society* (May 1971): 269–312.

———. "'Democracy and Burnt Cork': The End of Blackface and the Beginning of Civil Rights." *Representations* 46 (Spring 1994): 1–34.

Root, Deborah. "Speaking Christian: Orthodoxy and Difference in Sixteenth-Century Spain." *Representations* 23 (1988): 118–34.

Rutten-Pekelharing, C. J. *Waaraan moet ik denken? Wat moet ik doen? Wenken aan het Hollandsche Meisje dat als Huisvrouw naar Indie gaat.* Gorinchem: J. Noorduijn, 1923.

Said, Edward. *Culture and Imperialism.* New York: Knopf, 1993.

———. "Foucault and the Imagination of Power." *Foucault: A Critical Reader.* Ed. David C. Hoy. London: Basil Blackwell, 1986.

———. *Orientalism*. New York: Pantheon, 1978.

Sartre, Jean-Paul. *La Critique de la raison dialectique*. Paris: Gallimard, 1960.

Sawicki, Jana. *Disciplining Foucault: Feminism, Power and the Body*. London: Routledge, 1991.

Schama, Simon. *Patriots and Liberators: Revolution in the Netherlands, 1780–1813*. New York: Vintage, [1977] 1992.

Schaub, Uta Liebmann. "Foucault's Oriental Subtext." *PMLA* 104 (1989): 306–16.

Schumpeter, Joseph. *Imperialism and Social Class*. New York: Augustus Kelley, 1951.

Scott, David. *Formations of Ritual: Colonial and Anthropological Discourses on Sinhala Yaktovil*. Minneapolis: U of Minnesota P, 1994.

Segal, Daniel. "'The European': Allegories of Racial Purity." *Anthropology Today* 7.5 (Oct. 1991): 7–9.

Seidler, Victor. "Reason, Desire and Male Sexuality." *The Cultural Construction of Sexuality*. Ed. Pat Caplan. London: Tavistock, 1987.

Sevenhuijsen, Selma L. *De Orde van het Vaderschap: Politieke debatten over ongehuwd moederschap, afstamming en het huwelijk in Nederland, 1870–1900*. Amsterdam: CIP-Gegevens Koninklijke Bibliotheck, 1987.

Sewell, William. *A Rhetoric of Bourgeois Revolution: Abbé Sieyes and "What Is the Third Estate?"* Durham: Duke UP, 1994.

Shaffer, Elinor. "Book Review of *The History of Sexuality, Vol. I*." *Signs* (Summer 1980): 812–20.

Shapiro, Michael. *Child's Garden: The Kindergarten Movement from Froebel to Dewey*. University Park: The Pennslyvania State UP, 1983.

Shell, Marc. *Children of the Earth: Literature, Politics and Nationhood*. New York: Oxford, 1993.

Shell, Robert. "Tender Ties: Women and the Slave Household, 1652–1834." *The Societies of Southern Africa in the 19th and 20th Centuries*. Vol. 17. London: University of London, 1992.

Sheridan, Alan. *Michel Foucault: The Will to Truth*. London: Tavistock, 1980.

Showalter, Elaine. *Sexual Anarchy: Gender and Culture at the Fin de Siecle*. London: Penguin, 1990.

Shumway, David R. *Michel Foucault*. Boston: Twayne, 1989.

Sicroff, Albert A. *Les controverses des statuts de "pureté de sang" en Espagne du XVe au XVIIe siècle*. Paris: Didier, 1960.

Silverman, Kaja. "White Skin, Brown Masks: The Double Mimesis, or, With Lawrence in Arabia." *Differences* 1.3 (Fall 1989): 3–54.

Skurski, Julie. "The Ambiguities of Authenticity in Latin America: Doña Barbara and the Construction of National Identity." *Poetics Today* 15.4 (Winter 1994): 605–42.

Smith-Rosenberg, Carroll. *Disorderly Conduct: Visions of Gender in Victorian America*. New York: Oxford, 1985.

Snellebrand, I. J. Hissink. "Wat is te doen in het belang van de Indische paupermeisjes en tot versterking van het Nederlandsche element in Nederlandsch-Indie." *Indische Genootschap*. General Meeting of 22 November 1910.

Sommer, Doris. "Irresistible Romance: the Foundational Fictions of Latin America." *Nation and Narration*. Ed. Homi Bhabha. London: Routledge, 1990.

———. *Foundational Fictions: The National Romances of Latin America*. Berkeley: U of California P, 1991.

Spivak, Gayatri. "Can the Subaltern Speak?" *Marxism and the Interpretation of Culture*. Eds. Cary Nelson and Lawrence Grossberg. Urbana: U of Illinois P, 1988.

Sorum, Paul Clay. *Intellectuals and Decolonization in France.* Chapel Hill: U of North Carolina P, 1977.

Stallybrass, Peter and Allon White. *The Politics and Poetics of Transgression.* London: Methuen, 1986.

Stanton, Domna, ed. *Discourses of Sexuality: From Aristotle to Aids.* Ann Arbor: U of Michigan P, 1992.

Steedman, Carolyn. *Landscape for a Good Woman.* New Brunswick: Rutgers UP, 1986.

Stepan, Nancy Leys. "Race and Gender: The Role of Analogy in Science." *The Anatomy of Racism.* Ed. David Goldberg. Minneapolis: U of Minnesota P, 1990.

Stokes, Eric. *The English Utilitarians and India.* Oxford: Clarendon Press, 1959.

Stolcke, Verena. "Conquered Women." *Report on the Americas* 24.5 (1991): 25.

Stoler, Ann. *Carnal Knowledge and Imperial Power: Bourgeois Civilities and the Cultivation of Racial Categories in Colonial Southeast Asia.* Berkeley: U of California P, forthcoming.

———. "Carnal Knowledge and Imperial Power: Gender, Race and Morality in Colonial Asia." *Gender at the Crossroads of Knowledge: Feminist Anthropology in a Postmodern Era.* Ed. Micaela di Leonardo. Berkeley: U of California P, 1991: 55–101.

———. "In Cold Blood: Hierarchies of Credibility and the Politics of Colonial Narratives." *Representations* 37 (Winter 1992): 151–89.

———. "Rethinking Colonial Categories." *Comparative Studies in Society and History* 13.1 (1989): 134–61.

———. "A Sentimental Education: European Children and Native Servants in the Netherlands Indies." *Fantasizing the Feminine: Sex and Death in Indonesia.* Ed. Laurie Sears. Durham: Duke UP, 1995.

———. "Sexual Affronts and Racial Frontiers: European Identities and the Cultural Politics of Exclusion in Colonial Southeast Asia." *Comparative Studies in Society and History* 34.2 (July 1992): 514–51.

Stoler, Ann Laura and Frederick Cooper. "Between Metropole and Colony: Rethinking a Research Agenda." *Tensions of Empire: Colonial Cultures in a Bourgeois World.* Eds. Frederick Cooper and Ann Laura Stoler. Berkeley: U of California P, forthcoming.

Stoner, James. *Common Law and Liberal Theory.* Lawrence, Kansas: U of Kansas P, 1992.

Stratz, C. H. *De vrouwen op Java: eene gynaecologische studie.* Amsterdam: Scheltema and Holkemas, 1897.

Stuurman, Siep. "John Bright and Samuel van Houten: Radical Liberalism and the Working Classes in Britain and the Netherlands, 1860-1880." *History of European Ideas* 2 (1989): 593–604.

———. *Verzuiling, Kapitalisme en Patriarchaat: Aspecten van de ontwikkeling van de moderne staat in Nederland.* Nijmegen: SUN, 1983.

———. *Wacht op onze daden: Het liberalisme en de vernieuwing van de Nederlandse Staat.* Amsterdam: Bert Bakker, 1992.

Sullivan, Pierre. "Histoire et sexualité: à propos de l'oeuvre de Michel Foucault" *Revue Française de Psychoanalyse* 5 (1984): 1441–453.

Summers, Carol. "Intimate Colonialism: The Imperial Production of Reproduction in Uganda, 1907–1925." *Signs* 16.4 (1991): 787–807.

Swaisland, Cecile. *Servants and Gentlewomen to the Golden Land: The Emigration of Single Women from Britain to Southern Africa, 1820–1939.* Oxford: U of Natal P, 1993.

Swan, Jim. "Mater and Nannie: Freud's Two Mothers and the Discovery of the Oedipus Complex." *American Imago* 31.1 (Spring 1974): 1–64.

Taussig, Michael. *Mimesis and Alterity: A Particular History of the Senses.* New York: Routledge, 1993.

Thomas, Nicholas and David Arnold, eds. *Colonizing the Body: State Medicine and Epidemic Disease in 19th Century India.* Berkeley: U of California P, 1992.

Thomas, Nicholas. *Colonialism's Culture: Anthropology, Travel and Government.* Princeton: Princeton UP, 1994.

Taguieff, Pierre-André. "The Doctrine of the National Front in France (1972–1989): A 'Revolutionary' Programme? Ideological Aspects of a National-Populist Mobilization." *New Political Science* 16–17 (Fall/Winter 1989): 29–70.

——— . *La force du préjugé: essai sur le racisme et ses doubles.* Paris: La Découverte, 1988.

Takaki, Ronald T. *Iron Cages: Race and Culture in Nineteenth-Century America.* Seattle: U of Washington P, 1979.

Taussig, Michael. "Culture of Terror—Space of Death: Roger Casement's Putumayo Report and the Explanation of Torture." *Comparative Studies in Society and History* 26 (1984): 467–97.

Taylor, Jean. *The Social World of Batavia.* Madison: U of Wisconsin P, 1983.

Theleweit, Klaus. *Male Fantasies.* Minneapolis: U of Minnesota P, 1989.

Thompson, E. P. *William Morris: Romantic to Revolutionary.* N.Y.: Pantheon, 1977.

Thorne, Susan. "The Conversion of England and the Converserion of the World Inseparable: Missionary Imperialism and the Language of Class, 1750–1850." *Tensions of Empire: Colonial Cultures in a Bourgeois World.* Eds. Frederick Cooper and Ann Laura Stoler. Berkeley: U of California P, forthcoming.

Thwaite, Ann. *Waiting for the Party: The Life of Frances Hodgson Burnett, 1849–1924.* New York: Scribner.

Tiffany, Sharon and Kathleen Adams. *The Wild Woman: An Inquiry into the Anthropology of an Idea.* Cambridge: Schenkman, 1985.

Torgovnick, Marianna. *Gone Primitive: Savage Intellects, Modern Lives.* Chicago: Chicago UP, 1990.

Treub, M. W. F. "De Structuur der Indische Maatschappij." *Nederland in de Oost: Reisindrukken.* Haarlem: Tjeenk Willink, 1923.

Turkel, Shirley. *Psychoanalytic Politics: Jacques Lacan and Freud's French Revolution.* New York: Guilford Press, 1992.

Vaugh, Alden. "The Origins Debate: Slavery and Racism in 17th century Virginia." *Virginia Magazine of History and Biography* 97 (July 1989): 347–49.

Vaughan, Megan. *Curing their Ills: Colonial Power and African Illness.* London: Polity Press, 1991.

Veeneklaas, C. *Het Rassenconflict in de opvoeding in Indonesie.* Mededeelingen van het Nutsseminarium voor Paedagogiek aan de Universiteit van Amsterdam, no. 44. Batavia: J.B. Wolters, 1949.

Velde, Henk te. "How High did the Dutch Fly? Remarks on Stereotypes of Burger Mentality." *Images of the Nation: Different Meanings of Dutchness, 1870-1940.* Eds. A. Galema, B. Henkes and H. te Velde. Amsterdam: Rodopi, 1993.

Vicinus, Martha. "Sexuality and Power: A Review of Current Work in the History of Sexuality." *Feminist Studies* 8.1 (Spring 1982): 136.

Vrettos, Athena. *Somatic Fictions: Imagining Illness in Victorian Culture.* Stanford: Stanford UP, 1995.

Waal, J. H. F. van de. "Het Indoisme." *De Reflector* 39 (1916): 953.

Ware, Vron. *Beyond the Pale: White Women, Racism and History.* London: Verso, 1992.

Weber, Eugene. *From Peasants to Frenchmen.* Stanford: Stanford UP, 1976.

Weber, M. *From Max Weber: Essay in Sociology.* Eds. H. H. Gerth and C. Wright Mills. London: Routledge, 1948.

Weeks, Jeffrey. *Sex, Politics, and Society: The Regulation of Sexuality Since 1800.* London: Longman, 1981.

Weijl, S. and W. H. Boogaardt. *Pro en Contra: Het Concubinaat in de Indische Kazernes.* Baarn: Hollandia, 1917.

White, Hayden. "The Forms of Wildness: Archaeology of an Idea." *The Wild Man Within: An Image in Western Thought from the Renaissance to Romanticism.* Pittsburgh: U of Pittsburgh P, 1972.

———. "The Noble Savage Theme as Fetish." *Tropics of Discourse: Essays in Cultural Criticism.* Baltimore: Johns Hopkins UP, 1978: 183–96.

White, Luise. *The Comforts of Home: Prostitution in Colonial Nairobi.* Chicago: U of Chicago P, 1990.

———. Rev. of *Empire and Sexuality: The British Experience* by Ronald Hyam. *International Journal of African Historical Studies* 25.3 (1992): 664–65.

Williams, Patrick and Laura Chrisman, eds. *Colonial Discourse and Post-Colonial Theory.* New York: Columbia UP, 1994.

Williams, Raymond. *Keywords.* London: Croom Helm, 1976.

Wilson, Stephen. *Ideology and Experience: Antisemitism in France at the Time of the Dreyfus Affair.* London: Associated University Presses, 1982.

Wishy, Bernard. *The Child and the Republic: The Dawn of American Child Nurture.* Philadelphia: U of Pennslyvania P, 1967.

Wittgenstein, Ludwig. *Tractatus Logico-Philosophicus.* 1921. Atlantic Highlands, NJ: Humanities Press, 1961.

Wolff, Janet and John Seed, eds. *The Culture of Capital: Art, Power, and the 19th Century Middle-Class.* New York: St. Martin's Press, 1988.

Woodcock, George. *The British in the Far East.* New York: Atheneum, 1969.

Wright, Gwendolyn. *The Politics of Design in French Colonial Urbanism.* Chicago: Chicago UP, 1991.

Wright, Lawrence. "One Drop of Blood." *The New Yorker* (1994): 46–55.

Yazawa, Melvin. *From Colonies to Commonwealth: Familial Ideology and the Beginnings of the American Republic.* Baltimore: Johns Hopkins UP, 1985.

Young, Robert. *White Mythologies: Writing History and the West.* London: Routledge, 1990.

Index

Ann Laura Stoler is Professor of Anthropology and History at the
University of Michigan. She is author of Capitalism and
Confrontation in Sumatra's Plantation Belt, 1870–1979, and co-editor
with Frederick Cooper of Tensions of Empire: Colonial Cultures in a
Bourgeois World.

Library of Congress Cataloging-in-Publication Data
Stoler, Ann Laura.
Race and the education of desire : Foucault's History of Sexuality
and the colonial order of things / Ann Laura Stoler.
Includes bibliographical references (p.   ) and index.
ISBN 0-8223-1678-1 (cl : alk. paper). — ISBN 0-8223-1690-0 (pa : alk. paper)
1. Racism.   2. Indigenous peoples.   3. Foucault, Michel—Views on racism.
4. Foucault, Michel. Histoire de la sexualité.   I. Title.
HT1523.S76   1995
305.8—dc20   95-14487 CIP